OECD Reviews of Pension Systems: Mexico

OECD
BETTER POLICIES FOR BETTER LIVES

This work is published under the responsibility of the Secretary-General of the OECD. The opinions expressed and arguments employed herein do not necessarily reflect the official views of OECD member countries.

This document and any map included herein are without prejudice to the status of or sovereignty over any territory, to the delimitation of international frontiers and boundaries and to the name of any territory, city or area.

Please cite this publication as:
OECD (2016), *OECD Reviews of Pension Systems: Mexico*, OECD Publishing, Paris.
http://dx.doi.org/10.1787/9789264245938-en

ISBN 978-92-64-24592-1 (print)
ISBN 978-92-64-24593-8 (PDF)

The statistical data for Israel are supplied by and under the responsibility of the relevant Israeli authorities. The use of such data by the OECD is without prejudice to the status of the Golan Heights, East Jerusalem and Israeli settlements in the West Bank under the terms of international law.

Photo credits: Cover © Fbhenrg/iStock/Thinkstock

Corrigenda to OECD publications may be found on line at: *www.oecd.org/about/publishing/corrigenda.htm*.

Foreword

This review assesses the Mexican pension system on the basis of OECD best practices in pension design and presents various proposals to improve the Mexican pension system and guarantee its sustainability in the long term.

The defined contribution system of individual accounts introduced in the 1990s has been successful

The new defined contribution (DC) system of individual accounts, introduced in 1997 for private-sector workers and in 2007 for public-sector workers, has been relatively successful in increasing the capacity of the Mexican economy to finance pensions.

At the end of 2014, the system had assets backing-up pension benefits equivalent to 14.1% of GDP, putting Mexico in the middle range in the OECD area, after only 17 years of having the system in place. Moreover, private pension funds (AFORE), which manage the workers' savings that will finance their pensions, have achieved a performance of 12.5% on average annually since their introduction (6.2% in real terms).

The regulation and supervision of the system by the National Commission of the Retirement Savings System (CONSAR) has worked properly according to the best practices of OECD countries.

However, it needs important improvements

While these achievements are noteworthy, the OECD review has identified a number of areas that need improvements. The most important ones are:

- the transition process from the "old" to the "new" system;
- the level of mandatory contributions;
- the old-age safety net; and,
- the fragmentation of the pension system.

The review also recommends reforms in the regulatory framework of CONSAR and the National Insurance and Surety Commission (CNSF), especially regarding investment strategies and investment restrictions of AFORE and life annuities.

The review also highlights the low density of contributions resulting from informality as another important challenge facing the Mexican pension system. Reducing the size of the informal sector is a policy challenge that is out of the scope of this review, one that needs to be addressed by a range of labour market, tax and structural economic policies.

The transition process from the old to the new system needs to be smoothed to avoid disillusionment and opposition to the new system

One of the main challenges facing the Mexican pension system does not come from the DC system of individual accounts per se, but rather from the transition process from the old defined benefit (DB) pay-as-you-go (PAYG) system to the new funded DC system.

This transition process establishes that all individuals who were working or had contributed to the system at the time of the reform, retain the right to choose upon retirement whether their pension benefits are calculated based on the formula of the old DB system or based on the value of the assets accumulated in their retirement account in the new DC system. As this reviews shows, the DB formula of the old system provides a pension benefit that is not fully backed by contributions. It is much larger than what the accumulated savings can grant. Therefore, an individual who worked and contributed to the pension system one month before the introduction of the new system will receive a pension benefit much larger than that for an individual who entered the system one month later, although both individuals contributed the same and have the same work experience. This difference will obviously lead to disillusionment and opposition to the new DC pension system.

The review proposes a pro-rata mechanism to address this problem. All the rights acquired by workers up to today would be guaranteed, and from tomorrow onwards all workers would accumulate pension assets in the new system. Therefore, the pension benefit of a transitional worker would have two components, one based on the rights acquired under the DB formula, and the other one based on the assets accumulated in the DC individual accounts. This would smooth the convergence from the old system (generous and financially unsustainable) to the new system (balanced and financially sustainable).

Contributions to the system have to increase

Contributions to the system are too low to guarantee pension benefits of more than 50% of final salary. According to OECD calculations, a contribution rate of 6.5% may lead, in the best case scenario, to a replacement rate of only 26% for the average worker. This low replacement rate is mostly the result of the low mandatory contribution rate. As this review shows, a 50% replacement rate can be achieved with a 75% to 90% probability by contributing on average 13% to 18% over 40 years.

Therefore, the review recommends increasing the mandatory contribution rate, but gradually. This increase could be linked to salary increases in such a way that the worker would not suffer a reduction in disposable income.

Improve the old-age safety net by integrating and expanding it

Like all pension systems in OECD countries, the Mexican pension system has a non-contributory old-age social protection component for those individuals who, for various reasons, have been unable to accumulate enough rights or assets. This old-age safety net provides these individuals with a pension that puts them above a certain income threshold.

The review proposes to increase the level of the non-contributory benefit in order to alleviate poverty in old-age. Moreover, it highlights the importance of improving the link between the non-contributory safety net (*Pensión para Adultos Mayores*) and the minimum guaranteed pension (*Pensión Mínima Garantizada*).

It recommends, as well, improving the coordination of safety net programmes between different levels of government by conditioning part of the transfer to local governments on the adoption of the national scheme.

Eliminate the fragmentation of the system

Finally, the review recommends harmonising the rules for all pension plans, with the ultimate goal of establishing a truly national pension system equal for all Mexicans. This harmonisation should include the pension plans for private and public-sector workers, as well as the special regimes (for states, municipalities and universities, among others).

Table of contents

Tables

Figures

Boxes

Acronyms and abbreviations

AFORE	*Administradora de Fondos para el Retiro*	Specialised private pension manager
CNSF	*Comisión Nacional de Seguros y Fianzas*	National Insurance and Surety Commission
COFECE	*Comisión Federal de Competencia Económica*	Federal Economic Competition Commission
CONAPO	*Consejo Nacional de Población*	National Council of Population
CONSAR	*Comisión Nacional del Sistema de Ahorro para el Retiro*	National Commission of the Retirement Savings System
DB		Defined benefit
DC		Defined contribution
FOVISSSTE	*Fondo de la Vivienda del Instituto de Seguridad y Servicios Sociales de los Trabajadores del Estado*	Housing Fund of the Institute for Security and Social Services for State Workers
IMSS	*Instituto Mexicano del Seguro Social*	Mexican Institute of Social Security
INFONAVIT	*Instituto del Fondo Nacional de la Vivienda para los Trabajadores*	National Housing Fund Institute for Workers
IRN	*Indice de Rendimiento Neto*	Net Return Indicator
ISSSTE	*Instituto de Seguridad y Servicios Sociales de los Trabajadores del Estado*	Institute for Security and Social Services for State Workers
NPCC		National Pension Communication Campaign

PAYG		Pay-as-you-go
PMG	*Pensión Mínima Garantizada*	Guaranteed minimum pension
PAM	*Pensión para Adultos Mayores*	Pension for the elderly
RCV	*Subcuenta de Retiro, Cesantía en Edad Avanzada, y Vejez*	Retirement sub-account
SAOR	*El Sistema Administrador de Ofertas y Resoluciones*	Offers and Resolutions Management System
SAR	*Sistema de Ahorro para el Retiro*	Retirement Savings System
SB	*SIEFORE basica*	Basic SIEFORE
SIEFORE	*Sociedad de Inversión Especializada en Fondos para el Retiro*	Pension fund
UAIR	*Unidad para la Administración Integral de Riesgos*	Comprehensive Risk Management Unit
URV	*Unidad de Renta Vitalicia*	Annuity factor
VaR		Value at Risk
ΔCVaR		Difference of the Conditional Value at Risk

Executive summary

This review assesses the Mexican pension system according to the OECD best practices and guidelines, and draws on international experiences and examples to make recommendations on how to improve it. The main findings and recommendations are presented below.

Main findings

- The largest pension systems in Mexico have been reformed from a defined benefit (DB) to a defined contribution (DC) scheme. The main reforms so far include private-sector workers (*Instituto Mexicano del Seguro Social*, IMSS), federal government employees (*Instituto de Seguridad y Servicios Sociales de los Trabajadores del Estado*, ISSSTE) and some other government agencies. These reforms aimed at mitigating the growing liabilities of the DB system given pension promises and contribution rates. However, by allowing transitional workers to choose to retire with pension benefits determined by the old DB formula or the DC accumulation, and setting contribution rates in the new DC system as low as pre-reform rates, the fiscal adjustment is postponed.

- The substantial and fast demographic changes, the long transition of the past reforms and the numerous schemes that have not been reformed yet may lead to strong fiscal pressure for a long period, which may require a large financial effort starting in the mid-2030s.

- The fragmentation of the Mexican pension system is deeply entrenched and goes far beyond the striking difference between public and private-sector workers' schemes. Retirement conditions and benefits, as well as contribution rates, social quotas and government matching, are indeed different between public-sector workers affiliated to ISSSTE and private-sector workers affiliated to IMSS. Moreover, there are still many state government pension schemes and other occupational plans, such as the ones for the state oil company PEMEX and for state universities' employees that have very different terms of retirement conditions and benefits. This is a source of large inequalities.

- The combination of a relatively high level of the minimum pension in relation to contributions paid and wage conditions with a relatively short contribution period provides little incentive to contribute longer than the eligibility period, especially for low-wage workers.

- Mexico is among the three OECD countries offering the lowest old-age safety net for individuals not covered by the contributory pension system.

- There is an overlap between the federal non-contributory pension for old-age and the additional non-contributory pensions or aid programs offered by many local states without fiscal resources backing them up.

- The sharp drop in pension benefits to be expected after the transition period from the old DB system to the new DC systems ends, may lead to disillusionment and opposition to the new DC pension system in the population. This sharp drop is the result of low contribution rates, which were set at similar levels than before the reform, and high promises to transitional workers based on the old DB formula. Moreover, the low coverage rates and contribution periods compound this problem.

- The current investment regime of SIEFORE is too restrictive. Workers have very limited choices in the multi-fund system. Despite increased diversification, Mexico's pension funds are still significantly concentrated in debt relative to other OECD countries. The investment limits for equity and foreign securities are binding for most basic SIEFORE and thus prevent diversification and negative correlation between investments.

- Current mechanisms are not fostering enough competition among AFORE. Although fees charged by AFORE in Mexico have declined by more than 70 basis points in the last decade, they remain high in an international context. The incentives embedded in the registration, assignment and transfer processes are not enough to foster competition.

- There are large pots of assets that can be taken as lump sums instead of being used to finance retirement, which it will affect negatively retirement income adequacy and increase public pension liabilities.

- The lack of a thriving annuity market is due to a lack of demand. The demand for annuities will increase as the transition period ends.

- Annuity providers are ring-fenced subsidiaries of insurance companies. They cannot diversify risks (e.g. mortality) with other products or use the normal life business of the parent insurance company, and are subjected to a more restrictive investment regime. This increases the cost of annuities and reduces the pension payments for individuals. However, ring-fencing these annuity providers may increase the security that they will be able to fulfil their promises and obligations. Security has a cost.

- Insurance companies can only offer one annuity product, the traditional immediate life annuity.

- Mortality tables used by annuity providers sufficiently provision for expected mortality improvements. However, recent improvements in mortality have been slowing and Mexico currently has low life expectancy compared to other OECD countries. If this were to change and life expectancy were to catch up with other OECD countries, longevity risk could become a problem.

- Occupational DB pension funds are not subject to any minimum mortality requirements, including using tables accounting for future improvements in mortality.

Main recommendations

Improve the design of the public pension schemes

- Improve financial sustainability.
  - Implement parametric changes: increase contribution rates; reduce the matching contribution for public-sector workers; lower wage ceiling for private-sector scheme from 25 to 10 times the minimum wage for DB pensions; and scale back survivor's pension.
  - Increase the effective age at which people could retire: link the statutory retirement age to gains in life expectancy; continue to tighten early-retirement schemes; increase the contribution period required for a full pension in the old public-sector DB scheme and close the gender gap in the contribution period; and increase the age limit to get a full pension in the public sector faster and beyond 2028. However, consideration should be given to the fact that mid to low income individuals, as well as individuals with low educational attainment, have lower life expectancy at retirement and their improvements tend to be lower.
  - Harmonise the rules and ensure portability between the special pension schemes (e.g. state-owned companies, state pension schemes and public universities), with the ultimate goal of establishing a truly national pension system. Condition part of the transfers to local governments to the adoption of the national scheme and to the replacement of existing schemes. Make the level of the minimum pension under the 1973 Law converge with the minimum contributory pension (*Pensión Mínima Garantizada*, PMG, in the DC system) and delink it from the minimum wage.
- Increase safety-net levels, and better link the non-contributory components (including the *Pensión para Adultos Mayores*, PAM) with the PMG:
  - The level of the non-contributory benefit is too low to efficiently fight income poverty at older ages.
  - The link between the non-contributory PAM safety net and the minimum contributory pension PMG should be smoothed by: topping up the PAM by a new contribution-based minimum pension; setting the minimum pension benefit in line with contributions paid or as a function of the contribution period - the full rate should be reached with a longer than 1 250 weeks period; using the accumulated assets to finance the new integrated benefit rather than allowing lump sums; and progressively withdrawing the non-contributory component against the minimum pension. The withdrawal rate should be relatively low to limit disincentives to contribute.

Smooth out the transition period and increase coverage, contribution levels and contribution periods

- The first step to attenuate the sharp fall in replacement rates after the last transitional worker retires is to increase contribution rates, at least for private-sector workers. Everything else being equal, this would increase the pension income of workers who are fully in the DC system. This goal could be achieved through: i) increasing the mandatory contribution rate; (ii) earmarking for retirement part of the contributions to the National Housing Fund Institute for Workers (INFONAVIT); (iii) introducing automatic voluntary contributions with an opt-out option; and/or (iv) improving incentives for voluntary pension savings. The last option depends on the fiscal space available.

- To avoid that the increase in mandatory contribution rates would lead to a reduction in take home pay, which may affect disproportionally the low income, increases in mandatory contribution rates could be linked to increases in wages.
- The fall in replacement rates could be smoothed out further by applying a pro-rata system from today onwards for workers who can retire under the old DB formula. All the pension rights earned under the old DB formula would be kept, but from today onwards, workers would only earn pension benefits under the DC formula, so their retirement pension benefits would comprise two components, DB and DC.
- Consider introducing mandatory contributions for self-employed workers to increase coverage and lengthen contribution periods as part of informality is the result of workers moving in and out of self-employment. One of the main sources of low coverage is labour market informality.
- Public understanding and confidence in the pension system could be improved by better aligning public- and private-sector pensions; improving the information provided in pension statements; and organising well-designed National Pension Communication Campaigns to better promote pension savings and increase financial literacy.

Improve the design of the accumulation phase

- Allow more choice on investment strategies while keeping the default life-cycle strategy to protect those close to retirement against extreme negative outcomes (e.g. large falls in equity markets).
- Address high charges and increase competition among AFORE by improving the incentives in the registration, assignment and transfer processes. Consider other mechanisms to introduce competition and reduce charges like tender mechanisms (e.g. allocate new entrants to low cost pension providers).

Improve the design of the pay-out phase

- Early use of retirement savings should be avoided. Any exception should be allowed only under specific and exceptional circumstances. The general practice in most OECD countries is to allow early use of retirement savings in situations of extreme financial hardship, like long-term unemployment, and not once every five years when unemployed as it is the case in Mexico now. All the assets accumulated in the pension system should be combined with other retirement assets to buy a life annuity or get programmed withdrawals, or a combination of both.
- The operation of the annuity market should be improved by allowing additional annuity products that provide different types of guarantees, for example deferred life annuities. Different types of annuities bring in different levels of risks. In this context, the regulatory framework should align reserving and capital requirements with the different levels of risk, so that higher risks to fulfil promises require higher reserves.

- Encourage annuitisation as a protection against longevity risk. The OECD Roadmap for the Good Design of Defined Contribution Pension Plans suggests combining programmed withdrawals with deferred life annuities bought at the time of retirement to achieve flexibility and liquidity, as well as protection from longevity risk, as an appropriate default, as long as there are enough assets accumulated to have an annuity above the poverty threshold.

- Establish a specific regulatory framework to limit pensioners' choice of the insurance companies providing disability and survivors' benefits so that it balances premiums to be paid (by the social security institutes) and the extent of the protection provided. As a result, pensioners could not choose insurance companies that provide the same coverage at a higher cost.

- Assess the cost and benefits of having annuity providers ring-fenced from their parent insurance company.

- Occupational DB pension funds should be subject to minimum mortality requirements and should use mortality tables accounting for future improvements in mortality. At a minimum, they should use the same tables that annuity providers have to use, and ideally adjusted to their specific sub-population.

- Update regularly mortality tables and monitor closely mortality experiences for changing patterns, and especially for an acceleration of mortality improvements, to ensure that the mortality tables used by the industry remain adequate.

- Better account for future improvements in mortality and life expectancy and improve the management of longevity risk, following the recommendations in the 2014 OECD publication, *Mortality Assumptions and Longevity Risk.*

Chapter 1

Introduction to the Review of the Mexican pension system

This chapter briefly describes the objectives of the review of the Mexican pension system. It presents a brief historical background to the changes experienced by the Mexican pension system since the 1990s. This review provides recommendations, using OECD best practices in pension design, on how to improve the Mexican pension system with the ultimate goal of ameliorating the retirement income that people may receive from the pension system.

1.1. Objectives of the review

The National Commission of the Retirement Savings System (*Comisión Nacional del Sistema de Ahorro para el Retiro*, CONSAR), the Mexican pension regulator, requested the OECD to conduct a short and focused review of the Mexican pension system. The main motivation of the Mexican authorities for conducting this review is to understand the challenges facing the Mexican pension system, assess the system in light of the most common practices in the design of pension systems in OECD countries, and ultimately, increase awareness among different stakeholders of the challenges faced by the Mexican pension system.

The purpose of the review is therefore to provide recommendations, using OECD's best practices in pension design, on how to improve the Mexican pension system with the ultimate goal of ameliorating the retirement income that people may receive from the pension system. The detailed terms of reference for the review are reproduced in Box 1.1 below.

Box 1.1. **Terms of reference for the OECD review of Mexico's retirement income provision**

The National Commission of the Retirement Savings System (*Comisión Nacional del Sistema de Ahorro para el Retiro*, CONSAR), the Mexican pension regulator, requests the OECD to conduct a short and focused review of the Mexican pension system based on the OECD's best practices in pension design. The review will take account of current proposals to reform the current SAR Law (*Modificación de la Ley del SAR*).

Particular aspects for examination include:

- The adequacy of pensions given current levels of mandatory contributions, retirement age, voluntary savings, and short contribution densities.
- Mechanisms to increase coverage and the amount of contributions, in order to ensure adequate income in retirement with a particular focus on lower- and middle-income groups, independent workers and informal workers.
- Tax system and retirement savings. Fiscal and other incentives to promote participation and higher retirement savings.
- Improving the design of the overall pension system:
  - Improving the interaction between the labour market and the pension system, including mechanisms to work longer.
  - An analysis of the best way to design the basic pension to protect low-income groups in the light of the funded private pension system.
  - The need for two different sets of rules in the mandatory funded defined contribution system, one for public-sector workers (ISSSTE) and another one for private-sector workers (IMSS). Should they converge?
  - The convenience of maintaining a defined benefit pay-as-you-go system for State and public university employees.

Box 1.1. **Terms of reference for the OECD review of Mexico's retirement income provision** (cont.)

- Improving the design of the accumulation phase:
  - Approaches to promote low-cost retirement savings instruments.
  - Default investment strategies and life cycle strategies.
  - The wisdom of investment restrictions, in particular on foreign securities.
  - Risk-based supervision and the Value-At-Risk.
- Improving the design of the pay-out phase:
  - Different mechanisms to allocate assets accumulated at retirement: lump-sums, programme withdrawals and life annuities.
  - Pay-out phase and annuity markets.
  - Managing longevity risk (mortality tables, financial instrument to mitigate longevity risk, including longevity bonds).
- Policies to increase public understanding and the public's confidence in the pension system:
  - Strengthening the regulatory framework and governance of private pension funds (AFORE).
  - Pension statements and National Pension Communication Campaigns.

The review should also take account of the views of relevant stakeholders by way of a targeted consultation process.

A mission to Mexico took place 19-22 January 2015.

In addition, the review of the Mexican pension system considers current reform proposals under discussion. President Peña Nieto sent to Congress a reform proposal for the Social Security in 2013, which has three components:

- Universal pension;
- Unemployment insurance;
- Improvements to the Retirement Savings System (*Sistema de Ahorro para el Retiro*, SAR).

The Lower Chamber approved the reform proposal in April 2014. Its discussion and approval is since then pending in the Senate. The specific reform proposals related to the retirement savings system cover the following nine areas:

Reform proposal	Objective of the proposal
1. AFORE fee structure	Reduce fees and bring in more competition
2. AFORE switching model	Improve the quality of transfers and reduce business expenses of AFORE
3. Improve the assignment process of AFORE for new workers and non-continuous savers	Protect the interests of young workers and non-continuous savers
4. Incentives for voluntary pension savings	Encourage higher voluntary savings to reach higher pensions
5. AFORE's corporate governance	Strengthen investment decisions within AFORE to protect the savings of workers
6. Investment regime of SIEFORE	Introduce new investment alternatives to seek better returns
7. Facilitate the designation of beneficiaries	Make it easier for savers and their families to recover their savings in an AFORE
8. Better promotion and diffusion of savings for retirement	Better and more information for savers in the system
9. Better care and services to workers	Improve the experience of workers with their AFORE

1.2 Historical background to the changes experienced by the Mexican pension system since the 1990s

Mexico had a traditional defined benefit (DB) pay-as-you-go (PAYG) government run pension system until the mid-1990s.

The overhaul of the Mexican pension system started in 1992 with the creation of the Retirement Savings System (*Sistema de Ahorro para el Retiro*, SAR) for private- and public-sector workers affiliated respectively to the Mexican Institute of Social Security (*Instituto Mexicano del Seguro Social*, IMSS) and the Institute for Security and Social Services for State Workers (*Instituto de Seguridad y Servicios Sociales de los Trabajadores del Estado*, ISSSTE), introducing for the first time individual capitalisation accounts on a complementary basis to the DB PAYG public system.

In 1995, Mexico reformed its Social Security Law to address the growing actuarial deficit of the DB PAYG pension system for private-sector workers, and assure the system's financial sustainability. As a result, the IMSS DB system was definitely transformed into a defined contribution (DC) scheme, where workers own their accounts. Private-sector workers who were working or had contributed to the system at that moment still have the option at retirement of choosing their pension benefits according to the DB formula or according to the assets accumulated in their DC accounts.

In 2007, faced with large deficits as well the PAYG DB system for public-sector workers was also reformed, transforming the DB scheme into a DC scheme. The 2007 reform of ISSSTE gave public-sector workers who were working or had contributed to the system at that time the option to stay in the old DB system or to move to the new DC system. Those who chose the new DC system were granted a bonus that recognised their past tenure.

Mexico is consequently one of the few OECD countries that has reformed its mandatory pension system moving from DB PAYG to funded DC system and has made transparent its fiscal pension liabilities. The Mexican authorities argue that the reforms have led to substantial fiscal savings. Table 1.1 below shows fiscal savings of around 48.7 percentage points of GDP.

Table 1.1. **Actuarial deficit of reformed pension systems, as a % of GDP**

Institution	Before reform	After reform	Savings
IMSS	61.4	44.1	17.3
ISSSTE	45.6	23.0	22.6
Government companies (e.g. electricity)	8.6	6.0	2.6
IMSS workers (RPJ)	13.2	7.0	6.2
Total	**128.8**	**80.1**	**48.7**

Source: Mexican authorities.

1.3. Structure of the review

This review assesses the current Mexican pension system that has resulted from these reforms. The review also examines the period of transition between the old DB system and the new DC system that has resulted from allowing workers in the system at the time of the reforms to choose, either at retirement or at the time of the reform, between both systems.

The purpose of this review is therefore to identify areas that need to be improved and provide guidance on how to introduce these improvements to make the current Mexican pension system sustainable in the long term. Those improvements aim at ameliorating the fiscal sustainability of the system and the retirement income that people may receive from the system. The review uses the OECD's best practices on designing pension systems contained in the "OECD Roadmap for the Good Design of Defined Contribution Pension Plans" (OECD, 2012b), the *OECD Pensions at a Glance* (OECD, 2013), and the *OECD Pensions Outlook* (OECD, 2014b and 2012a).

The review is organised as follows. Chapter 2 describes succinctly the Mexican pension system. The Mexican pension system is mainly based on funded defined contribution individual accounts introduced in 1997. Therefore the "OECD Roadmap for the Good Design of Defined Contribution Pension Plans" (OECD, 2012b), endorsed and approved by pension regulators from OECD countries, is a key guide to assess the Mexican pension system.[1]

The Mexican pension system also has a public pension provision element. Public pensions first refer to the old defined benefit pension systems, which still cover workers who entered the labour market before the introduction of funded defined contribution individual accounts. The public pension provision also consists of a minimum guaranteed pension (*Pensión Mínima Garantizada*, PMG) and an alternative means-tested pension for people older than 65 (*Pensión para Adultos Mayores* or "65+").

1. The analysis supporting the Roadmap recommendations, contained in several chapters of the *OECD Pensions Outlook* 2012 and 2014 editions, would be also very useful.

Chapter 3 describes the Mexican public pension provision and presents proposals, based on best practices in other OECD countries, to reform the public pension system.

Chapter 4 addresses the implications of the transition period for the sustainability of the current pension system and provides recommendations. The transition period between the "old" DB system and the "new" DC system has resulted from allowing workers in the labour market or people having contributed to the system at the time the reforms were introduced to choose between both systems.

The coverage of the Mexican pension system as well as the level of contributions and the length of the contribution period, are the main factors explaining the potential problems with the amount of retirement income that the system may expect to deliver. Chapter 4 discusses how the combination of low contribution rates, low densities of contributions and high promises to transitional workers (those entitled to defined benefits) will lead to sharp declines in the amount of retirement income that people will receive once the last transitional worker has retired. The chapter then presents proposals based on OECD best practices on how to increase coverage and contribution levels (in both the mandatory and voluntary accounts). The review when discussing proposals to increase coverage/participation distinguishes among different types of informal workers. There are self-employed or independent workers who are not obliged to participate and other workers who despite having to participate and contribute they somehow fail to make contributions. The policies to increase coverage are different whether considering self-employed workers or workers who fail to make contributions.

Chapter 4 first looks at coverage distinguishing between people with active and inactive accounts. It provides information on mandatory and voluntary contributions and discusses the adequacy of having different mandatory contribution rates for private- and public-sector employees. The analysis also assesses the amount of contributions in an environment of uncertainty (financial market, labour market and demographic risks) necessary to achieve certain retirement income and/or replacement rates (*OECD Pensions Outlook 2012*, Chapter 6). The chapter then focuses on tax incentives to save for retirement. It describes the tax treatment of contributions, returns on investment and pension benefits and assesses different forms of implementing tax incentives and how current tax incentives combine with matching contributions. The chapter finally discusses options to increase coverage, contribution rates and contribution densities. Related to this, it discusses the pension statements and the National Pension Communication Campaigns.

Chapter 5 focuses on improving the design of the accumulation phase. The chapter addresses issues related to the costs and fees of pension funds and different approaches implemented to reduce these costs. The chapter also looks at different investment strategies, in particular the multi-funds age-related investment strategies of the AFORE and the defaults. It also discusses the different investment restrictions and the need for them. Other issues include risk-based supervision, governance and regulation in general. The chapter ends with some recommendations based on the OECD Roadmap for the Good Design of DC Pension Plans, the OECD Core Principles for Pension Fund Regulation, and the IOPS Principles for Supervision.

Chapter 6 discusses the current structure of the pay-out phase of the Mexican pension system and provides guidelines for improvements. The main recommendations are based on the OECD best practices contained in the "OECD Roadmap for the Good Design of DC Pension Plans" (OECD, 2012b), the *OECD Pensions Outlook* (OECD, 2014b) and the publication *Mortality Assumptions and Longevity Risk* (OECD, 2014a).

The chapter first introduces the main modalities that exist in Mexico to allocate assets accumulated in individual retirement accounts and thus finance retirement income. In this context, the chapter discusses the problems with the annuity market in Mexico and the type of annuity products available. The chapter also assesses the mortality tables used by annuity providers and pension funds, provides an assessment of the amount of longevity risk that they may be exposed to and discusses approaches to manage longevity risk in the context of the Mexican financial markets.

References

OECD (2014a), *Mortality Assumptions and Longevity Risk: Implications for pension funds and annuity providers*, OECD Publishing, Paris. DOI: *http://dx.doi.org/10.1787/9789264222748-en*

OECD (2014b), *OECD Pensions Outlook 2014*, OECD Publishing, Paris. DOI: *http://dx.doi.org/10.1787/9789264222687-en.*

OECD (2013), *Pensions at a Glance 2013: OECD and G20 Indicators*, OECD Publishing, Paris. DOI: *http://dx.doi.org/10.1787/pension_glance-2013-en.*

OECD (2012a), *OECD Pensions Outlook 2012*, OECD Publishing, Paris. DOI: *http://dx.doi.org/10.1787/9789264169401-en.*

OECD (2012b), "OECD Roadmap for the Good Design of Defined Contribution Pension Plans", *www.oecd.org/daf/fin/private-pensions/designingfundedpensionplans.htm.*

Chapter 2

The Mexican pension system today

This chapter succinctly describes the Mexican pension system. The Mexican pension system is mainly based on funded defined contribution individual accounts introduced in 1997 for private-sector workers and in 2007 for public-sector workers. The public pension component consists of the old pay-as-you-go defined benefit pension system, which still covers workers who entered the labour market before the introduction of funded defined contribution individual accounts, a minimum guaranteed pension and an alternative means-tested non-contributory pension for people older than 65.

2.1. Overview of the Mexican pension system

The Mexican pension system has four components: i) the federal and state non-contributory (first-tier) pension schemes, (ii) the mandatory defined contribution Retirement Savings System (*Sistema de Ahorro para el Retiro*, SAR), (iii) special pension schemes for certain public-sector employees and state universities, and (iv) individual and occupational voluntary pension plans.

The most important nationwide non-contributory scheme in Mexico, called the pension for the elderly (*Pensión para Adultos Mayores*), is funded by the federal budget. The programme started in 2007 and initially provided a pension to everyone aged 70 or over who lived in towns with populations up to 30 000 inhabitants. In 2012, the pension for the elderly was extended to all the country, and was granted to all those people who did not receive an old-age pension from any social security institution above a certain threshold. Starting in 2013, the programme was extended to cover all people aged 65 and over. In addition to the federal scheme, some states also have their own non-contributory scheme.

The main component of the Mexican pension system is the Retirement Savings System (SAR). This is a mandatory defined contribution (DC) fully funded system with individual accounts. All private-sector employees who entered the labour force on or after 1 July 1997 and most public-sector employees who entered the labour force on or after 1 April 2007 have an individual account in the SAR. Mandatory contributions from employees, employers and the government are deposited in these individual accounts which are invested in pension funds known as SIEFORE (*Sociedades de Inversión Especializadas en Fondos para el Retiro*) and managed by specialised private managers known as AFORE (*Administradoras de Fondos para el Retiro*).

The Retirement Savings System was created in 1992 when the revised Social Security Law was passed. This Law included for the first time funded DC individual accounts that were intended to complement the existing pay-as-you-go (PAYG), defined benefit (DB) public pension system. It mandated a 2% contribution from employers. The reform did not however address the financial unsustainability of the system. As a result, in December 1995 the Mexican Congress enacted a new Social Security Law. In April 1996, a second package established the legal and organisational framework (SAR Law).[1] The new SAR Law substituted the old PAYG DB system for a mandatory DC fully funded system with individual accounts for private-sector employees, complemented with a minimum pension guarantee by the government. It started on 1 July 1997, without any change for the affiliates who were pensioned before that date. In addition, workers who had accumulated pension rights before that date were granted the option to choose at retirement which system (the old DB system, under the 1973 Law, or the new DC system, under the 1997 Law) will be used to determine their pension benefits.

In December 2002, public-sector employees were given the right to voluntarily open an individual account in the AFORE of their choice. However, since the reform of the Law of the Institute for Security and Social Services for State Workers (ISSSTE Law) in 2007, all ISSSTE affiliates have been incorporated to a mandatory individual account pension system, with different rules than that for private-sector workers.[2]

Local governments, municipalities, public universities and state-owned companies (e.g. the oil company PEMEX) have their own pension scheme for their employees.

These systems have different features. Some are DB schemes, while others have migrated to DC schemes at least for new employees.

Voluntary contributions to individual accounts are allowed for employees contributing to the SAR, self-employed workers and informal workers. Some companies also offer to their employees access to occupational pension plans. Some of these plans are partially funded and may be defined benefit, defined contribution or hybrid. Finally, insurance companies and financial groups offer personal pension arrangements with various modalities.

2.2. Non-contributory pension for the elderly

The pension for the elderly (*Pensión para Adultos Mayores*) is a means-tested non-contributory safety net programme funded by the federal budget. It covers people aged 65 and older who do not receive an old-age pension or disability benefits higher than MXN 1 092 per month.[3] It provides a financial support of MXN 580 per month as of 2015. Several states have their own old-age safety net programmes, but the pension for the elderly is the most important nationwide safety net programme (see Chapter 3 for more details about safety nets).

2.3. The Retirement Savings System (SAR)

The Retirement Savings System comprises two social security schemes:

- the Mexican Institute of Social Security (*Instituto Mexicano del Seguro Social*, IMSS), which covers private-sector employees; and
- the Institute for Security and Social Services for State Workers (*Instituto de Seguridad y Servicios Sociales de los Trabajadores del Estado*, ISSSTE), which covers public-sector employees.[4]

Formal-sector employees (i.e. those paying social security contributions), except those covered by special regimes (see Chapter 3), must be enrolled to one of the aforementioned institutions (i.e. IMSS or ISSSTE) for old-age contributory pension entitlements. Once enrolled, formal-sector employees are eligible to select any AFORE of their choice. Workers can switch between AFORE once a year, given that they have been members of their current AFORE for at least one year.[5]

Self-employed workers do not have the legal obligation to become affiliates and make contributions into the compulsory pension system. They can nevertheless voluntarily open an individual account in the AFORE of their choice and make non-compulsory contributions since 2005.

The AFORE charge fees that are deducted from the workers' personal accounts. They can only charge fees on assets under management. They cannot charge, for example, workers any fee for switching to a different AFORE.

Additionally, the National Housing Fund Institute for Workers (*Instituto del Fondo Nacional de la Vivienda para los Trabajadores*, INFONAVIT) and the Housing Fund of the Institute for Security and Social Services for State Workers (*Fondo de la Vivienda del Instituto de Seguridad y Servicios Sociales de los Trabajadores del Estado*, FOVISSSTE) provide housing credits, where the accumulated funds left when reaching retirement are used to finance retirement.

Each individual retirement account, whether under the schemes for private and public-sector employees, comprises three sub-accounts:

- The retirement sub-account (*Subcuenta de Retiro, Cesantía en Edad Avanzada, y Vejez*, RCV): In this sub-account, workers, employers and the government make mandatory contributions to cover retirement insurance, severance at old-age and old-age.
- The voluntary savings sub-account: In this sub-account, the worker or employer freely decides to contribute in order to increase the balance in the employee's individual account.
- The housing sub-account: This sub-account comprises mandatory contributions that employers make to the housing fund managed by the relevant housing fund institute (INFONAVIT or FOVISSSTE), on behalf of their workers (5% of the salary). In case the worker obtains a loan from the housing fund institute, the resources in the sub-account will be used to pay the down payment and the following contributions to service the debt. Under the 1973 Law, any remaining balance at retirement is withdrawn as a lump sum; under the 1997 Law, any remaining balance is transferred from INFONAVIT to the AFORE to complement the employee's pension.

2.3.1. Private-sector employees affiliated to the IMSS

Private-sector workers affiliated to the IMSS are required to have an individual retirement account in the AFORE of their choice. They have the possibility to change AFORE under certain situations as regulated by the Mexican pension regulator (CONSAR). If a worker does not choose an AFORE, the SAR Law stipulates that his/her individual account must be assigned, on a temporary basis, to one of the AFORE that have achieved the largest net returns over a predetermined period. These workers are known as "assigned workers" to distinguish them from the rest of the workers affiliated to the IMSS that have made an active choice of an AFORE.

The total employee, employer and government contribution to the retirement sub-account is 6.5% of salary, of which 1.125% is paid by the employee, 5.15% by the employer and 0.225% by the government (Table 2.1). Contributions are based on the employee's basic salary for contributions, up to a ceiling of 25 times the minimum wage. The government supplements the total contribution with a social contribution called the social quota (*cuota social*) to support affiliates and thus increase the final account balance. This social quota is on top of the 0.225% contribution and depends on the salary level. It is provided for each day of contribution and is updated quarterly in line with inflation.

Table 2.1. **Contributions to the retirement sub-account for private-sector workers**

As a % of the basic salary for contributions, except for the social quota

	Employer	Worker	Federal government	Total
Retirement	2%			2%
Severance and old-age	3.15%	1.125%	0.225%	4.5%
Social quota*			Up to MXN 4.78 daily	Up to MXN 4.78 daily

Note: Social quota in force in November and December 2014. No social quota paid for income above 15 times the minimum wage.

The social quota was initially a flat-rate amount. However, since the amendment of the Social Security Law in May 2009, the amount of the social quota slightly decreases with income. In 2014, its amount declined from about 7% of earnings at the minimum wage to about 1.3% at 5 times the minimum wage and 0.4% at the ceiling of 15 times the minimum wage; for wages above this level no subsidy is paid. During the last quarter of 2014, 89.1% of the private-sector workers affiliated to the IMSS with an active account have received the social quota.[6] Table 2.2 provides the social quota in force in November and December 2014.

Table 2.2. **Social quota by wage level, November to December 2014**

Wage	Social quota (pesos per day)	Social quota as a % of the wage (upper limit)	Total contribution (6.5% + social quota)*
Up to 1 minimum wage	4.78130	7.11	13.61
Between 1.01 and 4 times the minimum wage	4.58208	1.70	8.20
Between 4.01 and 7 times the minimum wage	4.38286	0.93	7.43
Between 7.01 and 10 times the minimum wage	4.18364	0.62	7.12
Between 10.01 and 15 times the minimum wage	3.98442	0.39	6.89
Above 15 times the minimum wage	0	0	6.50

Note: * The 6.5% represents the total employee, employer and government contribution to the retirement sub-account.

2.3.2. Public-sector employees affiliated to the ISSSTE

Public-sector workers affiliated to the ISSSTE are required to have an individual retirement account in the AFORE managed by ISSSTE (PensionISSSTE) or any other AFORE of their choice. Individual retirement accounts are funded by contributions from the employee and the employer (state departments and related bodies), plus the social quota paid by the federal government.

The total employee and employer contribution to the retirement sub-account is 11.3% of salary, of which 6.125% is paid by the employee and 5.175% by the employer (state departments and related bodies) (Table 2.3). Contributions are based on the employee's basic salary for contributions, up to a ceiling of 10 times the minimum wage. The government supplements the total contribution with a flat-rate social quota. This amount is equivalent to 5.5% of the general minimum wage in Mexico City on 1 July 1997, updated quarterly in accordance with the National Consumer Price Index. It is paid for each day of contribution for workers earning less than 10 times the minimum wage. During the last quarter of 2014, 99.6% of the public-sector workers affiliated to the ISSSTE with an active account have received the social quota.

Table 2.3. **Contributions to the retirement sub-account for public-sector workers**

As a % of the basic salary for contributions, except for the social quota

	Employer	Worker	Federal government	Total
Retirement	2%	6.125%		8.125%
Severance and old-age	3.175%			3.175%
Social quota*			MXN 3.98442 daily	MXN 3.98442 daily

Note: Social quota in force in November and December 2014. No social quota paid for income equal to 10 times the minimum wage or above.

The new ISSSTE Law provides a portability scheme for the transfer of savings accumulated under the ISSSTE scheme to the new IMSS scheme, and vice versa, when workers switch jobs between the public and private sectors.[7]

2.3.3. Transitional workers

Transitional workers in the private sector are those employees who were working and contributing to the PAYG system in place before 1 July 1997. Although these workers began contributing to their new mandatory individual retirement account after this date, they retained the right to have their pension benefits at retirement calculated using the old DB formula. A lifetime switch option allows transitional generation workers to choose at retirement the higher of the acquired benefits under the old PAYG DB system and the accumulated balances in their individual retirement accounts under the new funded DC system. If they choose to receive benefits according to the old DB rules, some of the assets accumulated in the individual retirement account are transferred to the federal government to pay the DB benefits, while the rest of the assets (potentially accumulated in different accounts, including SAR IMSS 1992, INFONAVIT 1992, the retirement sub-account, INFONAVIT 1997, and voluntary contributions) are paid as a lump sum.[8]

All public-sector workers who were ISSSTE affiliates at the time the ISSSTE Law was approved in 2007 had the right to choose to switch to the new funded DC scheme or to remain in the old PAYG DB plan.[9] The affiliates had a time limit of six months to choose between these two options, starting 1 January 2008.

The ISSSTE affiliates who chose to move to the new DC system (only 14.2%) received a "recognition bond", paid by the federal government, acknowledging their rights for the periods of time in which they made contributions prior to the reform. This recognition bond was credited in the individual account of the affiliates, redeemable only when close to retirement. Those who had no account in an AFORE at the time of the reform were automatically registered with PensionISSSTE for the first three years. That period ended in December 2011. Since then, workers can transfer their individual accounts to any AFORE of their choice or stay in PensionISSSTE. Since that same date, PensionISSSTE is also able to receive the transfers of individual accounts of private-sector workers or self-employed workers.

New rules regarding the minimum retirement age and the contribution rate apply to ISSSTE affiliates who decided to remain in the old DB scheme (85.8%): the minimum retirement age is being increased gradually from 50 to 60 for men and from 48 to 58 for women by 2028; the contribution rate of workers for retirement increased gradually from 3.5% to 6.125% of the wage contribution base over the six years following the reform. In addition, contributions are directly paid to the ISSSTE to finance the PAYG system, except the 2% employer contribution for retirement insurance, which is deposited in an individual retirement account managed exclusively by PensionISSSTE.

2.3.4. Asset management

Specialised private asset managers (*Administradoras de Fondos para el Retiro*) known as AFORE manage the workers' individual retirement accounts where the IMSS and the ISSSTE deposit the contributions after collecting them. The AFORE place contributions in investment funds called SIEFORE. Thus, AFORE manage individual retirement accounts, while SIEFORE invest the assets generated in those accounts. Workers can choose their AFORE and are free to switch between them once a year.

Currently, AFORE must have four basic SIEFORE for investing the compulsory savings, and they may have additional SIEFORE for voluntary contributions and occupational pension plans. Each basic SIEFORE has a specific investment regime that depends on the age of the worker. This multi-fund system composes a life-cycle scheme. As members are getting older, their pension assets are invested in a more conservative investment regime (with lower exposure to equity and a greater proportion of fixed-income instruments) to reduce the volatility of their returns. Thus, a young worker will gradually move from basic SIEFORE 4 (SB4 up to 36 years old) to SB3 (from 37 to 45 years old), SB2 (from 46 to 59 years old) and finally SB1 (60 years and older). Nonetheless, any worker may opt to invest his/her resources in a more conservative fund than the default option.

2.3.5. Retirement benefits

There are different requirements for public and private-sector workers to be eligible for an old-age pension under the Retirement Savings System. Private-sector workers affiliated to the IMSS need to have contributed 1 250 weeks (24 years plus 2 weeks) and to have reached 65 years of age. Public-sector workers affiliated to the ISSSTE need to have contributed 25 years and to have reached 65 years of age. When the worker does not meet the previous requirements for obtaining an old-age pension, the IMSS or the ISSSTE gives a negative statement to the worker (*negativa de pensión*). In this case, the member can withdraw the total accumulated balance in the individual account all at once at age 65.

When a worker fulfils the age and contribution weeks requirements, retirement benefits are determined based on the accumulated balances in individual retirement accounts managed by the AFORE, plus any remaining balance in the housing sub-account managed by INFONAVIT or FOVISSSTE.

There is a minimum lifetime annuity payment to all workers (public or private) affiliated either to the IMSS or the ISSSTE who fulfil the requirements for a pension. The federal government guarantees this minimum in the event that the value of the worker's accumulated retirement account balances is not sufficient to finance a minimum pension level. The amount of this minimum guaranteed pension (*pensión mínima garantizada*, PMG) is lower for private-sector workers affiliated to the IMSS (equivalent to MXN 31 211.52 annually as of December 2014) than for public-sector workers affiliated to the ISSSTE (equivalent to MXN 48 650.04 annually as of December 2014). The PMG is adjusted every year to the Consumer Price Index. The guaranteed pension is paid in the beginning with the existing balance in the individual account, and when this balance is depleted, is funded from the federal budget.

In case the accumulated balances in the worker's individual retirement account are sufficient to finance a minimum pension level, the worker can choose between two pension modalities:

- Life annuity: The worker signs an irrevocable contract with the insurance company of his/her choice to buy an annuity. Under this contract, the worker transfers ownership of his/her funds in the individual account to the insurance company and the latter commits to pay him/her a monthly pension for life, indexed to inflation. A life annuity can only be bought by workers who have enough funds to obtain a pension that is equal to or higher than the guaranteed pension in effect at the time that he/she chooses this modality.

- Programmed withdrawals: In this case, the worker's balance in the individual retirement account is still managed by the AFORE and therefore continues to obtain the returns of the corresponding SIEFORE. The AFORE pays the pension through monthly withdrawals from the individual account until its balance is depleted. The amount of the monthly payment is adjusted annually taking into account the life expectancy of the pensioner at the time of the recalculation and the new balance in the individual account, which includes return earned in the last period and discounting the payments made. However, payments are not adjusted to inflation. The amount of the programmed withdrawal plan cannot be lower than the guaranteed pension. If in the periodic recalculation, the resulting amount were below the guaranteed pension, the AFORE would pay the pensioner a monthly amount equivalent to the guaranteed pension until the balance is depleted. Finally, the pensioner who opts for programmed withdrawals can buy at any time a life annuity if the life annuity value can be funded with the remaining balance.

Notwithstanding age, if the worker has accumulated enough assets to buy a life annuity equivalent to 1.3 times the minimum guaranteed pension, he or she has the right to buy such an annuity and withdraw the rest of the assets as a lump sum.

Table 2.4 summarises the different retirement benefit options for IMSS and ISSSTE affiliates.

Table 2.4. **Retirement benefit options for IMSS and ISSSTE affiliates**

Age	Required contribution period		Accumulated assets in individual account	Retirement income
	IMSS	ISSSTE		
65	< 1 250 weeks	< 25 years	Total balance	Lump sum
65	> 1 250 weeks	> 25 years	Life annuity* < PMG	PMG
65	> 1 250 weeks	> 25 years	Life annuity* > PMG	Programmed withdrawals or life annuity
	> 1 250 weeks	> 25 years	Life annuity* > 1.3 x PMG	Life annuity of 1.3 x PMG and rest as a lump sum

Note *: The life annuity that the individual can afford with his or her account balance.

Early retirement between 60 and 64 years old is possible provided that the worker is not employed and has contributed at least 1 250 weeks for private-sector workers (respectively 25 years for public-sector workers).

Private-sector workers are entitled to make partial withdrawals from the balance in their individual account in two cases: unemployment or marriage. Public-sector workers are entitled to make partial withdrawals from the balance in their individual account only in case of unemployment. These withdrawals also reduce weeks of contributions.

2.4. Special pension schemes

State-owned companies (e.g. the oil company PEMEX and the Federal Electricity Company), the Armed Forces, IMSS, teachers, Courts (e.g. the Supreme Court and the Federal Council of Justice), the Central Bank and the development banking institutions, have their own pension scheme for their employees. These systems have different features. Some are DB schemes, while others have migrated to DC schemes at least for new employees.

Local governments (31 sovereign states, one federal district and about 2 450 municipalities) and the 55 public universities also have their own pension schemes, mostly DB and without portability. Moreover, there is no interaction between the federal and the local systems.

2.5. Voluntary pension savings

Any worker can make four types of voluntary contributions into their individual accounts as follows:

- Short-term voluntary contributions: These contributions can be withdrawn partially or entirely before retirement. The minimum period to hold these contributions in the individual account is from two to six months after being made, depending on the AFORE.
- Complementary contributions to individual retirement accounts: These contributions can only be withdrawn at retirement as a lump sum or can supplement the worker's pension. They may be deducted from income tax up to four times the minimum annual salary or 10% of annual incomes, whichever is the lowest.
- Long-term voluntary contributions: These contributions can only be withdrawn at retirement age or in the event of disability or incapacity for remunerated work. They may be deducted from taxable income on the same fashion as the complementary retirement contributions.
- Contributions to special "savings for retirement" accounts: These contributions allow the deferral of tax payments until their withdrawal, which can be made after at least five years have elapsed from the date of the voluntary contribution. The maximum annual amount of contributions qualifying for tax exemption is MXN 152 000.

In addition, those public-sector employees who are affiliated to the ISSSTE benefit from a very generous matched-contribution scheme called Solidarity Savings (Ahorro Solidario). This scheme gives workers an attractive incentive to make voluntary contributions of between 1-2% of their earnings (capped at 10x the minimum wage), with the government adding 3.25 pesos for every 1 peso contributed. A recent reform proposal seeks to provide a similar matching scheme for private-sector workers. It would likely be far less generous, however, with the government only adding 20 cents for every 1 peso contributed, up to a 300-pesos annual limit (less than 1% of the minimum wage).

Notes

1. The Social Security Law establishes the mandatory pension scheme for private-sector employees, regulates coverage, contributions and the relationship between the old publicly-managed social security scheme and the mandatory private pension scheme. The SAR Law defines the structure and powers of CONSAR and regulates the establishment, operation and supervision of the AFORE and the SIEFORE.

2. The ISSSTE Law sets the mandatory pension system for Federal employees, regulates coverage, contributions and provides parametric reforms to the old system to regulate the provision of defined benefit pensions from the old system.

3. The amount is set according to the so-called "well-being lines" calculated by the social agency in charge of measuring poverty (CONEVAL). For more information, visit: www.coneval.gob.mx.

4. These two social security institutes provide not only pension-related services (old-age, severance at old-age and retirement insurance) but also health care services (including maternity, childcare and disability).

5. The worker can also change AFORE before one year under specific circumstances.

6. Active accounts are defined as those that received at least one contribution during the last three years.

7. There is no portability between any of the two old DB systems, neither between the old and the new schemes.

8. Resources in the housing sub-account are managed by the INFONAVIT and only appear in the AFORE statement for information purposes.

9. ISSSTE affiliates who started to contribute before 2007 but were inactive when the Law was passed did not have the right to choose between the two systems when re-entering the system. They automatically had to switch to the new DC scheme.

Chapter 3

The public pension system in Mexico

This chapter first describes the public pay-as-you-go defined benefit pension system. It presents and discusses the eligibility criteria for the contributory schemes and the benefit levels for both private and public-sector workers. It gives an overview of the financial prospects of pension provision and highlights the strong fragmentation of the pension system in Mexico. Secondly, the chapter focuses on issues related to the design of the minimum contributory pensions and of the elderly safety nets. It concludes with pension policy options to improve the design of the public provision.

The statistical data for Israel are supplied by and under the responsibility of the relevant Israeli authorities. The use of such data by the OECD is without prejudice to the status of the Golan Heights, East Jerusalem and Israeli settlements in the West Bank under the terms of international law.

3.1. Introduction

The preceding chapter laid out the main changes the Mexican pension system has been going through over the last two decades, in 1997 for the private sector and in 2007 for the public sector. Financial sustainability issues have been the main drivers of these structural reforms. Retirement-income adequacy will be reduced over time as a result, though safety nets for the most vulnerable older workers have also been provided albeit to a limited extent.

Overall, substantial demographic changes (Figure 3.1) will put fiscal pressure given the long transition of the past reforms and the numerous schemes that have not been reformed yet (see section 3.5). Mexico has been experiencing, as many other countries, continuous improvements in life expectancy and a very steep decline in birthrates over the last decades. The population aged over 65 years has been approximately doubling every 20 years although its growth is expected to slow after 2030. Overall it is projected to increase from 3.7 million in 1990 to 31.5 million in 2050, which implies an average annual growth rate of 3.6% compared to 1.0% for the total population. Hence, the Mexican population is expected to age at a much faster pace than OECD countries on average (Figure 3.2). While today the old-age dependency ratio is still below the OECD average level, it is projected to catch up fully by 2070.

Figure 3.1. **Demographic projections in Mexico**

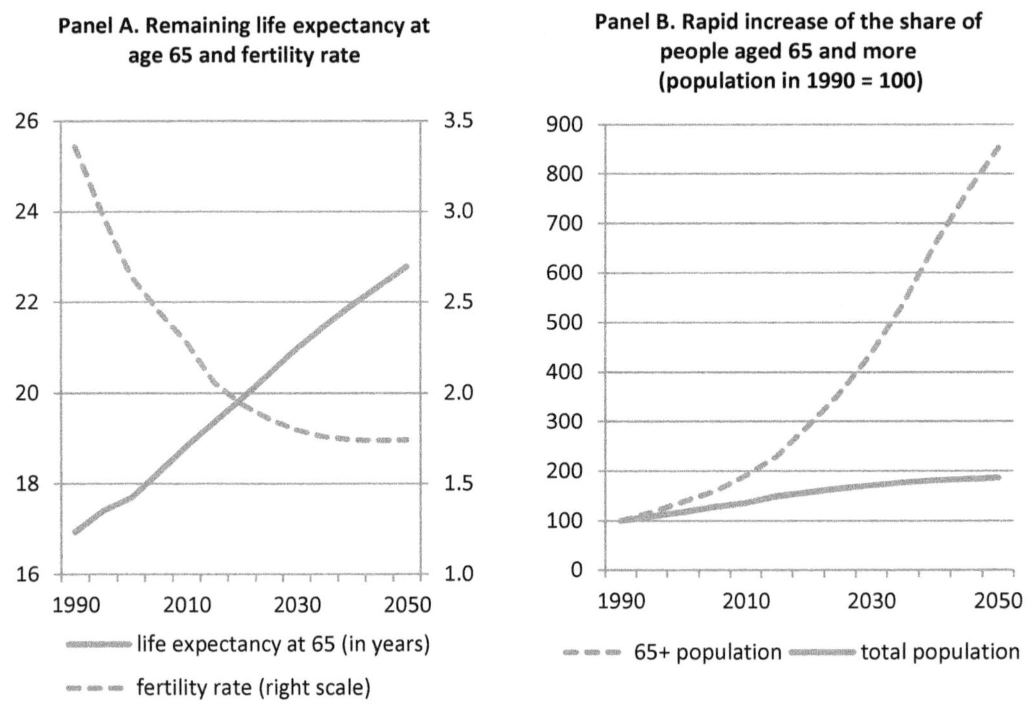

Source: United Nations data, World Population Prospects – 2012 Revision.

Figure 3.2. **Old-age dependency ratio, %**

Population aged over 65 divided by the 20-64 population

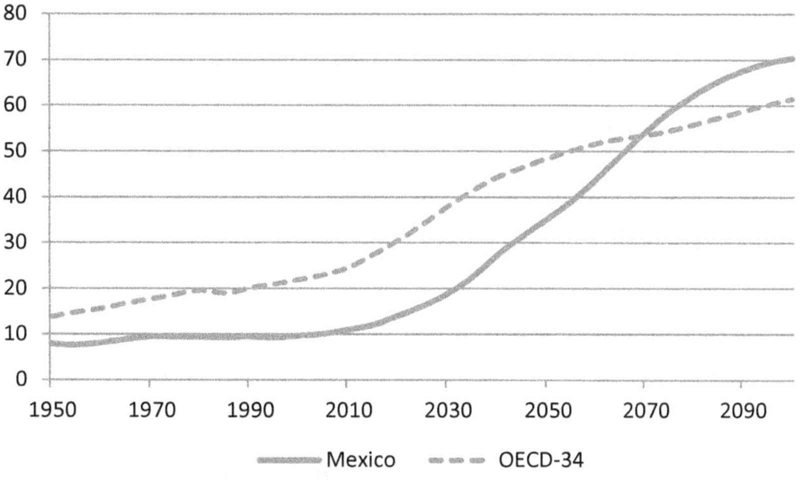

Source: United Nations data, World Population Prospects – 2012 Revision.

Addressing labour market informality is the biggest challenge for pension systems in Latin-American countries overall (OECD, 2014a), and it is also crucial for Mexico in order to ensure adequate pensions. As the contributory pension system covers formal sector workers who are in dependent employment and registered, a large part of the working-age population is not reached. According to the official definition of informality provided by the Statistical Office (INEGI) (which includes all employed population who work in unregistered economic units, workers in paid domestic work without social security, self-employed workers in subsistence agriculture, unpaid workers and subordinates who work without the protection of social security in registered economic units), 58% of the labour force worked in the informal economy in December 2014. Moreover, mobility between the formal and informal sectors is high, which generates significant contribution gaps.

As a result, only 25% of the population aged over 65 received an old-age contributory pension in 2010 (Villagómez and Ramírez, 2013). Informality generally means that transfers (including pension) are typically less redistributive, especially if safety nets are weak. Reducing the size of the informal sector is a policy challenge that goes far beyond the reach of pension reforms and needs to be addressed by a range of labour market, tax and structural economic policies. This report does not discuss the full range of policies needed but focuses on reforms to improve both the functioning of the contributory pension system and the safety nets for the protection of elderly Mexicans who remain outside of the formal pension system.

The pension system remains strongly fragmented as discussed below in more detail even though, according to Aguirre (2012), about 30% of the country's pension schemes have been reformed. As discussed in Chapter 2, the main components of the Mexican multi-tier pension system are:

- A means-tested safety net (65+ programme) financed by general taxation;

- Two main and significantly different systems which are mandatory and contributory. They are administered by IMSS (*Instituto Mexicano de Seguro Social*) and ISSSTE (*Instituto de Seguridad y Servicios Sociales de los Trabajadores del Estado*) covering private-sector and public-sector workers, respectively. Even the contribution rate and minimum pension schemes differ between IMSS and ISSSTE. Both systems were subject to a major structural reform replacing the pay-as-you-go defined benefit system by individual funded defined-contribution accounts which are phased in during a long transition period. The reform took place in 1997 for IMSS and 2007 for ISSSTE;
- Individual and occupational voluntary plans.

In addition, some states, local authorities and public universities, other public entities and various professions run their own independent pension systems. Overall, depending on data sources, between 40 and 45% of the economically active population are covered by the main contributory systems: 31-35% by IMSS, 5-6% by ISSSTE and 3-5% by state governments, municipalities, public universities and state-owned companies (Alonso et al., 2014; AMIS, 2014). Beyond its direct impact on public finance, such fragmentation is an obstacle to the optimal management of the overall system, to transparency, equity and the efficient labour mobility.

Since 1997 all private-sector workers have to choose an investment management company (AFORE) in order to open individual pension accounts (Chapter 2). Yet, anyone who had contributed at least once to the system prior to July 1997 can still decide at the time of retirement whether their benefit is paid according to the rules and formula of the old DB scheme, i.e. subject to the 1973 Law, based on their contributions made over their entire career or from their DC assets accumulated since 1997. This explains why individuals who started to contribute in the private sector before 1997 are generally referred to as "transitional workers".

Faced with financial difficulties in the parametric design of its public pension systems, Mexico made the choice of entirely replacing a (public) mandatory DB scheme by a (private) mandatory DC scheme, as Chile had done in 1981. In doing so, longevity risks have been shifted from the Mexican government to the annuity providers and to those retirees who choose to withdraw their pension as programmed withdrawals or who are not eligible to a pension. When introducing DC plans, other countries have often – although much less so in Latin America - reduced the generosity of the DB schemes, thus opting for a more balanced approach to diversify the sources of financing and to benefit from the complementarity of various schemes.

This chapter focuses on the public defined-benefit pension system, which will still be in place for a long period. The next section presents the eligibility criteria for the contributory schemes. Section 3.3 discusses the benefit levels for both the private and the public sectors. Section 3.4 gives an overview of the financial prospects of pension provision while section 3.5 highlights the strong fragmentation of the pension system in Mexico. Section 3.6 focuses on the minimum contributory pensions and on the elderly safety nets, and the last section concludes with some pension policy options currently available to improve the design of the public provision.

3.2. Age parameters and contribution periods

The normal retirement age to access a full pension is 65 years. The minimum contributory period to be entitled to a pension in the old private-sector system, which still applies to transitional workers, is only 500 weeks (about 10 years). The 1997 reform increased it to 1 250 weeks (about 24 years) for new entrants (in the defined-contribution system). Under the 1973 Law, contributions made for less than 500 weeks do not lead to any pension entitlement and are thus lost for the individual.

Early retirement is possible from age 60 for both men and women in the old system with a 5 percentage-point penalty for each year of anticipation. Despite this, in December 2014, about 80% of pensioners receiving a pension from IMSS based on the 1973 Law had retired before the age of 65. Working an extra year beyond the age of 65 increases the replacement rate by 0.6 percentage point at the minimum wage level, and by 2.5 points for wages exceeding 6 times the minimum wage.[1] Financial incentives to prolong the working life beyond 65 are thus very weak and far from actuarial neutrality.[2] [3]

Moreover, in the old system, survivor's benefits (i.e. benefits paid to the surviving spouse) amount to 90% of the deceased's pension, which is much higher than the OECD average of 64% and second only to the United States (100%) (OECD, 2014b). When one spouse dies, total household expenditure falls by about 25% due to household economies of scale (see e.g. James, 2009). While the primary goal of survivor pensions is to maintain or protect the survivor's standard of living on bereavement, 90% of their deceased partner's pension is awarded to the survivor, a proportion which tends to increase the survivor's standard of living substantially.

In the DB public-sector scheme, ISSSTE, the retirement age is not the key parameter for the decision to retire. Civil servants are eligible to a full pension after 28 years of contributions only for women and 30 years only for men. This implies that a male civil servant who had started his career at age 20 could retire with a full pension, i.e. with 100% of his final salary at age 50. Age requirements were added in 2010, starting from 49 years for women and 51 years for men. This age threshold will be increasing by one year every two years to 58 and 60 years respectively in 2028. While this is a fast adjustment pace, the retirement age will remain very low in 2028 given the starting point.

Each missing contribution year in the old ISSSTE scheme progressively reduces the replacement rate down to 50% with a 15-year contribution period. The age requirement was 56 until 2010 and has been increasing by one year every two years to reach 60 in 2018 onward. Early retirement is possible at age 60 with 10 years of contribution and a 40% replacement rate. The early-retirement replacement rate increases by 2 percentage points per year of anticipation up to 50% at age 65. Since 2010, the 60 age limit has been increasing by one year every two years and will reach 65 from 2018 onwards, which implies that this early-retirement route will be shut.

3.3. Pension benefits

3.3.1. Private-sector workers

Given that transitional workers can choose the system from which benefits are drawn upon retirement, it is crucial to compare the replacement rates provided by the old and the new systems.

Retirement benefits and conditions in the old system are very generous relative to the level of contributions paid (see Box 3.1 for a description of the rules for the old DB formula for private-sector workers). Figure 3.3, Panel A shows projected gross replacement rates at age 65 across various earnings levels for a worker having contributed during 45 years ("full career"), 35 years and 25 years. The reference wage is the average nominal wage of the last 250 weeks (about 5 years) capped at 25 times the minimum wage. The DB pension amount rises with the contribution period. Accounting for an 11% bonus which applies to all pensioners older than 60 years, the replacement rate is 100% for a full-career worker with earnings below the threshold of 25 times the minimum wage (about 6 times the average wage). At low-wage levels, it remains high, close to 100% for a worker having contributed for 25 years. However, for higher wages, the replacement rate declines more steeply with shorter contribution periods. Thus, for a worker with a reference wage equal to 3 times the average wage, the replacement rates are 100%, 83% and 56% with a 45-year, 35-year and 25-year contribution period, respectively. In 2010, the Supreme Court ruled that the reference-wage ceiling should be lowered to 10 times the minimum wage or about 2.5 times the average wage, which would reduce replacement rates of high-wage earners and lower public spending. The decision of the Supreme Court has, however, not been enforced yet. The ceiling of 10 times the minimum wage would be in line with the ceiling in the disability and death insurance scheme. The legislative response so far, which is now pending in the Senate, has been to try to harmonise these ceilings but at 25 times the minimum wage instead.

Under the 1973 Law, for a minimum contribution period of 500 weeks, workers can retire on minimum pension, which is equal to the minimum wage thus providing a high replacement rate. The implicit internal return on past contributions is thus very high especially given the low level of the contribution rates (Chapter 4). Moreover, a gross replacement rate of 100% actually implies a higher disposable income in retirement relative to income while working, as pensioners save on contributions and benefit from some tax exemptions.

Workers who started to contribute before 1997 can opt if they are eligible: either for the DB pension including the minimum pension; for the DC pension; or, if their cumulated DC assets are not enough to buy an annuity equivalent to the minimum guaranteed pension (PMG), for the PMG under the 1997 Law, which requires 1 250 weeks of contributions but generates a higher benefit level than the 1973 minimum pension (see sub-section 3.6.2 for more detail). That is why some pensioners have chosen the new regime. In December 2014, there were slightly more than 1.7 million of old-age pensions paid by IMSS, 43% of which were minimum pensions under the 1973 Law and less than 1% were the PMG.

Under the new scheme, the projected replacement rates are much lower even under the assumption that the accumulated assets yield very high returns (Figure 3.3, Panel B). Pensioners with earnings close to the minimum wage and who will have contributed enough to be eligible to the PMG are projected to have replacement rates around 60-70%. But as earnings increase, the gross replacement rate falls steeply below 35% for earnings above half the average wage and to 26% for the average-wage worker. Based on OECD pension model projections, a full-career worker earning below 0.65 times the average earnings (or about 2.5 times the minimum wage) throughout the whole career would receive the PMG. When the total 5 percentage-point INFONAVIT contributions (see Chapter 2) are taken into account (assuming the same return as in the DC accounts), the replacement rate increases by 15-20 percentage points beyond average earnings (Panel B).

Box 3.1. **Rules for the calculation of private-sector workers' pension when choosing the old DB formula**

A minimum of 500 weeks of contributions is required to get a pension under the old DB formula. The annual pension is composed of a basic amount and annual increments calculated according to the number of weeks of contributions in excess of the minimum 500 weeks. The basic amount and the increments are calculated by applying the following percentages to the average salary over the last 250 weeks of contributions:

Salary expressed as multiple of the general minimum wage in Mexico City	Basic amount (% of the salary)	Annual increment (% of the salary)
Up to 1	80.00	0.563
From 1.01 to 1.25	77.11	0.814
From 1.26 to 1.50	58.18	1.178
From 1.51 to 1.75	49.23	1.430
From 1.76 to 2.00	42.67	1.615
From 2.01 to 2.25	37.65	1.756
From 2.26 to 2.50	33.68	1.868
From 2.51 to 2.75	30.48	1.958
From 2.76 to 3.00	27.83	2.033
From 3.01 to 3.25	25.60	2.096
From 3.26 to 3.50	23.70	2.149
From 3.51 to 3.75	22.07	2.195
From 3.76 to 4.00	20.65	2.235
From 4.01 to 4.25	19.39	2.271
From 4.26 to 4.50	18.32	2.302
From 4.51 to 4.75	17.30	2.330
From 4.76 to 5.00	16.41	2.355
From 5.01 to 5.25	15.61	2.377
From 5.26 to 5.50	14.88	2.398
From 5.51 to 5.75	14.22	2.416
From 5.76 to 6.00	13.62	2.433
6.00 and above	13.00	2.450

For an incomplete year of contributions, half of the annual increment is taken into account between 13 and 26 weeks and the full increment for more than 26 weeks. The salary used to determine the income group and to which the percentages are applied to calculate the basic amount and the annual increment corresponds to the average salary over the last 250 weeks of contribution. Thus, for example, an individual with a 45-year career with an average salary over the last 250 weeks of contributions equal to four times the minimum wage has contributed 1 840 weeks (i.e. 35 years and 20 weeks) in excess of the 500 weeks and will get a replacement rate of 100% (20.65 + 35.5 × 2.235).

Figure 3.3. **Gross replacement rates for private-sector workers**

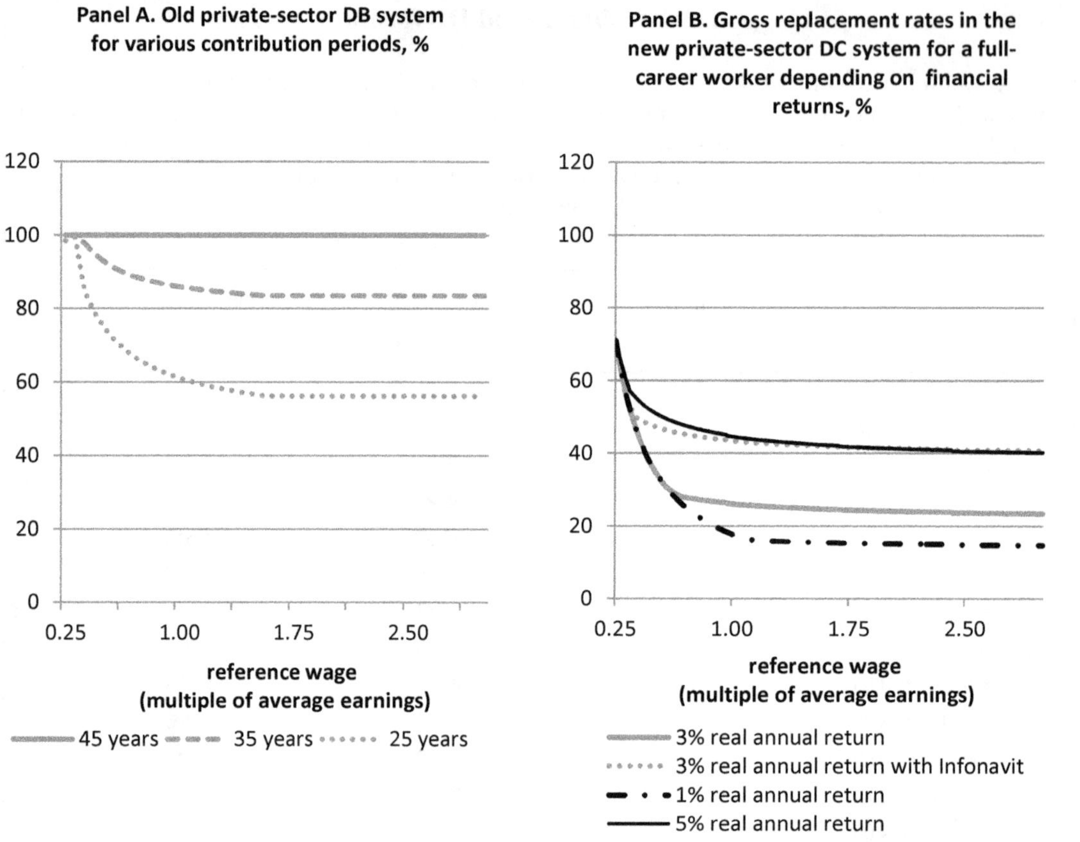

Note: For Panel B, the projected replacement rate applies for a private-sector worker entering the labour market at age 20 in 2014.

Source: OECD calculations.

This comparison shows that the old DB system yields higher benefits for everyone than what an actuarially fair scheme would deliver, and is therefore heavily subsidised by general government revenues.[4] Indeed, severe financial unsustainability was the prime reason for the 1997 reform, with future financial difficulties being compounded by expected demographic changes. The relative generosity of the old regime goes beyond the replacement rate levels. The eligibility conditions for a pension, including the minimum pension, are much tighter in the new regime. The reform is phased in over a long transition period and workers who entered just before 1997 might retire as late as in 2042 (if they joined the labour market at age 20) with the generous DB formula. Consequently, the reform introduced huge inequalities across cohorts.

Unsurprisingly, a vast majority of people who retired since 1997 chose to receive their benefits according to the old DB formula. This raises a number of problems. First, the long transition period means that the public finance pressure will still be felt over an extended period even though implicit liabilities for the post-transition workers have been substantially reduced. Second, as a result of flawed incentives there is an insufficient sense of ownership of their individual pension fund (AFORE) account by contributors who started to contribute before 1997, as many of them know they will end up choosing the DB pension. In that case, their individual accounts help finance the benefits through the transfer of resources to IMSS, but any gaps between the funds necessary to finance the pension promise and the value of the assets are borne by the federal government and of no consequence neither for the individual nor for the AFORE. This generates inadequate financial investment incentives for workers (especially in terms of the choice of the AFORE), induces poor discipline for the pension fund industry and transfers the costs of these inefficiencies to the public purse as the government has the responsibility to fund such gaps.

Third, the reform created huge inequalities between the transitional workers who can opt for the old system and those who entered after 1997 (see Chapter 4). Fourth, as expected replacement rates for new entrants are low, even for full-career workers due to the small mandatory contribution rate, the trust in the new system is undermined despite actuarial fairness. This feeling is further fuelled by generally poor financial literacy among the population (see e.g. Hastings and Tejeda-Ashton, 2008). In cross-country comparison, the projected replacement rates are the lowest across countries according to the OECD pension model (Figure 3.4). Even when taking into account the *cuota social* (a contribution subsidy up to 15 times the minimum wage in the private sector, see Chapter 2), the contribution rate for private-sector workers would have to increase from its current level of 6.5% to about 14.5% to raise the net replacement rate of full-career average-wage workers to the OECD average.

Figure 3.4. **Net replacement rate for the full-career average-wage worker, %**

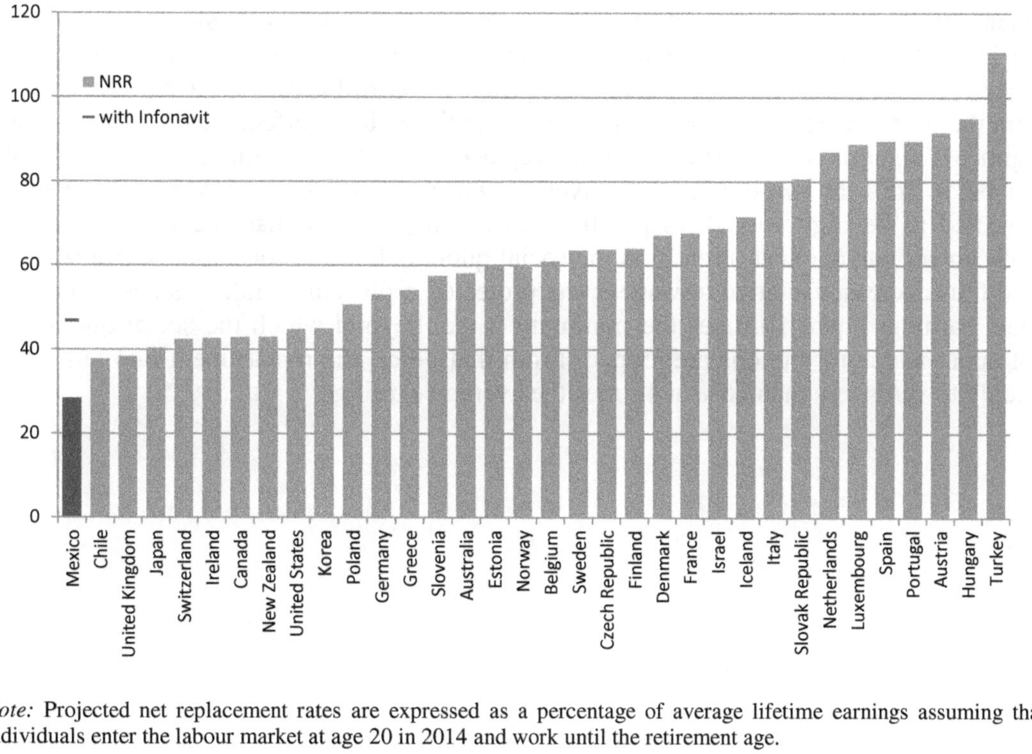

Note: Projected net replacement rates are expressed as a percentage of average lifetime earnings assuming that individuals enter the labour market at age 20 in 2014 and work until the retirement age.

Source: OECD (2015a).

3.3.2. Public-sector workers (main scheme)

In 2014, the number of ISSSTE retirees represented about one quarter of IMSS retirees. The number of active contributors to the ISSSTE pension system in the same year, however, was only about 6% of the contributors to the IMSS scheme. Beyond the downsizing of the public sector, the difference likely reflects the large employment flows between the formal private sector and the informal economy.

The 2007 reform modifying the pension system for civil servants avoided some of the weaknesses highlighted above in the 1997 IMSS pension reform. As with the IMSS reform, new entrants had to open individual DC accounts. But contrary to the IMSS reform, those who had contributed before were given six months to choose whether when retired their benefits will be paid according to the old DB pension formula or from their individual accumulated assets under the rules of the DC system. Those who opted for the new DC system received a recognition bond based on their past contribution, which was then deposited in their individual accounts. The contributions of those who remained within the DB scheme continue to directly finance the PAYG system (see Box 3.2 for a description of the rules for the old DB formula for public-sector workers). Yet, the recognition bond did not account fully for the option that was left to civil servants to remain in the old system until they retire; hence only 14% of pre-2007 civil servants chose to migrate to the new system. In any case, the choice that was given to them implies that the accrued and future pension liabilities of the civil servants who started their career before 2007 have thus not been reduced substantially.

Even for a full career (45 years) the replacement rates projected in the new DC scheme for civil servants are substantially lower than 100% of the final salary, which the old DB scheme pays after a 28 and 30 year career, for women and men respectively, except for low-wage earners (Figure 3.5). Low-wage full-career civil servants benefit from the PMG; its level is about 60% higher than the PMG in effect for the private-sector regime. While this represents a high gross replacement rate at the minimum wage, it falls just below 45% at two-thirds of the average wage, a level beyond which earnings are projected to be high enough to purchase an annuity greater than the PMG. Then the replacement rate declines slightly as the social quota is flat-rate for public-sector workers (and thus decreases relative to wages); the projected replacement rate reaches about 38% when earnings equal 10 times the minimum wage, beyond which the social quota does not apply and contributions are topped. From that point, the replacement rate falls more steeply towards less than 25% at 4 times the average earnings.

Box 3.2. **Rules for the calculation of public-sector workers' pension for those who chose to stay in the DB system**

Public-sector workers who left the public service voluntarily or were precluded from working after age 60 are entitled to a pension for severance at old-age if they have contributed at least 10 years. This pension corresponds to a fraction of the average basic salary of their last year of service, from 40% to 50% depending on the age at which they claim their benefits.

Public-sector workers aged at least 55 years old and who have at least 15 years of service are entitled to a retirement pension equivalent to a percentage of the average basic salary of their last year of service. This percentage varies from 50% to 95% for men for 15 to 29 years of service and from 50% to 85% for women for 15 to 27 years of service. Men with at least 30 years of service and women with at least 28 years of service are entitled to a full retirement pension, equivalent to 100% of the average basic salary of their last year of service. Starting 1 January 2010 there are new retirement age requirements for the pension benefits described above. This is summarised in the table below:

Number of years of contribution	Retirement age	Pension (as a % of basic salary)
≥ 10 and < 15	Increasing from 60 in 2009 to 65 as of 2018	40
≥ 10 and < 15	Increasing from 61 in 2009 to 66 as of 2018	42
≥ 10 and < 15	Increasing from 62 in 2009 to 67 as of 2018	44
≥ 10 and < 15	Increasing from 63 in 2009 to 68 as of 2018	46
≥ 10 and < 15	Increasing from 64 in 2009 to 69 as of 2018	48
≥ 10 and < 15	Increasing from 65 in 2009 to 70 as of 2018	50
15	Increasing from 55 in 2009 to 60 as of 2018	50
16	Increasing from 55 in 2009 to 60 as of 2018	52.5
17	Increasing from 55 in 2009 to 60 as of 2018	55
18	Increasing from 55 in 2009 to 60 as of 2018	57.5
19	Increasing from 55 in 2009 to 60 as of 2018	60
20	Increasing from 55 in 2009 to 60 as of 2018	62.5
21	Increasing from 55 in 2009 to 60 as of 2018	65
22	Increasing from 55 in 2009 to 60 as of 2018	67.5
23	Increasing from 55 in 2009 to 60 as of 2018	70
24	Increasing from 55 in 2009 to 60 as of 2018	72.5
25	Increasing from 55 in 2009 to 60 as of 2018	75
26	Increasing from 55 in 2009 to 60 as of 2018	80
27	Increasing from 55 in 2009 to 60 as of 2018	85
28 (men)	Increasing from 55 in 2009 to 60 as of 2018	90
29 (men)	Increasing from 55 in 2009 to 60 as of 2018	95
≥ 30 (men) ≥ 28 (women)	Men: increasing from 50 in 2009 to 60 as of 2028 Women: increasing from 48 in 2009 to 58 as of 2028	100

Figure 3.5. **Gross replacement rate in the reformed systems for full-career workers, %**

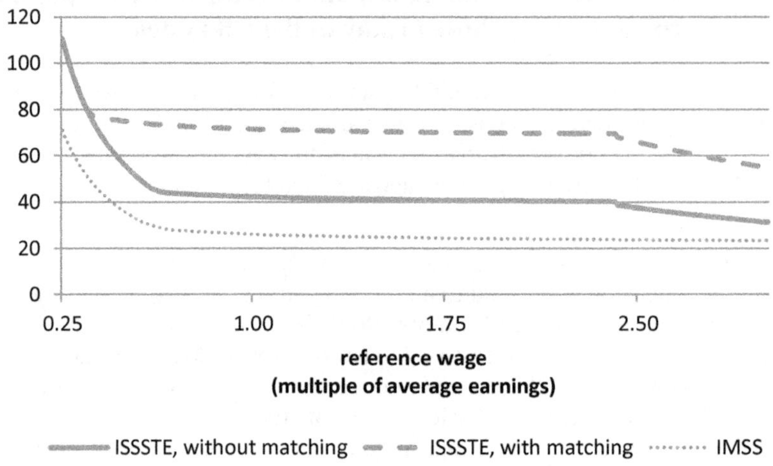

Source: OECD calculations.

In the reformed system, public-sector workers will continue to benefit from a higher old-age pension than private-sector workers with the same wage and career length, due to higher contribution rates, beyond the differential in the PMG. This not only is a source of inequality between the two groups of workers but also presents an obstacle to labour mobility between the public and the private sectors. These differences in expected benefits are exacerbated by the generous matching contributions scheme for voluntary pension savings which is available to public-sector workers: employees contribute voluntarily between 1 and 2% of their earnings up to 10 times the minimum wage and for each peso contributed, the government adds 3.25 pesos.[5] Accounting for this boosts the projected replacement rate by about 30 percentage points for the average-wage public-sector worker (Figure 3.5).

3.4. Financial pressure will grow

The current deficit of the overall pension system, excluding old-age safety nets (see below) beyond minimum pensions, slightly exceeds 0.5% of GDP, with pension expenditure amounting to about 3% of GDP and revenues to 2.5%. The schemes for private-sector workers account for slightly less than half of the spending, while they cover 77% of all retirees. Several smaller regimes, such as that applying to the Armed Forces, are paid directly by the federal government. Public pension spending is expected to increase to 3.4% of GDP by 2020, driven by a fast rise in ISSSTE pension spending.[6]

Overall, the governance of pension financing lacks consistency. For example, IMSS has been drawing down its financial pension reserves to cover operational deficits of its health accounts (Hernandez and Vernon, 2012), thus increasing net implicit pension debt through asset depletion (OECD, 2013).[7] This calls for a clearer legal and financial separation between health social security institutions and pension institutions (Vasquez Colmenares, 2012).

While the IMSS and ISSSTE pension systems should reach financial sustainability thanks to the reforms once the long transition period is completed, many of the unreformed local pension systems could face severe financial difficulties. According to

Fitch (2011), implicit pension liabilities are high in about half of the Mexican states. Moreover, about one third of all states have recently introduced non-contributory pension schemes, which are financed through taxes. Besides, states and municipalities have become heavily dependent on federal transfers to finance a growing share of overall public spending (OECD, 2013).

While the 1997 and 2007 pension reforms succeeded in reducing public implicit liabilities for the post-transition generations substantially, they opened a long transition period which has been generating explicit current costs for the public finance. Those transition costs include the payment of the pensions computed based on the previous regimes, the minimum pension guaranteed by the new laws and the public subsidies including the social quota (Alonso et al., 2014). Moreover, the 1997 reform increased the wage cap used in the DB formula to 25 times the minimum wage instead of 10 times before the reform, thus increasing both benefits and implicit liabilities. As the current contributions fund individual accounts, transition costs have to be financed outside the pension system through taxes and transfers.

There are various estimates of the transitional cost of the 1997 reform, i.e. for the private-sector system. The financial deficit of the regime applied to private-sector workers is generally projected to increase from its current level (slightly more than 0.5% of GDP) and peak at 1 to 1.4% of GDP in the 2040s from which it would decline steadily after 2070 (see for example Alonso et al. (2014), Casal and Hoyo (2007) and Tapen (2012)). For ISSSTE and the special regime benefiting workers in IMSS itself (IMSS-RJP), Tapen (2012) projects that the deficit will grow from about 1.2% of GDP in 2010 to almost 3% of GDP in the mid-2030s (Figure 3.6, Panel A). In addition, for the non-reformed systems of States, the Armed Forces and PEMEX alone, the current deficit would grow from about 0.25% of GDP in 2010 to 2.5% of GDP in 2055.

Under unchanged policies the combination of the transition costs of the reformed systems and the growing financial imbalances of the non-reformed systems will exert strong pressure on public finances for a long period, with an expected cumulative deficit of this subset of the overall pension system of about 6% of GDP in the mid-2030s according to Tapen (2012) (Panel B). This is likely to prove unsustainable. The public sector will be representing a disproportionate share of these growing imbalances relative to its size in the economy and even to its share of formal employment. Without further or new reforms to the old systems those costs will turn explicit as most PAYG schemes are too generous in Mexico, i.e. far from what contributions can finance, and because new contributions are used to finance individual accounts rather than the pensions of current retirees. Increasing the contribution rate would improve the financial sustainability of the old regimes and the income prospects of pensioners in the new systems. In any case, policy action is needed to reduce both the transition costs and the generosity of the unreformed systems.

Figure 3.6. **Projected deficit of the pension system**

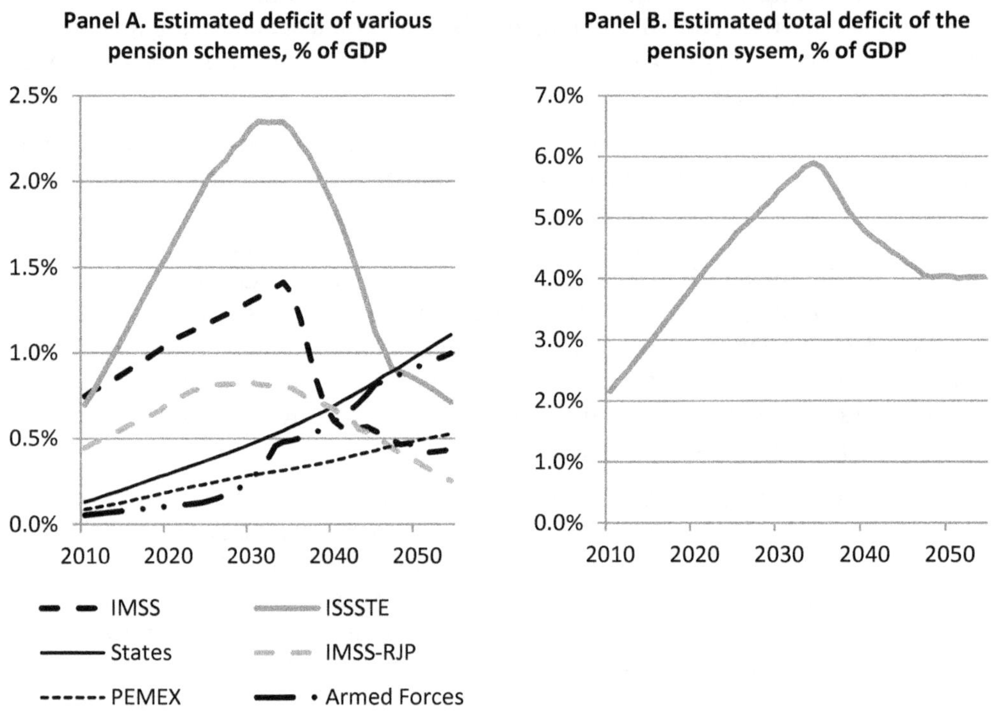

Source: Tapen (2012).

3.5. Deep-seated fragmentation

The fragmentation of the Mexican pension system is deeply entrenched and goes far beyond the striking differences between the IMSS and ISSSTE schemes; different professional groups are treated very differently in terms of retirement conditions and benefits. It is a source of large inequalities. There is no coordination across the various plans which are run by different institutions, thus generating overlaps. Special regimes include those covering the Armed Forces, the oil company PEMEX, the Federal Electricity Company (CFE), IMSS itself for its employees (IMSS-RJP), teachers, Courts (e.g. the Supreme Court and the Federal Council of Justice), the Central Bank and the development banking institutions, which are entities of the federal public administration. The pension schemes were reformed for new IMSS-RJP and CFE workers in 2008 to reduce implicit liabilities.

Some local governments, i.e. those of 31 sovereign states, one federal district and about 2 450 municipalities, and the 55 public universities have their own pension schemes, mostly of the DB type, with no portability of entitlements between them. In particular, there is no interaction between the federal and the local systems. According to the Office of the Auditor General, there are more than 250 identified pension schemes either operated directly or subsidised by the federal government (Tapen, 2012), and little is known about what is taking place in the small municipalities. Most of them lack a formal pension system, and pension obligations for municipal employees are paid through current expenditure (OECD, 2013). Among the 2 450 municipalities, about 1 100 are estimated to have their own scheme. Over the last two decades, 14 states reformed their pension system, as well as 27 public universities, one of which adopting a DC regime. Some states and public universities have agreements with ISSSTE or IMSS, so that they are covered by them.

Some pension programs might come under strong financial pressure (Villagómez, 2014). Although exact information is lacking, the level of financial solvency of the pension schemes appears to be very heterogeneous across states and universities. According to IMCO (2012), pension projections indicate dire financial prospects in more than half of the states. Moreover, the sovereign autonomy enjoyed by municipalities over their political and fiscal development feeds the fragmentation of the pension system. Indeed, municipalities while playing a small role compared to what happens in other OECD countries, focusing on the provision of local services such as waste management or water supply (see OECD, 2013, and especially Figure 3.3 therein), increasingly depend on transfers from the federal government. This creates a disconnection between revenues and expenditures and damages accountability, in particular in the pension area.

3.6. Minimum social benefits for the elderly

3.6.1. Relative old-age income

The old-age poverty rate (at half of median equivalised income) in Mexico was above 30% in 2013 and the second highest in the OECD (Figure 3.7). Old-age poverty is also high compared to the poverty rate for the total population, which stood at about 20%. On the other hand, the relative income of those over 65 was fairly high on average in the late 2000s compared with other OECD countries. It reached on average 96% of the mean income of the total population compared with 87% on average across OECD countries (Figure 3.8); this places Mexico among OECD countries with the highest average relative income of the elderly. Overall, the combination of these indicators implies considerable inequalities among the elderly in Mexico.

At the same time, there is room to expand the budget allocated to old-age safety nets provided that financial resources are raised. Indeed, among OECD countries Mexico spends the lowest share of its GDP on old-age and survivors: recipients received a total of 1.8% of GDP in 2011 compared with an OECD average of 8.4% (Figure 3.9, Panel A). Moreover, the non-contributory safety net (called *70 y más* then) represented about 6% of this small spending in 2011 (Panel B) but has since been expanding at a fast pace (see below).

Figure 3.7. **Old-age poverty rate, %, 2013**

Percentage of those aged 65 and over with income lower than half median equivalised income

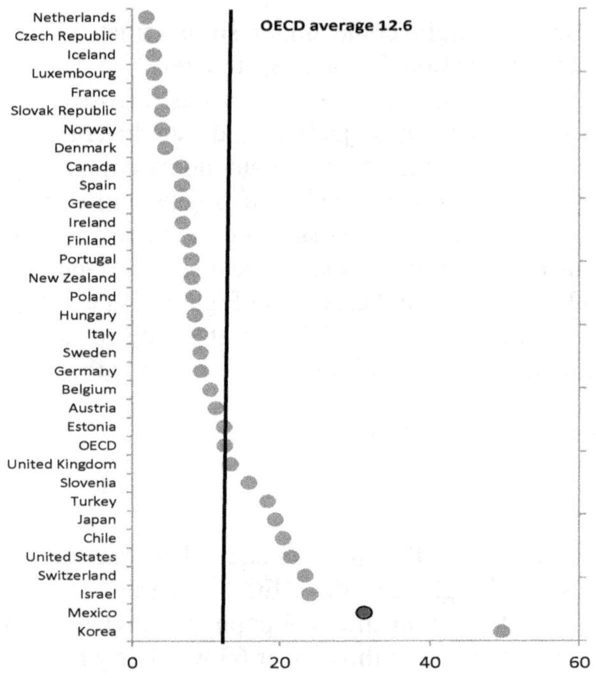

Source: OECD Income Distribution Database, *www.oecd.org/social/income-distribution-database.htm.*

Figure 3.8. **Relative income of the over 65s, late 2000s**

Income of individuals over age 65 in % of the mean income of the total population

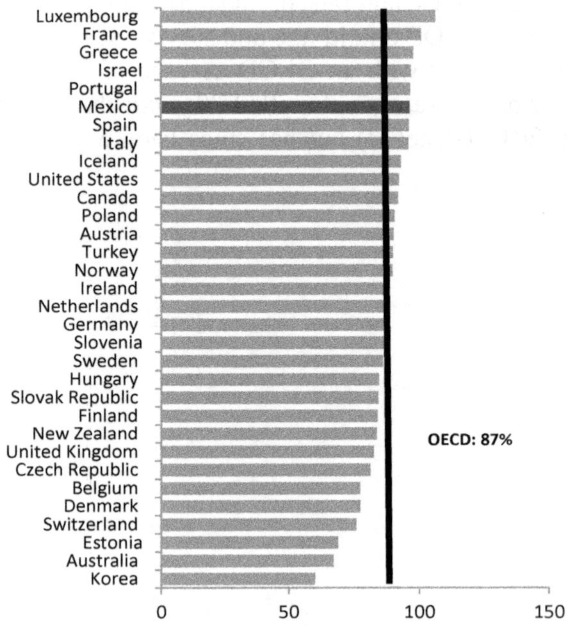

Source: Authors' calculations: OECD Income Distribution Database, *www.oecd.org/social/income-distribution-database.htm.*

Figure 3.9. **Old-age pension spending**

Panel A. Pension expenditures in benefits, OECD countries, % of GDP | **Panel B. Breakdown of expenditures by schemes, Mexico, % of spending**

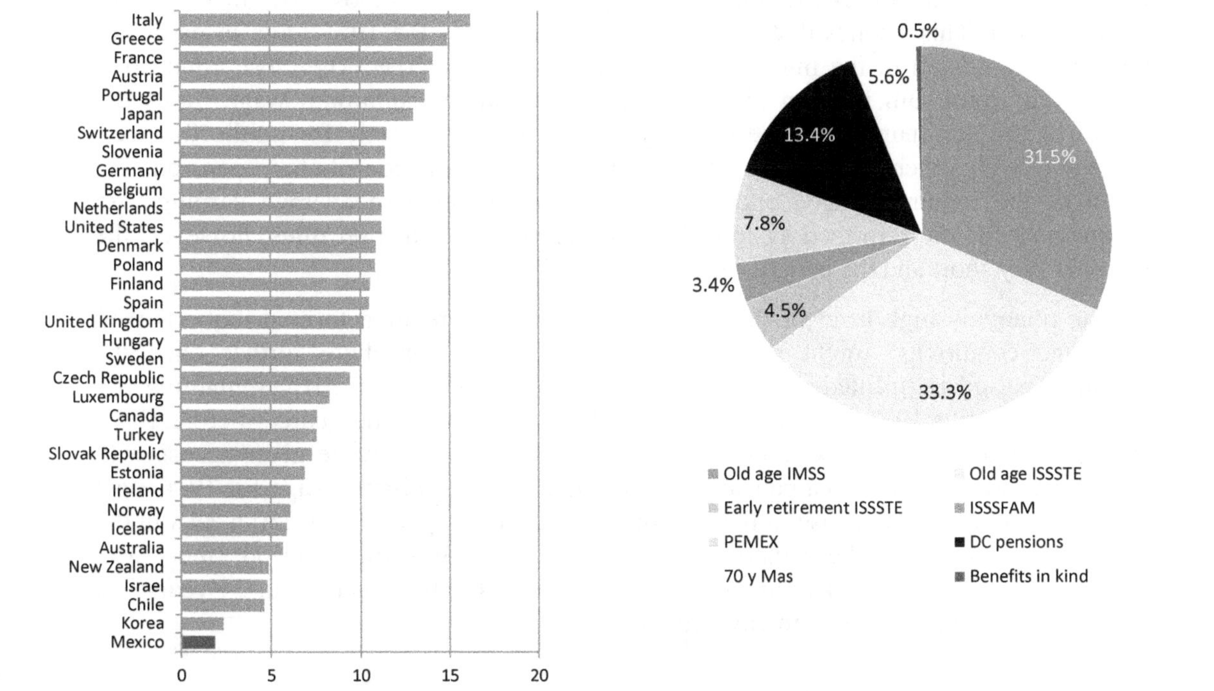

Source: OECD SOCX database.

3.6.2. Minimum pensions

Private-sector workers having reached the retirement age of 65 are entitled to a minimum pension, provided they have contributed for a minimum period. Under the 1973 Law, its level is equal to the Federal District minimum wage subject to 500 weeks of contribution. For individuals covered by the 1997 Law, the *pension minima garantizada* (PMG) was fixed at the 1997 minimum wage level, is price-indexed and subject to a much longer contribution period of 1 250 weeks. Receipt of the minimum pension also gives access to health care. In December 2014, about 740 000 private-sector retirees were receiving the 1973 minimum pension and about 15 000 the PMG, which in total represented 44% of the 1.7 million IMSS retirees (out of 8.2 million people aged over 65, or 21%).

The minimum wage has not kept pace with consumer price inflation since 1997 while the PMG is price indexed.[8] Therefore, the 1973 minimum pension is currently about 20% lower than the private-sector PMG. For ISSSTE, the PMG was set at twice the minimum wage level in 2007 and is CPI indexed. As a result, it was worth about 60% higher than the PMG for private-sector retirees in 2014. Retirees eligible to the PMG but whose assets are insufficient to buy an annuity equivalent to the PMG receive the PMG, which is paid by the AFORE until the individual account is depleted and then by the social security system financed by general taxation.

On the one hand the ratio of the minimum pension to the minimum wage is very high. On the other hand Mexico has the second lowest minimum wage in relative terms among

OECD countries: in 2013, the minimum wage was equal to 37% of the median wage compared with an OECD average of about 50% (ranging from 36% in the Czech Republic to 69% in Turkey). About 13% of the employed population earn the minimum wage. Since the mid-1970s the minimum wage has fallen by almost 70% in real terms (Tapen, 2012). This implies that some pensions covered by the 1973 Law, in particular those closely related to the minimum pension, also fell by 70%. The close connection between the minimum pension in the old regimes and the minimum wage limits the growth of the minimum wage inefficiently as any upside is costly for public finances. Compared with other OECD countries having a minimum contributory pension, the length of the required period and the benefit level relative to average earnings are intermediate for the reformed system. For workers under transition rules, however, the period is very short and the benefit relatively low (Figure 3.10).

The relatively high level of the minimum pension (in relation to contributions paid and wage conditions) might provide a disincentive to contribute further once the eligibility period is fulfilled, especially for low-wage workers. In 2015, remaining life expectancy at 65 is 19.4 years in Mexico. For those who started their career before 1997, having worked for 500 weeks (about 10 years) at the minimum wage gives access with limited past contributions to a pension benefit equal to the minimum wage for 19.4 years on average. While the increase in the minimum contributory period to 1 250 weeks in the new system improves the situation, despite the long transition period, the PMG entitlement after 1 250 weeks remains overly generous. On the other hand, 24 years is a very long period to be eligible to any pension.

Figure 3.10. **Eligibility and benefit level of the minimum pension**

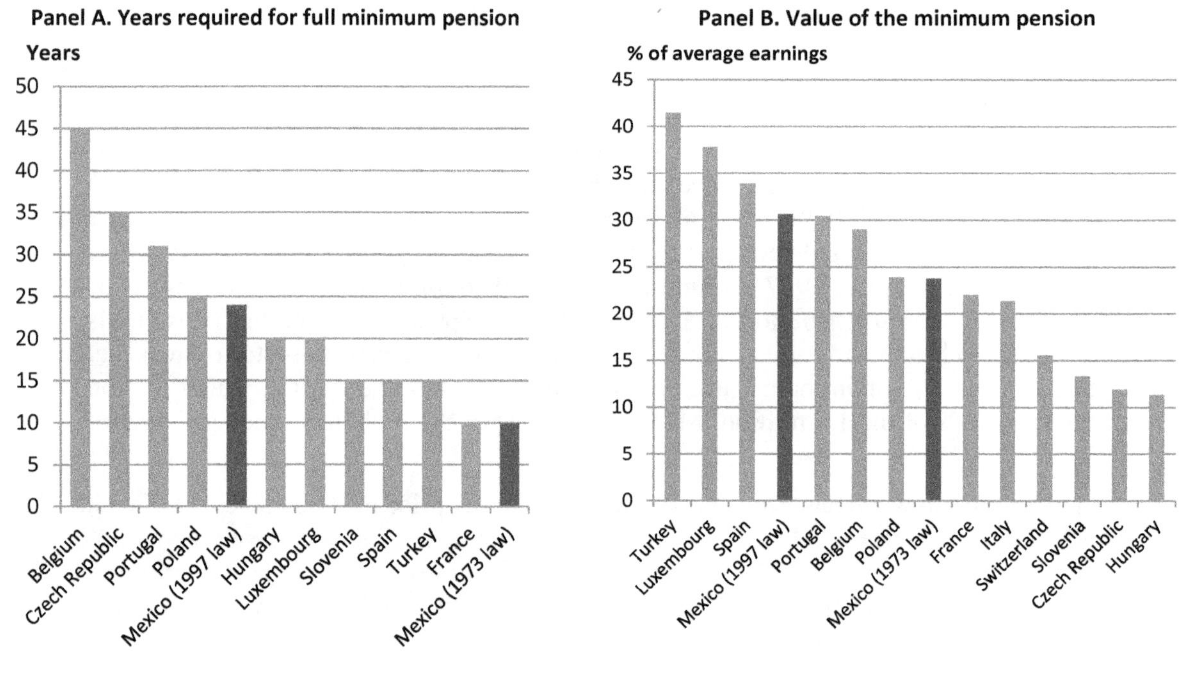

Source: OECD (2015a).

However, to be entitled to a pension, the defined-benefit system requires that at retirement the individual has not been inactive for more than a fourth of her past contribution period. For example, if the worker left the workforce at age 55 with 20 years of past contributions, she has to wait 5 years to obtain a pension at age 60, which is the minimum retirement age. However, if she only had 12 years of contribution, she then loses the right to a pension. Maintaining the latter requires to restart contributing. As a result, many workers, especially women, lost their pension rights in the defined-benefit scheme. In the defined-contribution system, below 1 250 weeks of contributions, the individual account balance is recovered as a lump sum even if there is a large period without contributions before retirement.

According to the standard economic and financial assumptions used in the OECD pension model, a man (woman) entering the labour market in the private sector in 2015 at age 20 would have to work a full career at about 60% (65%) of average earnings, i.e. about 2.3 (2.6) times the minimum wage, in order to receive a pension greater than the PMG.[9] If the contribution period is limited to 1 250 weeks instead of the full career, a man (woman) would have to earn 220% (250%) of the average wage to start getting more than the PMG.

The current rule with the 1 250 weeks cut-off creates a large discontinuity even when taking into account that individuals receive a lump sum when they have contributed for less than 1 250 weeks. With the actuarial conversion of the lump sum, moving just above the cut-off would about double the benefit (from about half to one PMG) for someone earning twice the minimum wage (i.e. about half the average wage) (Figure 3.11). On top of that, when the contribution period is shorter than 1 250 weeks individuals are subject to longevity risks when managing their lump sum. Beyond the cut-off period there is no incentive in terms of pension benefit to continue contributing as the half-average-wage worker will never be able to finance more than the PMG. For the average-wage worker, the benefit jumps from about three quarters to one PMG, and the contribution period has to reach 37 years for the benefit to exceed the PMG. This implies that workers could be contributing for about 13 additional years without any added benefit. For high-wage workers, working a few years beyond the 1 250 cut-off generates a lower amount because of eligibility to the non-contributory safety net is lost. This last point is discussed in greater detail in the following sub-sections, which suggest an integrated approach that avoids the damaging impact of these discontinuities.

Figure 3.11. **Benefit level as a function of the contribution period for different levels of earnings throughout the career**

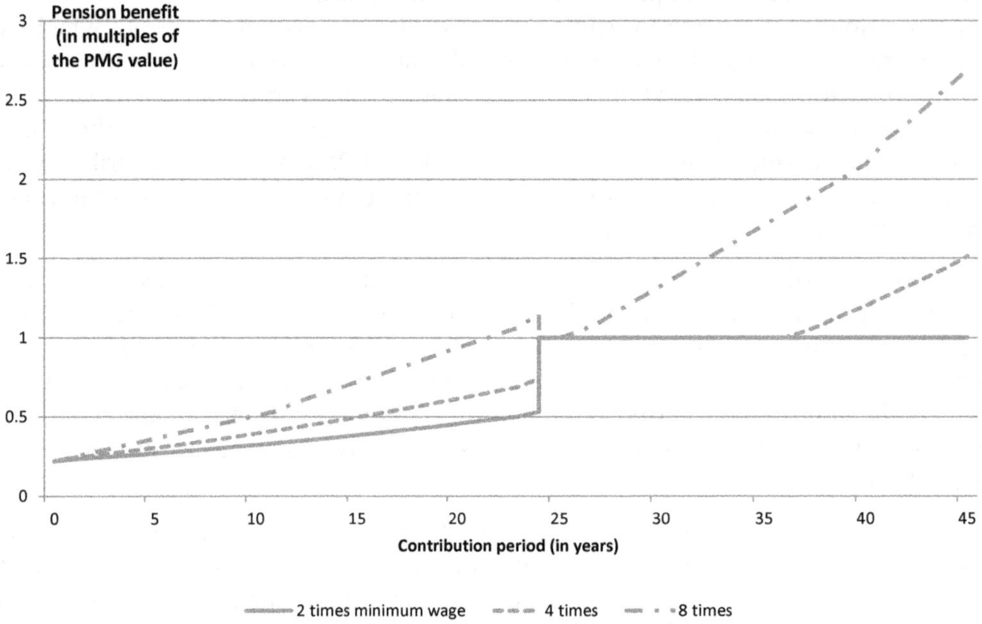

Note: The simulations are run by taking into account the non-contributory component (*Pensión para Adultos Mayores*, PAM; see section 3.6.3) and are based on the case of a private-sector male worker born in 1995 contributing for a given period at the end of his career in 2060. For individuals having contributed less than 1 250 weeks, the lump sum is assumed to be annuitized in order to facilitate comparison, thus ignoring longevity risks.

Source: OECD calculations.

This suggests first that minimum pension levels should be reduced relative to the minimum wage. Ideally, in the case of Mexico (see above), that should probably occur via an increase in the minimum wage and a looser connection between the two in the old regimes. Second, the price indexation of the PMG raises complex issues. On the one hand, in the long term the price indexation of first-tier pensions is not the best strategy because it induces a declining trend in the minimum pension replacement rate towards zero provided the economy generates real wage gains. On the other hand, the price indexation of the PMG should help reduce its level relative to wages. Also, given fast population ageing, price indexation is likely to generate a higher level of public spending on minimum pensions in Mexico as a percentage of GDP (OECD, 2015b). Combined with the high PMG-to-minimum-wage ratio, this implies that over the medium term price indexation should probably be maintained on top of increases in the eligibility age in relation with life expectancy gains. Finally, the first-tier benefit scheme should avoid a cut-off period (see below).

3.6.3. Safety nets

The combination of low coverage, low contribution density and low replacement rates in a country where poverty rates are already high raises social challenges (Villagómez, 2014). Efforts to close the coverage gap have generally led to the development of non-contributory pensions in Latin American countries including Mexico. While such schemes can help reduce old-age poverty, especially in countries with large informal sectors, it is important to design them in a way which is fiscally sustainable (OECD, 2014a).

The most important nationwide non-contributory scheme in Mexico is the *Pensión para Adultos Mayores* (PAM). In 2014, PAM had about 5.4 million of beneficiaries which represented more than 60% of the population aged over 65, compared with 3.0 million for *70 y más* in 2012. The related public expenditure, financed by general taxation, has been increasing at a fast pace albeit from a low level, and reached 0.25% of GDP compared to 0.11% in 2012 and 0.05% in 2007. The PAM applies to people who are at least 65 and do not receive another old-age or disability pension from a social security institute above a certain threshold currently equal to about half of the minimum wage. This mean-tested benefit extended the *70 y más* programme in 2013 by lowering the eligibility age from age 70 to 65. *70 y más* itself had replaced in 2007 a scheme created in 2003 which targeted rural residents. The means-test largely disconnects the PAM from the contributory schemes since minimum pension levels are above the PAM eligibility income threshold.

The amount of the benefit is about equal to 22% of the private-sector PMG or less than 15% of the median wage. This places Mexico along with Korea and Turkey amongst the OECD countries offering the lowest level of old-age protection for individuals not covered by contributory pensions (Figure 3.12). While most developed countries have the means to finance higher safety net benefits (Figure 3.13), it seems that the level of economic development alone cannot explain the low degree of protection in Mexico, which is insufficient to alleviate poverty.

Figure 3.12. **Value of basic and minimum pensions, 2014**

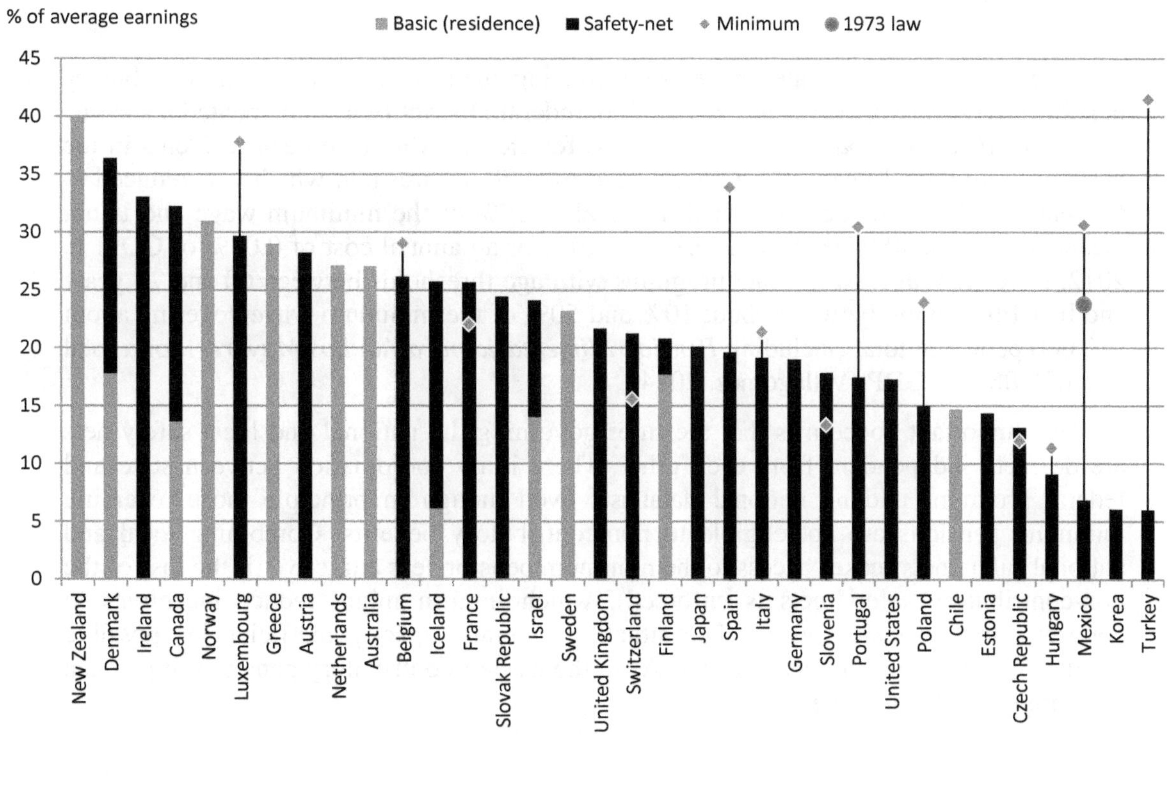

Source: OECD, (2015a).

Figure 3.13. **Old-age safety net level and economic development, 2014**

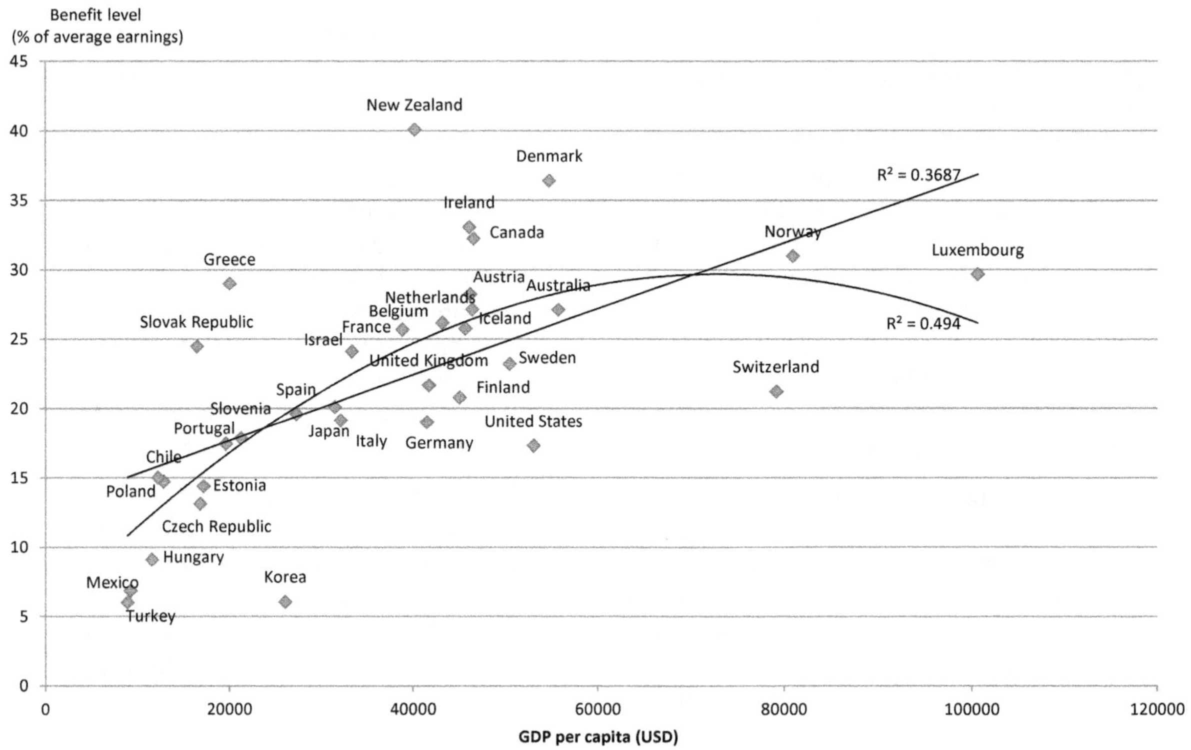

Source: OECD calculations.

Since 2000, several states have been creating their own old-age non-contributory benefit programs (Rofman et al., 2013). The Federal District first implemented a scheme (*Pensi6n Alimentaria para Adultos Mayores*) for elderly who have been residents in the area for more than 3 years and who are aged over 70, a threshold which was reduced to 68 years in 2008. The benefit, which is equal to 50% of the minimum wage and is not means-tested, had 480 000 beneficiaries in 2013 for an annual cost of 0.03% of GDP. In 2012, there were at least 13 state programs with age thresholds between 60 and 70 years and benefits varying between about 10% and 50% of the minimum wage covering about 930 000 people in total (including *Pension Alimentaria para Adultos Mayores)* for a total cost of 0.06% of GDP (Villagomez, 2014).

One important concern is that the rules governing the national and local safety nets are de facto independent from each other. There is no coordination between state and federal programs and no national database, even though in principle those receiving minimum pensions are not eligible to non-contributory benefits. Combining local and national safety nets makes access to the minimum pension less attractive (if the loss of the non-contributory safety nets is enforced), which in turn might reduce incentives to contribute to the pension system. This situation generates opacity, inefficiencies, possible duplications and therefore inequalities. As in the case of contributory pensions, it paints a very fragmented landscape.

3.6.4. The draft Universal Pension Law

Access to a universal pension was introduced in the Mexican constitution as a principle but it is so far not operational. In October 2013, the President presented draft legislation, the Universal Pension Law, to the Congress. It was voted by the House of Representatives in March 2014 but remains to be approved by the Senate; at this stage, there appears to be no plans for such a debate.

The draft legislation removes the means test in the strict sense and replaces it with a pension test. It stipulates that: i) the universal pension would be financed by taxation at the federal level; ii) through a transition period the PAM would converge towards the universal pension; iii) the benefit would increase from 580 pesos in 2015 (the PAM level) to 1 092 pesos by 2030 and then be indexed to price inflation; iv) the eligibility age threshold is initially set at 65 years, and would then increase every five years by 87% of the change in life expectancy at birth – as a result it would reach 67 in 2024 and 70 in 2054 ; v) eligibility conditions would also include 25 years of residence in the country and no contributory pension.

This last condition implies that this benefit would not strictly qualify as a universal old-age non-contributory pension. Moreover, one substantial limitation comes from the missed opportunity to reduce fragmentation: there is no provision about the consolidation and replacement of non-contributory local pensions. The fiscal cost of a fully universal pension, i.e. paid to everyone aged over 65, would amount to about 0.35% of GDP in 2015 and would roughly double to 0.7% of GDP in 2030 due to population ageing. Given the importance of fighting old-age poverty, these orders of magnitude are manageable. However, they would add up to the public finance pressure induced by the remaining financial difficulties of the contributory schemes which are highlighted above.

The planned increase of the benefit level is equal to 4.3% per year on average between 2015 and 2030 in nominal terms, compared with the central inflation target of 3% by the Central Bank. If the Bank of Mexico succeeds in its mandate, this would imply a cumulated rise in real terms of just over 20% throughout the period, raising the safety-net level from 22% of PMG with the PAM today to 27% in 2030. Other measures proposed in the same draft legislation, which might be responsible for its setting aside, include assigning a share of the INFONAVIT contributions to finance retirement and unemployment benefits.

3.6.5. Towards an integrated structure of first-tier pensions within the overall pension system

There are concerns that non-contributory pensions may have unintended consequences. In theory, non-contributory pensions create an incentive to go informal and save less because, by increasing retirement income, the safety net modifies the decisions that determine the trade-off between saving and consumption through the lifetime. A universal pension encourages more consumption today as the access to that benefit later is not affected by less saving today. A non-contributory pension that is gradually withdrawn as retirement income rises amplifies this effect, as such a withdrawal increases the effective marginal taxes. This suggests using relatively low withdrawal rates to minimise crowding-out effects on labour supply and contributory pensions. Indeed, the cliff due to the loss of the non-contributory subsidies in case of a full abrupt withdrawal (as in Mexico for PAM) or even large withdrawal rates could lower contribution density (Beyer and Valdés-Prieto, 2004).

On the other hand, there is a trade-off between a lower level of distortions thanks to small withdrawal rates and the cost for public finances of not tightly targeting, which tends to reduce the level of the safety net for a given level of spending allocated to the programme. Based on the Universal Pension Law individuals who do not comply for a contributory pension would get a lump sum from their accumulated assets in their individual accounts and be eligible to the "universal" pension. It might be more appropriate to use their account to partially finance an integrated benefit. Taking into account the public finance cost, Valdés-Prieto (2009) suggests that it is optimal to opt for a scheme with a relatively low but strictly positive withdrawal rate.

To avoid the detrimental effects of the discontinuities highlighted in Figure 3.11 on incentives and equity, policy makers in Mexico should aim at better aligning the non-contributory component with the first-tier contributory pension, i.e. minimum pensions, as Chile did for example in 2008. This should be done in a way that provides a smooth benefit pattern as a function of either contributions or contribution periods in order to reduce the incentives not to contribute to the formal system. In Mexico, there is some evidence that the *70 y mas* programme lowered labour force participation of beneficiaries and of younger individuals who live with them through income effects (Juarez and Pfutze, 2014). Such a strategy might require adjusting both the level of the safety net and the minimum pensions.

An integrated framework would be consistent with the proposal of Villagómez and Ramírez (2014), who recommend the implementation of a proportional pension based on the length of the contributory period. While their proposal has the advantage of smoothing the benefit pattern, Valdés-Prieto (2009) highlighted that a benefit that is withdrawn based on the length of the contribution period is less efficient than one based on contributory pensions (and other income). The reasons are that the former could create disincentives to contribute and generate vertical inequities for example between part-time and full-time workers who could have the same contribution period but with very different contributed amounts.

3.7. Policy options to improve the public pension provision

The priorities for the Mexican pension system are twofold. Reforms should aim at ensuring financial sustainability and improving the governance and transparency by streamlining the numerous schemes. Another key objective should be to raise the old-age benefits of the most vulnerable and better align the old-age safety net and the contributory first-tier pension scheme.

3.7.1. Improve financial sustainability

Financial sustainability challenges for pension provision arise in Mexico from the long transition periods of the schemes that have been reformed since the mid-1990s and from the implicit liabilities in non-reformed systems. Chapter 4 provides several options to reduce the transition costs of old schemes.

Some parametric changes could also generate significant net public saving, which in turn would create fiscal space to expand the non-contributory pension scheme. While the increase in contribution rates in the private DC schemes is needed to raise retirement-income adequacy, it would also increase the revenues of the public DB schemes. Moreover, the matching contribution for civil servants is overly generous (for each peso voluntarily contributed, between 1 and 2% of earnings below 10 times the minimum wage, the government adds 3.25 pesos) and exacerbates the differences between public-sector and private-sector pensions; it should be drastically reduced. The way the benefits are computed could be modified beyond changes in the DB formula. For example, the 2010 Supreme Court ruling, according to which the reference-wage ceiling for DB pensions should be lowered from 25 to 10 times the minimum wage, could be enacted, thereby lowering public spending. In addition, the survivor's pension should be scaled back, given that the current replacement of 90%, the second highest in the OECD, goes way beyond protecting the standard of living of the survivor. The saving potential is limited though as survivors' pension expenditure amount to only 0.3% of GDP given low pension coverage more generally.

Given the fast projected pace of population ageing in Mexico, policy makers should strive to increase the effective retirement age down the road. First, the statutory retirement age should be linked to gains in life expectancy. Second, exiting the labour market early should be discouraged. Early retirement rules should be tightened by increasing the age limit (60 years both in the private sector and in case of dismissals in the public sector) and, in the old system, the benefit penalty for retiring early (5 percentage points for each year of anticipation in the private sector). Moreover, in the public sector (old law), the contribution period of 28 years for women and 30 years for men for a full pension should be substantially increased. It is conditional on reaching an age threshold which will reach 60 in 2028. This age limit should increase at a faster pace and continue beyond 2028 (before the old public-sector system expires at the beginning of the 2050s) while the gender gap should be closed.

Finally, numerous pension schemes at different levels of governments and sectors should be reformed with a view to harmonising the rules and ensuring portability to remove obstacles to labour mobility. Ultimately, establishing a truly national pension system should be the key objective. Hence, the fragmentation of the pension system should be reduced and its governance and financial prospects upgraded by: conditioning part of the transfers to local governments on the adoption of the national scheme in order to replace existing schemes; eliminating special regimes benefiting firms and universities among others; and starting the gradual convergence of IMSS and ISSSTE parameters. In particular, the eligibility period in the old private-sector scheme is very short (500 weeks) and should be raised to get the minimum pension in full (see below). There should also be a convergence between the minimum pension level under the 1973 Law and the PMG, both in the private and public sectors, with the converged benefit level being delinked from the minimum wage. Moreover, pension and health social security institutions should be clearly separated both legally and financially.

3.7.2. Increase safety net levels, and better link the non-contributory with contributory first-tier components

The level of the non-contributory benefit (PAM) is too low to efficiently fight old-age poverty. With high poverty rates, the low level of social expenditures in Mexico leaves some room to progressively improve safety nets for the elderly.

Moreover, the non-contributory safety net should be integrated within the first-tier scheme:

- The PAM would be topped-up by a new contribution-based minimum pension benefit;

- The minimum pension benefit would grow steadily with the contributions paid up to a ceiling or with the contribution period, and the full rate be reached after more than 1 250 weeks. This would broaden the access to the first-tier contributory benefit;
- Accumulated assets in individual accounts of pensioners who cannot finance a pension higher than the full-rate minimum would be used to finance the new integrated benefit rather than to provide lump sums;
- Continuity between the non-contributory and first-tier schemes would be ensured by progressively withdrawing the non-contributory component against the new progressive minimum pension. The withdrawal rate should be relatively low to limit disincentives to contribute. With the current levels of the PMG and the PAM, the withdrawal rate would be equal to the PAM / PMG ratio which is currently 22%. Chile uses a withdrawal rate of 30% and Finland 50% while Norway and Sweden have two large rates instead of a unique rate (Valdés-Prieto, 2009);
- The coordination of minimal old-age protection between the federal and local governments should be enhanced via financial transfer incentives and improved monitoring.

Notes

1. In this chapter the minimum wage refers to that applied in the federal district as this is the reference used in pension parameters.
2. Actuarial neutrality is a central concept to work incentives around retirement ages. There are two main interrelated but different definitions, capturing changes in pension benefits at the margin. According to the first (se e.g. Duval, 2003), the pension system is neutral if the cost in terms of foregone pensions and contributions paid for working an additional year is exactly offset by an increase in future benefits. According to the second (see e.g. Queisser and Whitehouse, 2006), the system is actuarially neutral if the present value of accrued pension benefits for working an additional year is the same as in the year before (meaning that benefits increase only by the additional entitlement earned in that year). The main difference between the two definitions is that contributions paid or benefits earned during the additional year are not considered in the second one. In any case, although that depends on the pension parameters, including mortality rates, actuarial neutrality is typically associated with an increase of 6-8% in future annual pensions for working an extra year.
3. As explained in sub-section 3.6.2 below, the level of minimum pension under the 1973 law is well below that under the 1997 law. This creates some incentives to contribute up to 1 250 weeks.
4. Actuarially fairness means that the present value of lifetime contributions equals the present value of lifetime benefits (Queisser and Whitehouse, 2006).
5. A recent reform proposal would provide a matching contribution for private-sector workers. The proposed terms are much less generous though than those applied to the public sector as the matching would be 20 cents for each peso that is contributed up to a 300-pesos annual limit, corresponding to less than 1% of the minimum wage.
6. *Source:* Criterios Generales de Política Económica 2015.

7. According to Hernandez and Vernon (2012), financial pension reserves had been drawn also to subsidise theatres and a football team, but this does not happen any longer since the reform to the Social Security Law in 1995.

8. In addition, in 2002, both the 1973 and 1997 Law minimum pension were revalued by 11% in real terms.

9. According to the standard economic and financial assumptions used in the OECD pension model, the PMG would at retirement be equal to 18% of the average wage compared to 32% today as the PMG is price indexed while productivity gains translate into real wage growth.

References

Aguirre, F.M. (2012), *Pensiones ... y con qué?*, Fineo (ed.).

Alonso, J., C. Hoyo and D. Tuesta (2014), "A model for the pension system in Mexico: diagnosis and recommendations", *Journal of Pensions, Economics and Finance*, Vol. 14, No. 1.

AMIS (2014), "Evolucion de los seguros de pensiones derivados de la seguridad social", *mimeo*, Marzo 2014.

Beyer, H. and S. Valdés-Prieto (2004), "Proposal to increase the density of contribution", *Report for the national Office of Women (SERNAM)*, March, Santiago.

Casal, J. and C. Hoyo (2007), "Costo fiscal de la reforma a Ley del Seguro Social en Mexico", *document interno*, CONSAR.

Duval, R. (2003), "The retirement effects of old-age pension and early retirement schemes in OECD countries", *OECD Economics Department Working Papers*, No.24, Paris.

Fitch (2011), "Marco Institucional de los Gobiernos Subnacionales en México", Fitch Ratings, International Public Finance Mexico, September.

Hastings J.S. and L. Tejeda-Ashton, "Financial literacy, information, and demand elasticity: survey and experimental evidence from Mexico. 2008", *NBER Working Papers*, No. 14538.

Hernandez, A. and A. Vernon (2012), "The Reformed Mexican Social Security System: 15 years of experience", mimeo.

James, E. (2009), "Rethinking Survivor Benefits", World Bank, *Social Protection and Labour Discussion Paper*, No. 928.

Juarez, L. and T. Pfutze, "The Effects of a Non-Contributory Pension Program on Labor Force Participation: The Case of 70 y Mas in Mexico", *Banco de México Working Papers*, No 2014-12.

IMCO (2012), "Pensiones estatales: Otra bomba de tiempo", *http://imco.org.mx/indice_estatal_2010/PDFS/Pensionesestatales.pdf.*

OECD (2013), *OECD Economic Surveys: Mexico 2013*, OECD Publishing, Paris. DOI: *http://dx.doi.org/10.1787/eco_surveys-mex-2013-en.*

OECD/IDB/The World Bank (2014a), *Pensions at a Glance: Latin America and the Caribbean*, OECD Publishing, Paris. DOI: *http://dx.doi.org/10.1787/pension_glance-2014-en.*

OECD (2014b), *OECD Economic Surveys: Poland 2014*, OECD Publishing, Paris. DOI: *http://dx.doi.org/10.1787/eco_surveys-pol-2014-en.*

OECD (2015a), *Pensions at a Glance*, forthcoming, OECD Publishing.

OECD (2015b), *OECD Urban Policy Reviews: Mexico 2015: Transforming Urban Policy and Housing Finance*, OECD Publishing, Paris. DOI: *http://dx.doi.org/10.1787/9789264227293-en.*

Queisser, M. and E. R. Whitehouse (2006), "Neutral or Fair?: Actuarial Concepts and Pension-System Design", *OECD Social, Employment and Migration Working Papers*, No. 40, OECD Publishing, Paris. DOI: *http://dx.doi.org/10.1787/351382456457.*

Tapen, S. (2012), "Estimating future pension liability of the Mexican Government", *Study commissioned by the Inter-American Development* Bank.

Valdés-Prieto, S. (2009), "The 2008 Chilean Reform to First-Pillar Pensions", *CESIfo Working Papers*, No. 2520.

Vasquez Colmenares, G. (2012), "Nueva seguridad social y la crisis de las pensiones", *ECONOM/Aunam*, Vol. 10, No. 28.

Villagomez, F .A. (2014), "Mexico : un esquema multiplar fragmentado", *Como fortalecer los sistemas de pensiones latinoamericanos*, Estudio internacional de SURA Asset Management.

Villagomez, F .A. and D. Ramirez (2014), "Pension universal proporcional. Una propuesta para Mexico", *El Trimestre Economico*, Vol. LXXXI (4), No. 324.

Villagomez, F .A. and D. Ramirez (2013), "Mas alla de las pensiones contributivas : Mexico", T.Rofman, I. Apella and E. Vezza (eds), *Mas alla de las pensiones contributivas*, Banco Mundial.

Chapter 4

Smoothing the transition period and increasing pension contributions in Mexico

The sharp drop in pension benefits to be expected after the transition period from the old defined benefit (DB) system to the new defined contribution (DC) system may lead to disillusionment with the new DC pension system. This sharp drop is the result of low contribution rates, which were set at levels similar to those existing before the reform, and high promises to transitional workers based on the old DB formula. In this context, people with similar labour histories separated by a few months would have drastically different pension benefits. Moreover, the low coverage rates and contribution periods compound this problem. This chapter explains how this situation comes about and presents alternatives to smooth-out the transition period. The chapter also discusses approaches to increase coverage, contribution levels and contribution periods.

The statistical data for Israel are supplied by and under the responsibility of the relevant Israeli authorities. The use of such data by the OECD is without prejudice to the status of the Golan Heights, East Jerusalem and Israeli settlements in the West Bank under the terms of international law.

The Mexican pension system faces a potentially explosive challenge stemming from a combination of low contribution rates and high promises to transitional workers. As the previous chapter argued, the pension benefits granted under the old defined benefit (DB) formula are high relative to the contribution levels. Moreover, pension benefits under the defined contribution (DC) rules will be lower than what people may expect, and definitively much lower than those under the old DB formula. This two together translate into a sharp fall in pension benefits after the transition period ends. In this context, people with similar labour histories separated by a few months would have drastically different pension benefits. Moreover, short contribution periods and low contribution densities compound the problem.

This chapter explains how this potentially explosive situation comes about and presents alternatives to smooth-out the transition period. The chapter also discusses approaches to increase coverage, contribution levels and contribution periods. The discussion in the chapter draws directly from the OECD's best practices contained in the OECD Roadmap for the Good Design of Defined Contribution Pension Plans and the OECD Pensions Outlook 2012 and 2014.

The chapter starts illustrating the sharp falls in replacement rates that are expected for private and public-sector workers after the last transitional workers retire. It then shows that short contribution periods and low contribution densities compound the problem. In section three, the chapter shows that voluntary contribution levels are not sufficient to offset the fall in replacement rates.

The chapter then assesses two policies commonly implemented to promote higher voluntary retirement savings in OECD countries (OECD, 2012): the tax treatment of retirement savings and the pension statement. The analysis argues that the tax treatment of retirement savings in Mexico fails to create the appropriate incentives for people to make additional voluntary contributions. In addition, the pension statement that CONSAR requires AFORE to provide to members contains a lot of relevant information, but it does not seem to engage members and encourage them to take active steps to improve retirement income adequacy by, for example, increasing contributions and/or postponing retirement. The chapter ends presenting proposals to increase mandatory and/or voluntary contributions, to smooth-out the transition period, to increase coverage and contribution densities, and to improve the public's understanding and confidence in the pension system.

4.1. Sharp falls in replacement rates are expected after the last transitional worker retires

4.1.1. Private-sector workers

Private-sector workers who were working and contributing to the PAYG system in place before 1 July 1997 have the right to choose a pension calculated according to the old DB formula upon retirement. Although these workers began contributing to their new mandatory individual retirement accounts after this date, they retained the right to choose between getting their pension benefits calculated using the old formula at retirement or using the DC balances. The rules for the old DB formula for private-sector workers were described in Box 3.1 (Chapter 3). A worker with a final salary equal to four times the minimum wage for example, can expect to replace 100% of that final salary after 45 years of contributions. Moreover, the previous chapter argued that those replacement rates are generous given contribution rates and contribution periods.

Pension benefits from DC individual accounts, given current mandatory contributions and realistic rates of return on portfolio investment, may be much lower than those from the DB formula. Hence, private-sector workers who entered the labour market after July 1997 will have much lower benefits despite having the same contribution rates and contribution period. According to the OECD pension model (OECD, 2015b), a private-sector average earner entering the Mexican labour market in 2014 and contributing to the pension system continuously from 20 to 65 years old can expect to replace 26% of his/her final gross earnings, assuming a real rate of return after administrative charges of 3% per year, compared with 100% under the old DB formula. For a minimum-wage earner, the replacement rate would increase to 71%.[1,2]

According to the OECD pension model, in order to achieve a replacement rate in the new DC system equivalent to 100% under the old DB formula over a 45-year contribution period for the average earner, one would need to assume a real rate of return of 8% or a contribution rate of 29%.

Given the difference in retirement income and replacement rates between the DB formula and the DC rules, it is expected that the vast majority of transitional private-sector workers will choose the old DB formula when claiming their benefits at 65. Indeed, over the period 2003 to 2014, less than 1% of the workers have chosen the DC rules (Chapter 3).[3] Therefore, it is likely that by the year 2042, most transitional workers will have retired and chosen the old DB formula. There would be a sharp fall in replacement rates once the last transitional worker retires and all new retirees get their pension benefits according to the assets accumulated in their DC accounts. Using CONSAR model for projecting DC replacement rates, Figure 4.1 illustrates the fall in replacement rates that one can expect for private-sector workers with 40 years of contributions earning above the minimum wage up to six times the minimum wage and retiring over the next 45 years. The higher the lifetime earnings level the sharpest the fall. The difference would reach about 60 percentage points for people earning six times the minimum wage. On the contrary, replacement rates for workers earning the minimum wage will not fall when the transition period is over. Workers earning the minimum wage can choose between the minimum guaranteed pension (PMG) in the DC system and the minimum pension in the old DB system, which it is lower. The PMG represents 129% of the minimum wage.

Figure 4.1. **Evolution of replacement rates for private-sector workers retiring at 65 between 2015 and 2060, with 40 years of contributions and earning 1 to 6 times the minimum wage**

As a % of final salary

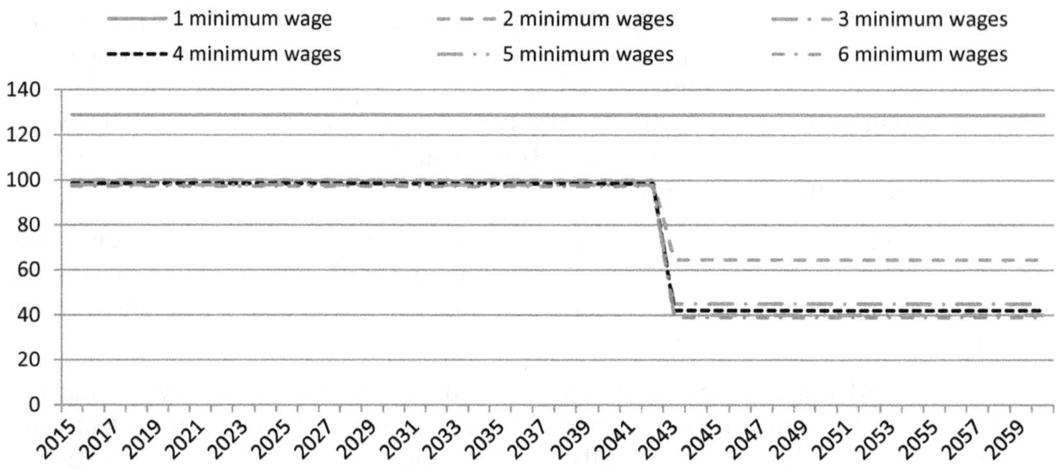

Note: The replacement rates for people retiring under the new DC system (as of 2043) are calculated assuming a 40-year career with a flat salary, 1.19% fees, 5.19% real rate of return and the progressive social quota in force during the period November to December 2014. After the transition period is over, only private-sector workers earning one to two times the minimum wage would receive the minimum guaranteed pension.

Source: CONSAR.

A combination of low contribution rates to mandatory individual retirement accounts and high promises to transitional workers explains this potentially explosive situation. Contribution rates to the retirement sub-account vary from just over 7% to 13.6% depending on the social quota. The contribution rate for private-sector workers is 6.5% of the basic salary for contributions. When adding the progressive social quota, the total contribution rate increases for people under 15 times the minimum wage, up to 13.6% for very low-income workers (see Table 4.1). During the last quarter of 2014, 89.1% of the private-sector workers affiliated to the IMSS with an active account received the social quota.[4]

Table 4.1. **Contribution rates for private-sector workers, according to multiples of the minimum wage**

	1 minimum wage	3 minimum wages	5 minimum wages	10 minimum wages
Retirement, severance and old-age	6.5	6.5	6.5	6.5
Worker	1.125	1.125	1.125	1.125
Employer	5.150	5.150	5.150	5.150
Federal government	0.225	0.225	0.225	0.225
Social quota*	7.106	2.270	1.303	0.622
Total	**13.606**	**8.770**	**7.803**	**7.122**

Note: The calculation uses the progressive social quota in force during the period November to December 2014.

Source: Author's calculations.

The contribution rate in the Mexican pension system is low by international standards. Figure 4.2 shows the total contribution rate in Mexico for a worker earning three times the minimum wage (8.77%) in comparison with other countries. It ranks last among the selected OECD and non-OECD countries with available information on the contribution rate to mandatory pension plans. In many other Latin American countries, mandatory contribution rates are around 10% (for example, Bolivia, Chile, Dominican Republic, El Salvador, and Peru). In 14 countries, the contribution rate to the mandatory pension system ranges from 16% to 20%. Italy and Hungary are extreme cases where the contribution rate to the mandatory pension system is above 30%.

Figure 4.2. **Contribution rates in mandatory pension plans, selected OECD and non-OECD countries, 2012 or latest available data**

1. The contribution rate to mandatory occupational pension plans varies across age groups, from 7% between 25 and 34 years old to 18% beyond 55 years old. The graph uses the rate of 10% (for people aged 35 to 44).

2. Numbers for Mexico include state contributions and the social quota for workers with a wage equivalent to 3 times the minimum wage.

Source: OECD (2013) and OECD/IDB/The World Bank (2014).

4.1.2. Public-sector workers

All public-sector workers who were ISSSTE affiliates at the time the ISSSTE Law was approved in 2007 had the right to choose to switch to the new funded DC system or to remain in the old PAYG DB system. Those workers who decided to remain in the DB system continued contributing to the ISSSTE to finance the PAYG system, but some rules of the DB system were changed. The minimum retirement age is being increased gradually from 50 to 60 by 2028 and the contribution rate of workers for retirement, severance at old-age and old-age has increased from 3.5% to 6.125% of the basic salary for contributions over the six years following the reform. The rules for the current DB formula for public-sector workers were described in Box 3.2 (Chapter 3). Men with at least 30 years of service and women with at least 28 years of service are entitled to a retirement pension equivalent to 100% of the average basic salary of their last year of service.

Pension benefits from DC individual accounts, given current mandatory contributions and realistic rates of return, may be much lower than those from the DB formula, for the same contribution rate and contribution period. Hence, public-sector workers who entered the labour market from April 2007 and those from the transitional cohort who chose to get their benefits according to the DC rules can expect much lower benefits. According to estimations from CONSAR, a public-sector worker entering the Mexican labour market in 2014, earning four times the minimum wage and contributing to the pension system continuously for 40 years can expect to replace 65.6% of his/her final earnings, assuming flat salaries. With three times the minimum wage, the replacement rate increases to 68.1%.[5] These estimations do not account for the Solidarity Savings state matching contribution.[6] Replacement rates obtained according to the new DC rules are therefore lower than replacement rates obtained according to the current DB formula (100%), for the same contribution rate and contribution period.

As the majority of public-sector workers who were affiliated to the ISSSTE in April 2007 chose the DB system, a sharp fall in replacement rates is expected after the last transitional worker retires. Indeed, of the 2 072 518 affiliates to the ISSSTE in April 2007, only 294 736 chose the new DC system (14.2%). Therefore, it is likely that by the year 2052, most transitional workers will have retired under the current DB formula, while the generation who entered the labour market after April 2007 will start retiring with the new DC rules. Using CONSAR model for projecting DC replacement rates, Figure 4.3 illustrates the fall in replacement rates that one can expect for public-sector workers with 40 years of contributions earning three to six times the minimum wage and retiring over the next 65 years.[7] The higher the lifetime earnings level the sharpest the fall. The difference would reach 37 percentage points for people earning six times the minimum wage. Replacement rates for public-sector workers earning one or two times the minimum wage will not fall. Public-sector workers earning the minimum wage that chose in 2007 to stay in the old DB system get the minimum pension in the old DB system that represents 100% of the minimum wage. However, once the transition period is over public-sector workers that joined after 2007 will be getting the PMG that for public-sector workers is 200% of the minimum wage. Those earning two times the minimum wage get 100% of their wage under the old DB formula and the PMG once the transition is over, which also represents 100% of their income (two times the minimum wage).

Figure 4.3. **Evolution of replacement rates for public-sector workers retiring at 65 between 2015 and 2080, with 40 years of contributions and earning 1 to 6 times the minimum wage**

As a % of final salary

Note: The replacement rates for people retiring under the new DC system (as of 2053) are calculated assuming a 40-year career with a flat salary, 1.19% fees, 5.19% real rate of return and the social quota in force during the period November to December 2014. After the transition period is over, only public-sector workers earning from one to two times the minimum wage would receive the minimum guaranteed pension.

Source: CONSAR.

The fall in replacement rate is less dramatic for public-sector workers than for private-sector workers, thanks to higher contributions rates to their DC individual accounts. Table 4.2 shows how the contribution rate of 11.3% increases for those getting the social quota. The impact of the flat social quota on the total contribution rate decreases rapidly with income. During the last quarter of 2014, 99.6% of the public-sector workers affiliated to the ISSSTE with an active account received the social quota. However, there will be a reduction in replacement rates of more than 30 percentage points for certain income groups once everyone retires under the DC rules.[8]

Table 4.2. **Contribution rates for public-sector workers, according to multiples of the minimum wage**

	1 minimum wage	3 minimum wages	5 minimum wages	10 minimum wages
Retirement, severance and old-age	11.3	11.3	11.3	11.3
Worker	6.125	6.125	6.125	6.125
Employer	5.175	5.175	5.175	5.175
Social quota*	5.921	1.974	1.184	0.592
Total	17.221	13.274	12.484	11.892

Note: The calculation uses the social quota in force during the period November to December 2014.

Source: Author's calculations.

4.2. Low coverage rates and contribution densities compound the problem

The percentage of the working-age population having an individual retirement account as of December 2014 was 60%. This amounts to a total of 52 728 388 Mexicans. Of those, 51 242 289 are private-sector workers affiliated to the IMSS (97.2%), 1 222 947 are public-sector workers affiliated to the ISSSTE (2.3%) and 263 152 are self-employed workers (0.5%).[9]

The distribution of accounts by age, gender and income is different for private- and public-sector workers (see Figure 4.4 and Figure 4.5). Public-sector workers having an account are those who decided to switch to the new DC system in 2008 and all the new entrants in the public service since 1 April 2007. This explains why, compared to private-sector workers, ISSSTE account holders are younger. The proportion of women is also higher among ISSSTE account holders than among IMSS account holders, probably due a higher proportion of women working in the civil service. Finally, the distribution of account holders is more skewed towards low income levels (close to 60% of IMSS account holders have wages below 3 times the minimum wage, while close to 70% of ISSSTE account holders have wages below 3 times the minimum wage).

Figure 4.4. **Accounts administered by AFORE by age and gender**

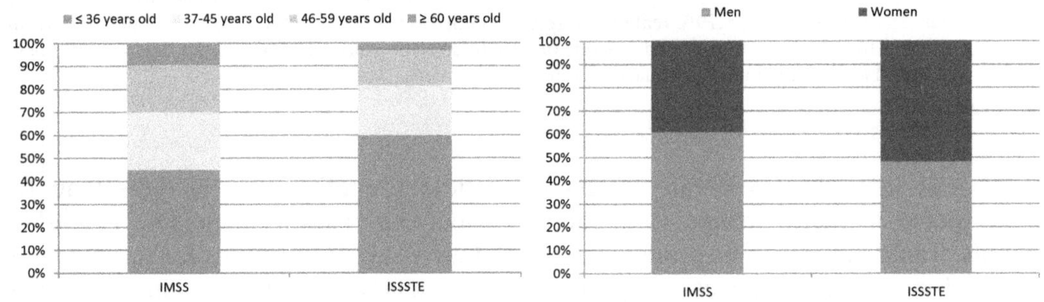

Notes: Preliminary data for the last quarter of 2014. IMSS: Includes IMSS workers registered to an AFORE and assigned workers with money deposited in a SIEFORE. The breakdown by gender does not include assigned workers when their gender is not known. ISSSTE: Includes workers who have only contributed to the ISSSTE and do not have a social security number (pure ISSSTE workers) and workers currently contributing to the ISSSTE and have a social security number because they already have contributed to the IMSS in the past (mixed ISSSTE workers).

Source: CONSAR.

Figure 4.5. **Accounts administered by AFORE by income level**

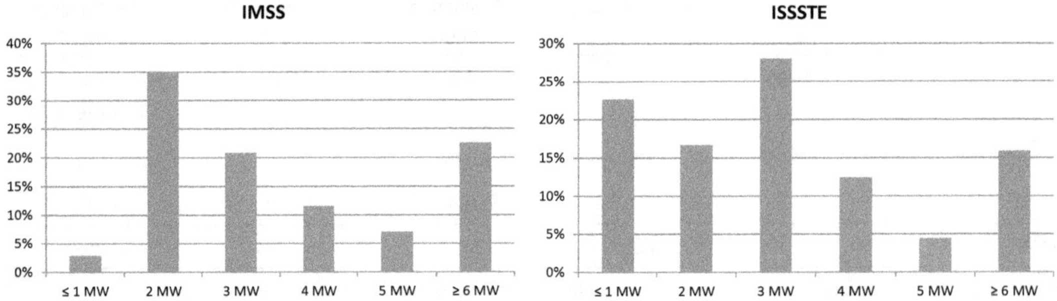

Notes: MW = minimum wage. Data refer to the last quarter of 2014. IMSS: Includes workers currently contributing to the IMSS. ISSSTE: Workers who have contributed at least once during the last three years; includes workers who have only contributed to the ISSSTE and do not have a social security number (pure ISSSTE workers) and workers currently contributing to the ISSSTE and who have a social security number because they already have contributed to the IMSS in the past (mixed ISSSTE workers).

Source: CONSAR.

The number of active retirement accounts is below half of all accounts. According to CONSAR numbers that define active accounts as those in which at least one contribution had been made during the last three years, only 44.5% of the accounts were active during the fourth quarter of 2014.

Workers with active accounts therefore only represent 30.0% of the working-age population. The proportion of active accounts is much larger among public-sector workers affiliated to the ISSSTE (78.5%) than among private-sector workers affiliated to the IMSS (49.0%) given more stable employment and lesser labour market informality.

The percentage of active accounts in Mexico is low when comparing internationally. Indeed, Bosch et al. (2013) compared the proportion of workers contributing to the pension system around 2010 in 19 countries of the Latin America and the Caribbean (LAC) region. With 34.7% of workers contributing to the pension system in 2010, Mexico is 10 percentage points below the LAC average (see Figure 4.6).

The main reason for the discrepancy between the number of workers having an account and the number of workers actively contributing to it is that many workers contribute intermittently to their individual retirement account. Indeed, the frequency or density of contributions for all account holders, according to CONSAR (2012), was about 38.2% in 2012 to both the IMSS and the ISSSTE. Additionally, the density of contributions is below 10% for 47.9% of workers (Figure 4.7). This means that out of 100 weeks of work, these individuals only contribute 10 weeks or less. At the other extreme, just a quarter of account holders contribute all the time or nearly all the time (90% to 100%) to their individual retirement account.

Figure 4.6. **Contributors or affiliates of pension systems in Latin America and the Caribbean, around 2010**

As a percentage of total workers (aged 15-64)

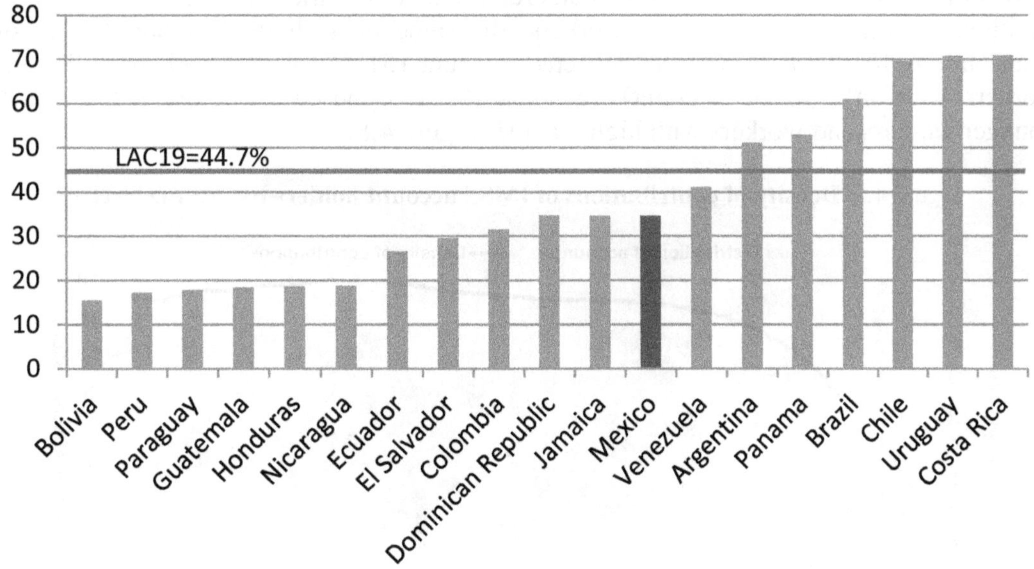

Source: Bosch et al. (2013).

Figure 4.7. **Distribution of density of contributions**

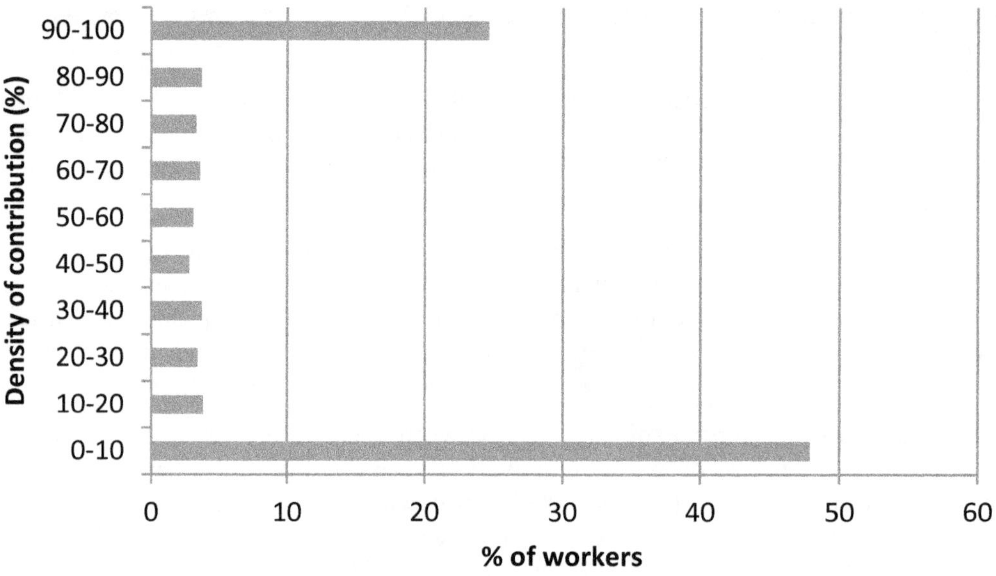

Note: Density of contributions calculated as the time a worker has been affiliated to a social security institution (IMSS and ISSSTE) as a percentage of total time that he/she could have been affiliated since he/she began to work.

Source: 2012 National Survey of Labour Paths (*Encuesta Nacional* de *Trayectorias Laborales*).

The frequency or density of contributions varies according to different socio-economic characteristics. Data on all IMSS account holders as of December 2013 show an average density of contributions of 44.4%, which is slightly higher for transitional workers (47.2%) than for workers who entered the labour market after 1997 (42.6%). In addition, for this last category of workers, the same data show a higher density of contributions for workers with a registered account (51.2% as opposed to 31.9% for workers with an assigned account), men (54.1% as opposed to 47.6% for women), younger workers and workers with high income (Figure 4.8).

Figure 4.8. **Density of contributions of IMSS account holders by income level**

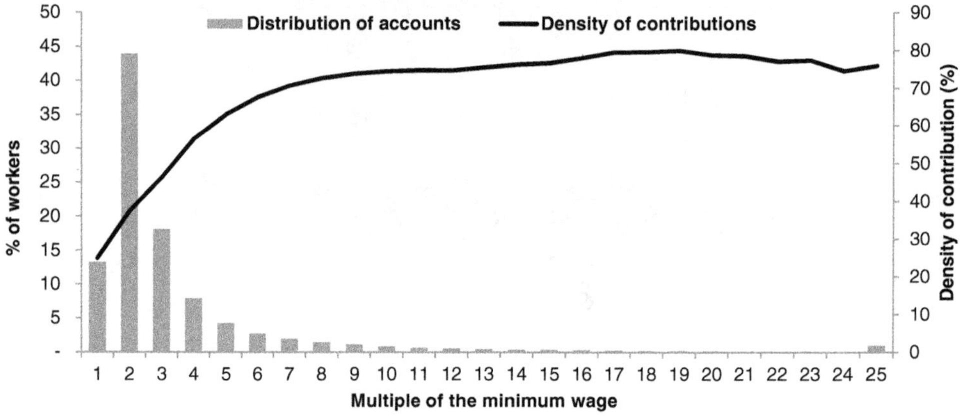

Source: CONSAR presentation "Sistema de ahorro para el retiro: Análisis de densidad de cotización histórica, cuentahabientes IMSS", June 2015, mimeo.

The density of contributions for workers with active accounts is larger than for all account holders. Figure 4.9 below shows that between the first quarter of 2013 and the first quarter of 2014, workers who have contributed to their individual retirement account during the last three years, contribute around 69% of the time. This means that on average, they contribute 69 weeks for every 100 weeks of work.

Figure 4.9. **Density of contributions in active individual retirement accounts, IMSS**

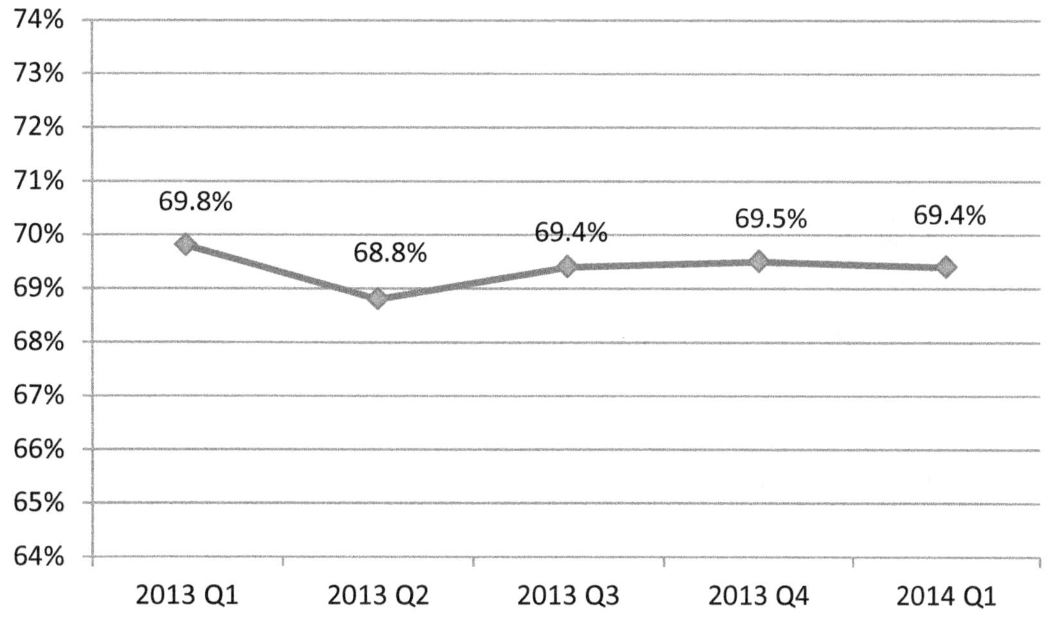

Note: Density of contributions during the last 36 months for workers who have contributed at least once during that period.

Source: CONSAR.

Finally, the low proportion of pension contributors, of active accounts, and of low densities of contributions is related to the level of formality and the transition to and from formality.[10] As shown in Figure 4.10, during the last quarter of 2014, there were 20.8 million formal workers, most of them salaried workers. At the same time, there were 28.9 million informal workers, representing 58.1% of all workers. Informal workers are common among salaried workers, self-employed workers and unpaid workers. They do not pay social security contributions, let alone pension contributions. Additionally, the number of people switching between informality and formality and vice versa during a 1-year period is around 13% according to the Mexican National Survey of Occupation and Employment (ENOE), and 24% over a five-year period.

Figure 4.10. **Formal and informal workers by type of employment, third quarter of 2014**

Millions of workers

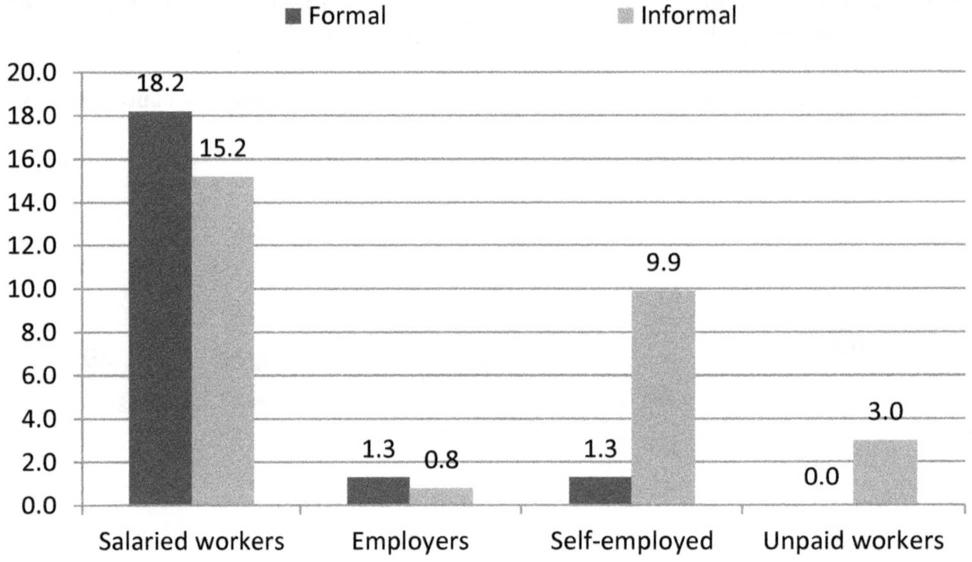

Source: National Survey of Occupation and Employment (ENOE).

4.3. Voluntary contribution levels are not sufficient to offset the fall in replacement rates

4.3.1. Voluntary contributions in the Retirement Savings System (SAR)

Voluntary savings made by workers and employers in the SAR are not high enough to complement the contribution rates in the mandatory accounts and prevent large replacement rate differences between workers retiring under the old DB formula and workers that would retire under the new DC rules. At the end of December 2014, total voluntary savings accumulated in the system only represented 1.1% of the net assets of SIEFORE (see Figure 4.11). There were 2 270 417 accounts with voluntary contributions and 299 132 accounts with solidarity savings at the end of August 2014.[11]

Figure 4.11. **Evolution of net assets and total voluntary savings**

Millions of pesos

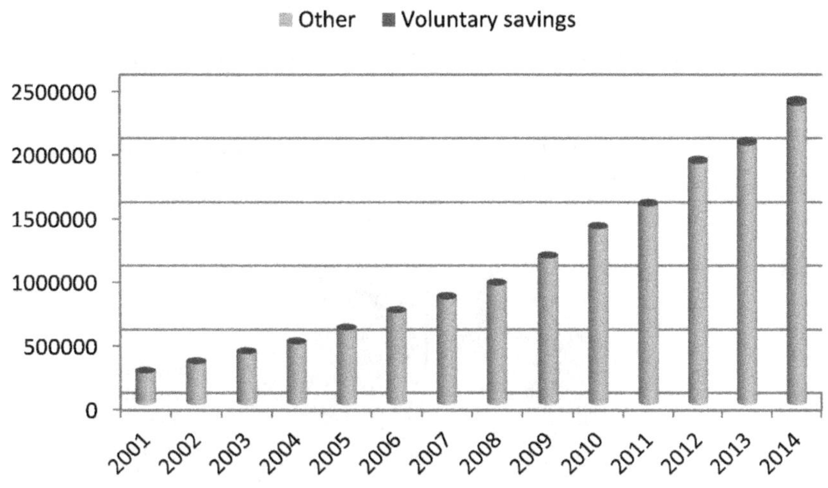

Source: CONSAR.

Despite that, Figure 4.12 shows that the solidarity savings for public-sector workers affiliated to the ISSSTE have been increasing rapidly since the programme was introduced in 2010, accounting for 33.2% of total voluntary savings as of December 2014. The direct and very generous government incentive (the government contributes 3.25 pesos for each peso contributed by the worker) explains this rapid growth. At the end of August 2014, about one-fourth of public-sector workers had a solidarity savings account, meaning that they had made a contribution under this programme at least once since 2010. As 76% of all contributions into solidarity savings accounts come from the state (by definition of the matching), the cost for the federal government may prove to be quite high (at the end of 2014, the total balance of solidarity savings accounts, including returns, was MXN 8 622 million).

Figure 4.12. **Evolution of voluntary savings and solidarity savings accumulated in the system, 2001-2014**

Millions of pesos

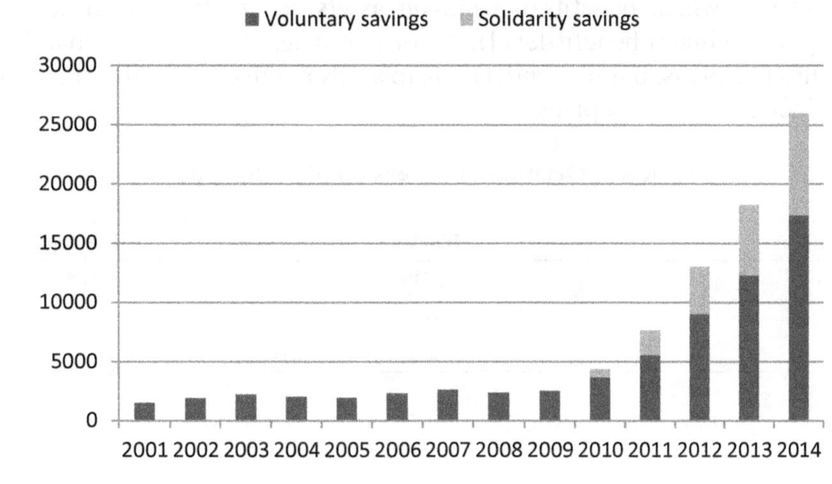

Source: CONSAR.

More than half of voluntary savings are done by employers through complementary contributions to individual retirement accounts. Short-term voluntary contributions by workers represent 33% of voluntary savings (see Figure 4.13).

Figure 4.13. **Composition of voluntary savings, December 2014**

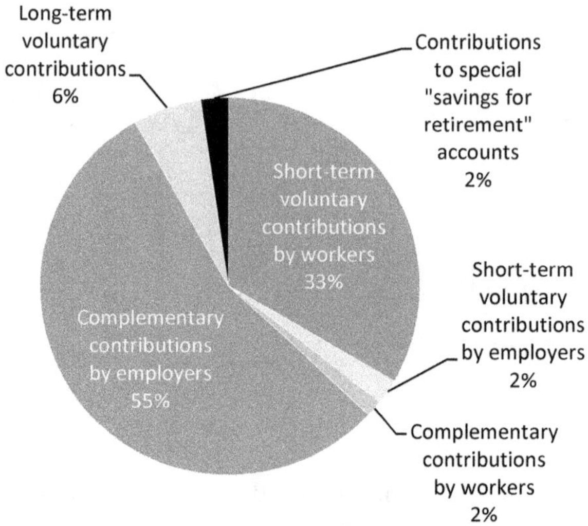

Source: CONSAR.

4.3.2. Voluntary participation in occupational pension plans

Voluntary savings can also be done through occupational pension plans. These plans are not regulated by CONSAR, but employers have to register their plans with CONSAR in order to obtain fiscal benefits. The available statistics on occupational pension plans may therefore provide a partial view of this system, as it is up to the employer to register the plan or not.

At the end of May 2014, there were 1 930 occupational pension plans registered with CONSAR offered by 1 727 employers (some employers offer more than one plan). These plans can be DB, DC or hybrid (plans combining features of pure DB and DC plans, for example, a plan in which benefits depend on assets accumulated with some kind of guarantee, e.g. a minimum benefit level). As of that date, slightly more than half of the plans were pure DB plans, but the tendency is towards a reduction in the creation of such plans and an increase in hybrid plans.

Table 4.3. **Occupational pension plans by type**

Type of plan	Number	Percentage
DB	1 019	52.8%
DC	241	12.5%
Hybrid	670	34.7%

Source: CONSAR.

Voluntary savings in these plans may not address the sharp fall in replacement rates. Indeed, active members of occupational pension plans only represent 1.6% of the Mexican working-age population. The plans registered in 2014 cover 1 352 507 persons, of which 1 254 225 are active employees, 73 807 are pensioners and 24 475 are employees with deferred rights. The average age of active employees is 36.2 years old, while the average seniority in the job is 7.9 years. Pensioners are 65.8 years old on average. The median wage is 5.4 times the minimum wage for all active employees and is lower for people who entered the labour market after 1997 (median wage at 4.6 times the minimum wage) than for people from the transitional generation (median wage at 6.8 times the minimum wage), mostly reflecting age differences.

The plans managed MXN 496 068 million in 2014, representing 2.7% of GDP. During 2013, MXN 25 464 million have been contributed to such plans, 86% coming from employers. During the same year, MXN 24 710 million have been paid to beneficiaries.

There are concerns about the appropriate protection of members and barriers to setting up occupational pension plans. For example, there are concerns about the protection of workers' rights accrued in occupational pension plans as the regulation is far from clear on this. Ex-employees may not keep deferred rights in the plans and some of them may lose their rights when leaving the company.[12] In addition, workers have no recourse in case of sponsor insolvency when assets in the occupational plan are not sufficient to cover the liabilities.

In addition, the obligation of employers to pay a legal dismissal payment may reduce incentives to create occupational pension plans. Indeed, the Labour Law defines a legal dismissal payment of 3 months' salary plus 20 days' salary per year of service to be paid by employers upon the dismissal of employees without cause, such as dismissal due to old-age. This legal indemnity reduces the incentive to create occupational pension plans because employers have to pay the dismissal cost independently of any other benefit (pension) they may grant.

4.4. The tax treatment of retirement savings fails to provide the appropriate incentives to make additional voluntary contributions

The previous section has shown that voluntary contributions fail to offset the fall in replacement rates. The literature suggests (OECD, 2012a and 2012b) that a different tax treatment of private pension plans with respect to other saving vehicles may promote voluntary retirement savings. This section reviews the tax treatment of retirement savings in Mexico.

The design of the Mexican personal income tax system does not seem to create the appropriate incentives to make additional voluntary contributions. The tax treatment of pension contributions, investment income of pension funds and pension benefits varies according the type of contributions made and how amounts are withdrawn. This creates a complex system that many individuals may not be able to understand in order to take advantage of tax deductions/exemptions.

4.4.1. Tax treatment of contributions

In the Mexican personal income tax system, individuals pay taxes from the first peso of income earned. Marginal tax rates vary from 1.92% to 35% (Table 4.4).

Table 4.4. **Personal income tax brackets**

Lower limit (pesos)	Upper limit (pesos)	Fixed tax payment (pesos)	Tax rate applied on the excess to the lower limit (%)
0.01	5 952.84	0.00	1.92%
5 952.85	50 524.92	114.29	6.40%
50 524.93	88 793.04	2 966.91	10.88%
88 793.05	103 218.00	7 130.48	16.00%
103 218.01	123 580.20	9 438.47	17.92%
123 580.21	249 243.48	13 087.37	21.36%
249 243.49	392 841.96	39 929.05	23.52%
392 841.97	750 000.00	73 703.41	30.00%
750 000.01	1 000 000.00	180 850.82	32.00%
1 000 000.01	3 000 000.00	260 850.81	34.00%
3 000 000.01	--	940 850.81	35.00%

Source: Mexican Ministry of Finance.

Mandatory employer contributions to the retirement sub-account, as well as state contributions and social quotas are not considered as taxable income for the employee. The same applies to mandatory employer contributions to the housing sub-account. However, mandatory employee contributions to the retirement sub-account are not tax exempt.[13]

The tax treatment of voluntary savings contributions depends essentially on whether these savings have a long-term perspective or not. Short-term voluntary contributions, which can be withdrawn at any time after a period from two to six month depending on the AFORE, are not tax-exempt. They are made from after-tax income and therefore taxed at the individual's marginal rate of income tax. The same applies to solidarity savings. All the other types of voluntary personal contributions have a long-term perspective and are tax-deductible up to different limits, as described in Table 4.5.

Voluntary employer contributions to individual retirement accounts or to occupational pension plans are never considered as taxable income for the worker. However, the maximum deductible amount of contributions to occupational plans (12.5% of the employee's salary and up to 53% of total contributions to the occupational plan) includes both employee and employer contributions.[14]

There is a general limit in the income tax system for personal deductions. This limit is equal to the minimum between four times the minimum annual wage and 10% of the taxpayer's total gross income. The general deduction limit applies to the sum of all tax-deductible contributions.[15]

Table 4.5. **Tax treatment of pension contributions by workers, by type of contribution**

Type of contribution	Tax treatment	General deduction limit applies (lowest of 4 MW or 10% of taxable income)
Mandatory contributions to individual retirement accounts (IRAs)	Not deductible	
Short-term voluntary contributions	Not deductible	
Complementary contributions to IRAs	Deductible up to the lowest of 5 MW or 10% of taxable income	Yes
Long-term voluntary contributions to IRAs	Deductible up to the lowest of 5 MW or 10% of taxable income	Yes
Contributions to special "savings for retirement" accounts	Deductible up to MXN 152 000 per year	Yes
Solidarity savings	Not deductible	
Contributions to private occupational pension plans	Deductible up to 12.5% of salary (includes both employee and employer contributions)	Yes
Contributions to personal pension plans	Deductible up to the lowest of 5 MW or 10% of taxable income	Yes

Note: MW = minimum annual wage (MXN 70.10 in 2015).

Source: Mexican Ministry of Finance.

The fiscal incentive provided through the tax deductibility of some voluntary savings contributions is not an enticement for the majority of the population. Indeed, only workers with income above MXP 400 000 per year (18 times the minimum wage in the geographic area "A") are legally required to file an income tax return.[16] For workers with an income below that threshold receiving a salary from one employer only, this employer must declare the taxes withhold directly from the worker's salary. In that case, workers do not file an income tax return and therefore the deduction of their pension contributions is not direct. They have to ask the employer to make the contribution on their behalf and by this mechanism they can benefit from the fiscal deduction. According to the National Survey of Occupation and Employment (*Encuesta Nacional de Ocupación y Empleo*, ENOE), during the third quarter of 2014, only 6.7% of the employed population had a wage above five times the minimum wage (i.e. around MXN 123 000). A tiny proportion of workers is therefore required to file an income tax return and is likely to deduct pension contributions directly.

4.4.2. Tax treatment of investment income

Investment income is always tax-exempt as long as it stays invested. Upon withdrawal, investment income remains tax-exempt when generated by mandatory contributions to individual retirement accounts, long-term voluntary contributions to individual retirement accounts, contributions to special "savings for retirement" accounts, and contributions to occupational and personal pension plans.

The real interests earned from investing short-term voluntary contributions, complementary contributions to individual retirement accounts and solidarity savings is considered as taxable income upon withdrawal and taxed at the individual's marginal rate. A provisional withholding tax of 0.6% of the amounts contributed applies.[17]

4.4.3. Tax treatment of pension income

The tax treatment of pension income depends primarily on two factors: the form of payment and whether the individual is entitled to a pension when money is withdrawn (see Table 4.6). When workers reach retirement age and get benefits in the form of an annuity or programmed withdrawals, these benefits are tax-exempt up to an amount equivalent to 15 times the minimum wage. Benefits above this limit are taxed at the marginal rate. This limit applies to the sum of benefits paid by the federal government (DB benefits to transitional workers), by AFORE (individual retirement accounts), by occupational pension plans and by personal pension plans.

Workers entitled to a pension may also take their benefits in the form of a lump sum (for example, when they comply with the contribution period requirement and have accumulated enough assets to buy a life annuity equivalent to 1.3 times the minimum guaranteed pension, they have the right to buy such an annuity and withdraw the rest of the assets as a lump sum). In that case, the amounts withdrawn enjoy a yearly tax exemption of 90 times the minimum wage. The excess amount is considered as taxable income and is taxed at the average annual rate applicable to ordinary income.[18] However, lump sum payments originated from short-term voluntary contributions are tax-free, once the tax levied on real interests has been deducted.

Table 4.6. **Tax treatment of pension withdrawals, by type of contribution and form of payment**

Type of contribution	Annuity / programmed withdrawal	Lump sums	Withdrawal while not entitled to a pension
Mandatory contributions to individual retirement accounts (IRAs)	Exempt up to 15 MW; Excess taxed at marginal tax rate	Exempt up to 90 MW annually; Excess taxed at average tax rate	Exempt up to 90 MW for each year of contribution; Excess taxed at marginal tax rate with a temporary withholding tax of 20%
Short-term voluntary contributions	Not applicable	Exempt	Exempt
Complementary contributions to IRAs	Exempt up to 15 MW; Excess taxed at marginal tax rate	Exempt up to 90 MW annually; Excess taxed at marginal tax rate;	Taxed at average tax rate with a temporary withholding tax of 20%
Long-term voluntary contributions to IRAs	Exempt up to 15 MW; Excess taxed at marginal tax rate	Exempt up to 90 MW annually; Excess taxed at average tax rate	Taxed at average tax rate with a temporary withholding tax of 20%
Contributions to special "savings for retirement" accounts	Not applicable	Taxed at marginal tax rate	Taxed at marginal tax rate
Solidarity savings	Exempt up to 15 MW; Excess taxed at marginal tax rate	Exempt up to 90 MW annually; Excess taxed at average tax rate	Exempt up to 90 MW for each year of contribution; Excess taxed at marginal tax rate with a temporary withholding tax of 20%
Contributions to private occupational pension plans	Exempt up to 15 MW; Excess taxed at marginal tax rate	Exempt up to 90 MW annually; Excess taxed at average tax rate	Taxed at 30%
Contributions to personal pension plans	Exempt up to 15 MW; Excess taxed marginal tax rate	Exempt up to 90 MW annually; Excess taxed at average tax rate	Taxed at marginal tax rate with a temporary withholding tax of 20%

Note: MW = minimum wage.

When the worker gets a lump sum payment because he/she does not fulfil the requirements for obtaining a pension from his/her retirement sub-account (*negativa de pensión*), this payment is tax-exempt up to 90 times the minimum wage for each year of contribution. The excess amount is considered as sporadic taxable income and is subject to a temporary 20% withholding tax. The 20% withholding tax becomes final when the taxable income is less than MXN 123 580.20.

Amounts withdrawn before retirement from personal pension plans and retirement accounts constituted by complementary contributions and long-term voluntary contributions are considered as taxable income. A temporary withholding tax of 20% is applied on the capital and the updated interest income generated by that capital.

Finally, amounts withdrawn from the special "savings for retirement" account are considered as taxable income. However, the tax rate applied cannot be higher than the one in force at the time of the deposit.

Table 4.7 summarises the tax treatment of private pensions in Mexico. It shows that different types of contributions enjoy different tax treatments, even when they have a long-term perspective. For example, complementary contributions to individual retirement accounts and long-term voluntary contributions can both be withdrawn at retirement age only, but investment income is taxed for the former and not for the latter. This creates confusion for individuals who may have difficulties to choose the option that best suits them.

Table 4.7. **Tax treatment of private pensions, by type of contribution**

Type of contribution	Contributions	Investment income	Pension income
Mandatory contributions to individual retirement accounts (IRAs)	T	E	E
Short-term voluntary contributions	T	T upon withdrawal	E
Complementary contributions to IRAs	E	T upon withdrawal	E
Long-term voluntary contributions to IRAs	E	E	E
Contributions to special "savings for retirement" accounts	E	E	T
Solidarity savings	T	T upon withdrawal	E
Contributions to private occupational pension plans	E	E	E
Contributions to personal pension plans	E	E	E

Note: E = exempt up to a limit; T = taxed.

4.5. Low pension awareness

The main link between workers and their individual retirement account is the pension statement. This document has to be sent by the AFORE to each affiliate at least three times a year (in January, May and September). The main objective of the pension statement is to provide savers with clear and simple information to help getting information on the amount accumulated for retirement. It also allows comparing net returns between AFORE, therefore encouraging competition in the sector.

There are four different formats of pension statement for different types of workers:[19]

- "Generation AFORE": Public and private-sector workers who entered the labour market after the respective reforms took place (1 April 2007 and 1 July 1997 respectively), as well as public-sector workers who chose the DC system in 2008;
- "Transitional generation": Transitional private-sector workers who were working and contributing to the PAYG system in place before 1 July 1997;
- "Mixed IMSS-ISSSTE transitional generation": Transitional workers who have worked both in the public and private sectors and contributed to both the IMSS and the ISSSTE; and
- "Transitory DB regime": Public-sector workers who chose to remain in the old DB system in 2008.

All the pension statements include the following common information:

- The period covered by the pension statement;
- Personal data on the worker (name, personal ID code number, social security number);
- Contact details of the AFORE managing the individual account;
- Total amount of savings accumulated in the individual retirement account;
- A comparative indicator showing the net performance of each AFORE called the "Net Return Indicator" (*Indice de Rendimiento Neto*, IRN). The position of the worker's AFORE is highlighted to emphasise the relative performance of the AFORE;
- The asset allocation of the retirement savings;
- All the movements in the accounts that happened during the period covered by the statement by date (i.e. contributions paid by the worker, the employer and the state, returns earned on the portfolio, withdrawals made from the account and commissions paid to the AFORE managing the account); and
- An area where CONSAR and the AFORE can make publicity.

Two blocks in the pension statement are specific to each type of worker. For workers affiliated to the ISSSTE who have chosen the DC system in 2008 and transitional workers who have contributed both to the IMSS and the ISSSTE, the pension statement provides the amount in pesos of the recognition bond that recognizes their rights for the periods of time in which they made contributions in the ISSSTE until December 2007.

The last part of the pension statement is a general summary table of the worker's retirement savings over the period covered by the statement. For workers fully in the new DC system (generation AFORE), it has three lines for each of the main sub-accounts: the retirement sub-account, the voluntary sub-account and the housing sub-account. For the retirement sub-account and the voluntary sub-account, the table provides the account balance at the beginning of the period, the contributions paid, the withdrawals made, the returns earned, the commissions paid and the account balance at the end of the period. For the housing sub-account, the table provides the account balance at the beginning of the period, movements during the period and the account balance at the end of the period. For transitional workers, the table separates the resources that the worker will be able to withdraw as a lump sum upon retirement from those that will be used to finance his/her pension.[20] For IMSS workers, the resources used to finance the pension correspond to the resources accumulated since 1997 coming from the severance at old-age and old-age contributions plus the social quotas. For ISSSTE workers, they correspond to the resources accumulated since 2008 coming from the retirement, severance at old-age and old-age contributions plus the social quotas, plus the solidarity savings, plus any resources left in the housing sub-account (FOVISSSTE). Finally, for public-sector workers who chose to stay in the old DB scheme (transitory DB regime), the table provides the contributions realised during the period for retirement insurance, severance at old-age and old-age, as well as the detailed information for the voluntary sub-account and the housing sub-account.[21]

Although the pension statement provides a lot of information to workers, it does not seem to engage members and encourage them to take active steps to improve retirement income adequacy by, for example, increasing contributions and/or postponing retirement. One of the reasons is because not all workers contributing to the pension system receive a pension statement. In particular, assigned workers with money deposited in a SIEFORE (i.e. workers contributing but who have not chosen an AFORE) may not receive their pension statement because the AFORE does not know their address. At the end of 2014, 20% of the 52 728 388 individual retirement accounts were assigned accounts with money deposited in a SIEFORE. According to the National Survey of Labour Paths (CONSAR, 2012), only 62.4% of workers having an account with an AFORE receive their pension statement regularly.[22]

In addition, the pension statement does not engage members because a large proportion of them do not even read it. The same survey shows that less than half of workers having an account with an AFORE consult their pension statement. The interest for the pension statement increases with age, as 42.4% of workers younger than 27 having an account with an AFORE consult their pension statement, while 53.0% do so among those aged 45 to 54. In addition, 24.3% of workers having an account with an AFORE do not understand what an AFORE is.

Furthermore, one could argue that transitional workers that will be better-off choosing their pension benefits according to the old DB formula may not have any incentive to increase contributions. Indeed, increasing contributions will not improve their pension benefits under the old DB formula. For those using the DC rule, the increase in contributions necessary to achieve the same replacement rate than in the DB formula is quite large.

The lack of interest in the pension system is linked to the low financial literacy of the Mexican population. According to the 2013 National Survey on the knowledge and perception of the Retirement Savings System, targeting private-sector workers affiliated to the IMSS aged 18 to 65, 66% of workers are not in the habit of saving. Of those who save, around 70% do so to face emergencies and only 7.2% save for retirement outside the AFORE. More than half of workers have not thought about how are they going to fund their retirement. About 56% of them hope they will get a pension replacing fully their salary, but only 27% actually save to reach that target. Finally, a large proportion of workers do not know the performance of their AFORE (67.5%) or the commission charged by their AFORE (74.2%).

Some recent new steps have been taken by CONSAR to increase interest in the pension system and stimulate additional savings. Starting in 2014, CONSAR requires

AFORE to send an annual pension report which contains an estimate of the future pension level, as well as voluntary savings scenarios. In addition, CONSAR launched at the beginning of 2015 two new simulators on its webpage for IMSS affiliates and self-employed workers to provide them with the opportunity to calculate their pension with different scenarios of retirement ages, densities of contributions and voluntary savings.

4.6. Proposals to smooth-out the transition period and to increase coverage, contribution levels and contribution periods

The main objective of any proposal to address the problems facing the Mexican pension system is to increase contributions and address the transition period. The level of contributions in the Mexican pension system is low by international standards and this level may lead, in the best case scenario, to pension benefits that may only replace around 30% of final salary. Moreover, because transitional workers can choose to get their pension benefits using the more generous old DB formula, that could give them on average a replacement rate of 100%, there will be as a result a sharp fall in replacement rates once the last transitional worker retires. Therefore, there is a need to address this and smooth-out the transition period.

This section ends with a discussion on how to increase coverage and density of contributions, and on how to improve the public confidence in and understanding of the pension system. The discussion on increasing coverage focuses on those groups, considered informal, for whom it is not compulsory to save for retirement (e.g. the self-employed).

4.6.1. Increase contribution levels

The first step to attenuate the sharp fall in replacement rates after the last transitional worker retires is to increase contribution rates, at least for private-sector workers. Everything else being equal, this would increase the pension income of workers who are fully in the DC system. This section discusses four options to reach this goal: i) increase the mandatory contribution rate; (ii) earmark for retirement part of the contributions to the National Housing Fund Institute for Workers; (iii) introduce automatic voluntary contributions with an opt-out option; and/or (iv) improve incentives for voluntary pension savings.

Increase mandatory contribution rates

This section discusses first whether there is room to increase mandatory contribution rates. It then describes how to increase overall contributions and how high they may need to increase to achieve different target replacement rates taking into account the risks facing saving for retirement (financial, labour market and demographic risks).

As seen in Figure 4.2, Mexico is one of the countries among the OECD and Latin America with the lowest mandatory pension contribution rates, especially for private-sector workers (around 8.5% for an average earner when including the social quota). In addition, the tax wedge on labour income in Mexico is low in OECD comparison (see Figure 4.14). There seems therefore to be room for increasing mandatory contribution rates in Mexico, in order to enhance workers' chances to reach higher retirement income.

Figure 4.14. **Average tax wedge on labour, 2013 (1)**

At 67% of average worker earnings, single person without children

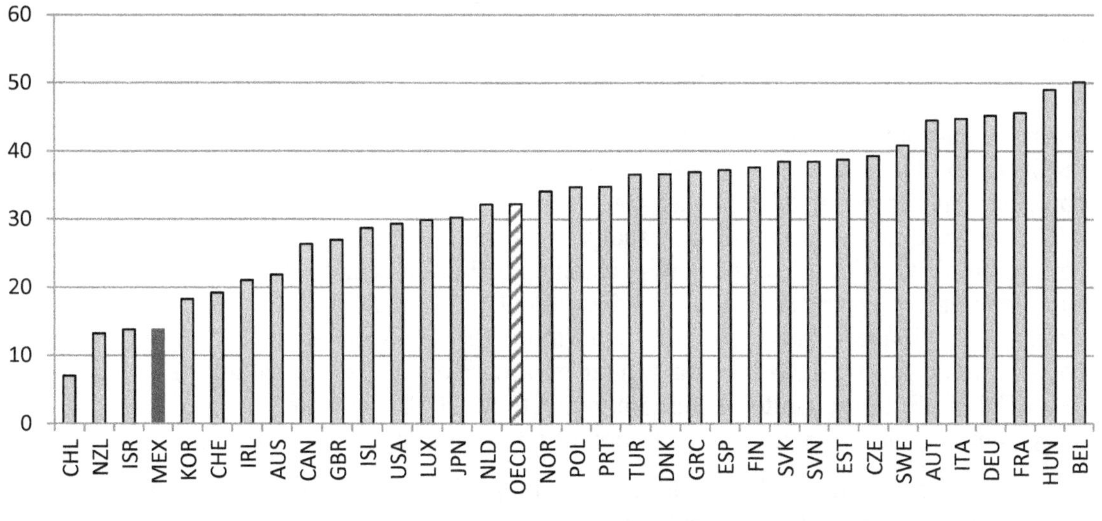

1. The tax wedge on labour is measured as the difference between total labour compensation paid by the employer and the net take-home pay of employees, as a ratio of total labour compensation. It therefore includes both employer and employee social security contributions.

Source: OECD, Taxing Wages Database.

Increases in mandatory contribution rates need however to be considered in the broader labour market context. As shown in section 4.2, there is a large share of workers that are informal (do not contribute to social security), nearly 60% of all workers in Mexico. Moreover, there are important transitions from formality into informality and vice versa. Consequently, increasing mandatory contribution rates to the pension system may encourage some private-sector workers to move into informality to avoid paying those increased social security contributions. However, OECD work on informality in low-income OECD countries shows that other factors, apart from higher taxes on labour, can affect informal employment (OECD, 2008). In particular, binding minimum wages, preferential tax treatments for self-employed workers and complex tax systems may encourage informal employment. The work concludes that combined with enhancing incentives for formalisation and improving workers' perception of the value of the benefits they are likely to receive from social protection schemes, effective enforcement of labour, tax and social security regulations is essential to combat informal employment.

Therefore, any reform to the pension system, especially one increasing the mandatory contribution rate, would need to be accompanied by a well-designed communication campaign (OECD, 2014, Chapter 5). The national pension communication campaign should explain the main goal of increasing contribution rates: to increase pension income and ensure a better standard of living during retirement.

Contribution rates can be increased by expanding workers' contributions, employers' contributions or both. On the one hand, increasing workers' contributions would reduce their disposable income which for certain income strata is already low. On the other hand, employers are already paying most of the contributions (5.15 percentage points out of the 6.5% rate) and increasing their contributions may increase their labour costs and affect their international competitiveness, and in the medium to long-term would reduce disposable income as well.[23]

There is no unique distribution of pension contributions between employers, workers and the state. Figure 4.15 shows that, among selected OECD and non-OECD countries, the share of total contributions paid by employers varies from 100% in Australia to 0% in Bolivia, Chile, the Netherlands and Peru. In countries with a mix of sources to finance pension contributions, employer contributions represent between 91% in Estonia and 36% in Slovenia. On average across the countries represented in Figure 4.15, employer contributions represent 54% of the total pension contribution, employee contributions 44% and state contributions 2%. Usually, only employers and workers make pension contributions. Outside Mexico, state pension contributions can be found in the voluntary automatic-enrolment pension plans in New Zealand and the United Kingdom. In New Zealand (KiwiSaver plans), the state contributes 50 cents for every dollar of member contribution (minimum 3%, with a similar minimum employer contribution) annually up to NZD 521.43. In the United Kingdom, by October 2018, the state will contribute 1% of wages out of a minimum total contribution of 8% in automatic-enrolment plans.

The employees in Mexico do not seem to be paying as much of the total contribution rate as they do in most OECD countries. Indeed, one can observe in Figure 4.15 that the share of total contribution paid by private-sector workers is among the lowest, only in Estonia and Australia private-sector employees pay a lower share of total contributions (0% in Australia, 9.1% in Estonia and 12.8% in Mexico).

The increase in contribution rates could be done in a gradual automatic manner to allow all stakeholders to adjust to the cost of the change. In 2012, Australia enacted an increase in mandatory pension contributions from 9% to 12%. Initially, the increase was phased-in between July 2013 and July 2019. The full 12% contribution rate is now expected to apply from 1 July 2025. Under the new schedule, the contribution rate is planned to stall for 7 years at 9.5% (until 2021) and then increase by 0.5% each year until it reaches 12% by July 2025. The United Kingdom will phase in, between October 2012 and October 2018, the minimum contribution levels to the new automatic-enrolment voluntary scheme. The minimum total contribution rate (i.e. including employee, employer and state contributions) will be 2% until September 2017, then 5% between October 2017 and September 2018, and it will be 8% from October 2018 onward. Meanwhile, the minimum employer contribution rate will stand at 1%, 2% and then 3% respectively during those three periods.[24] Chile introduced a gradual increase in the salary subjected to the contribution rate for the self-employed, who are not obliged to contribute to the mandatory DC pension system. Starting from 1 January 2012, self-employed workers are expected to contribute 10%, just as employees in general, on 40% of their covered earnings in 2012, 70% in 2013 and 100% in 2014. The success of this measure has been limited so far as participation is voluntary.

Figure 4.15. **Distribution of the total pension contribution between employers, employees and the state in selected OECD and non-OECD countries, 2012 or latest available data**

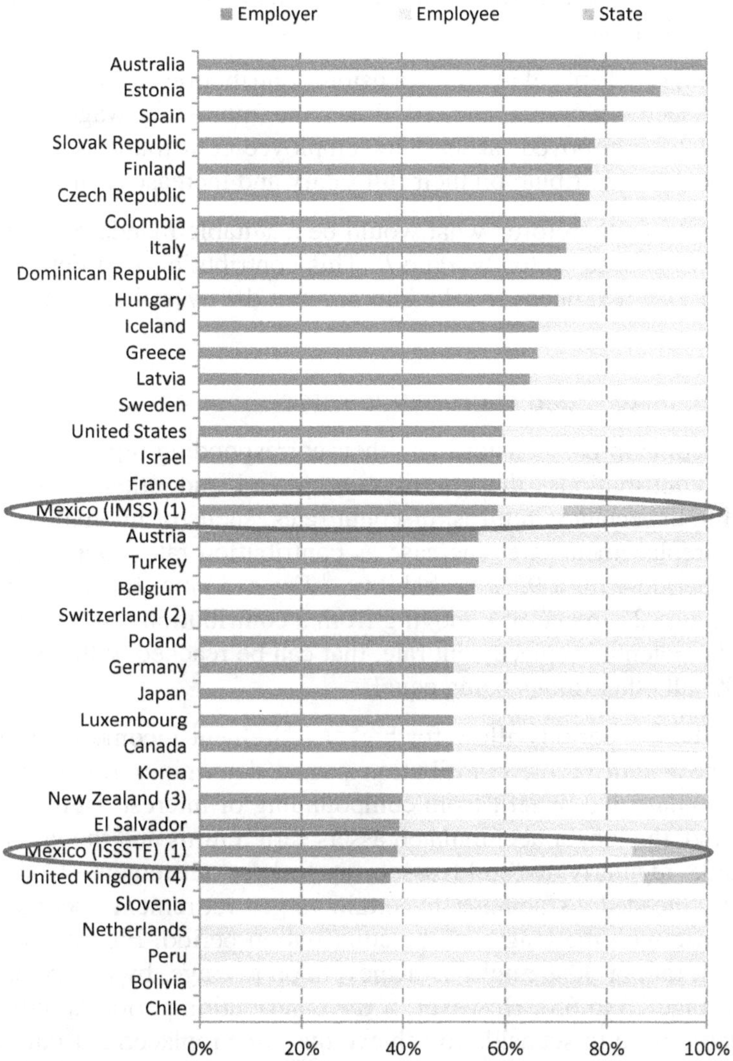

1. State contributions include the social quota for workers with a wage equivalent to 3 times the minimum wage.
2. The contribution rate to mandatory occupational pension plans varies across age groups, from 7% between 25 and 34 years old to 18% beyond 55 years old. The graph uses the rate of 10% (for people aged 35 to 44).
3. Numbers refer to minimum contribution rates to KiwiSaver pension plans.
4. Numbers refer to minimum contribution rates to automatic-enrolment pension plans.

Source: OECD (2013) and OECD/IDB/The World Bank (2014).

Increases in mandatory contributions could alternatively be tied to growth in wages. Contributions would thus increase only if wages increase and therefore they will do so without leading to a reduction in workers' disposable income. Part of the wage increase would go to increase the workers' disposable income and the other part to increase their pension contribution. The share of the increase of wages going to higher contributions should be set clearly as a result of negotiations between the parties concerned. Obviously, the smaller the share of the growth in wages going to higher contributions, the longer it will take to reach the contribution rate that will provide a level of retirement income concomitant with people's expectations. This increase would be applied at the individual level, meaning that two individuals working in a different industry may experience different wage increases and therefore may not contribute at the same rate in all periods. Each individual would have a different pace of increase, until reaching the targeted mandatory contribution rate.

Caps on earnings when calculating pension contributions (25 times the minimum wage for private-sector workers and 10 times the minimum wage for public-sector workers) could also be removed, at least for employee contributions. This would allow high-income earners to contribute on their full salary and increase their replacement rate.

The next question is therefore "what would be a suitable mandatory contribution rate for both public and private-sector workers?" This contribution rate depends first on the target replacement rate and needs to take into account the overall structure of the pension system.

Target retirement income and contribution rate

Retirement income in DC pensions and their corresponding replacement rates depend on the level of contributions, the contribution period and other parameters that are uncertain (e.g. life expectancy, returns, discount rates, spells of unemployment).[25] Figure 4.16 shows how replacement rates increase as contribution rates increase, depending on the contribution period with a 95% probability.[26] For example, for a contribution period of 40 years (from age 25 to age 65), moving from a contribution rate of just below 9% to 13% increases the potential replacement rate, that can be reached with a 95% probability, from 20% to 30% all other things being equal.

Longer contribution periods allow for higher retirement income for a given level of contributions. The length of the contribution period determines for how long amounts contributed accumulate and benefit from compounding of interest. Hence, the longer the contribution period, the longer accumulated assets earn returns and the less money people need to put aside regularly to build assets to finance retirement. Consequently, the contribution rates needed to achieve a certain target retirement income with a 95% probability decrease with the length of the contribution period. Figure 4.16 shows that a target replacement rate of 30% might be achieved, on average, by contributing 13% over a 40 year period (age 25 to 65). However, if the contribution period is only 30 years, the amounts one would need to set aside to achieve the same replacement rate with the same probability would equal around 18% of wages. For a contribution period of only 20 years, a 30% replacement rate cannot be achieved with 95% probability with a contribution rate lower than 20%.

Increasing contributions raises the probability of reaching a given target retirement income and the associated replacement rate. Using the same methodology as for Figure 4.16, Table 4.8 shows the contribution rates needed to achieve different target replacement rates with various pre-established probabilities based on a 40-year career, a portfolio composed of 60% long-term government bonds and 40% equities, and a stochastic model. The table shows that, to reach a target replacement rate of 60% with a 90% probability, one needs to contribute 21.75% of his/her wage over 40 years. With a 15.5% contribution rate, the likelihood of reaching a 60% replacement rate falls to 75%. If policy makers set as a goal of the pension system to provide a pension income replacing 70% of the last salary with a 90% probability, the contribution rate needs to increase to 25.25%.

Figure 4.16. **Replacement rates reached with 95% probability according to different contribution levels and contribution periods**

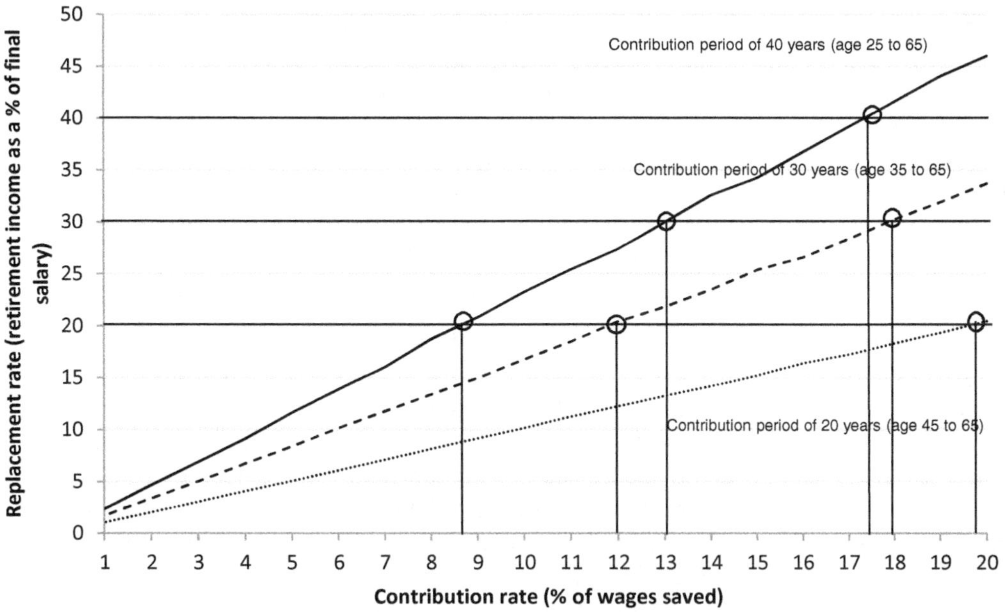

Note: Contribution and replacement rates at the 5th percentile when assets are invested in a portfolio comprising 40% equities and 60% fixed income, assuming stochastic investment returns, discount rates, inflation, labour market conditions and stochastic life expectancy at age 65.

Source: OECD (2012a).

Table 4.8. **Contribution rates needed to achieve different target replacement rates with a given probability**

		Target replacement rate (RR)							
		30	40	50	60	70	80	90	100
Probability of reaching the target RR	50	5.3	7.0	8.8	10.3	12.0	14.0	15.5	17.3
	75	7.8	10.5	13.0	15.5	18.0	20.8	23.5	26.0
	90	11.0	14.5	18.0	21.8	25.3	28.8	32.3	36.3
	95	12.8	17.3	21.8	25.8	30.5	35.0	39.0	43.3
	99	17.3	23.3	28.5	34.5	39.3	45.8	51.5	57.0

Note: OECD calculations, which result from assuming uncertain investment returns, inflation, discount rates, life expectancy and labour market conditions. People contribute over a 40-year period, assets are invested in a portfolio comprising 40% in equities and 60% in long-term government bonds, and people are assumed to buy a nominal life annuity at age 65.

Source: Authors' calculations.

Therefore, contribution rates to achieve target replacement rates of the magnitude of those granted by the old DB formula and with a high probability are unrealistic. The pension benefits granted by the DB formula are too generous given current contribution rates. Therefore, the only way to smooth-out the transition period without increasing contributions to levels that are unrealistic would be to adjust downward the retirement income granted by the DB formula going forward and increase in parallel the contribution rates to the levels of other similar countries (e.g. 10% for all workers). Before elaborating this proposal, let's review additional proposals to increase contribution further without increasing labour cost, that is, using contributions already being disbursed.

Earmark for retirement part of the contributions to the National Housing Fund Institute for Workers

As a way to alleviate the country's pension gap, the current reform proposal approved by the Lower Chamber and pending approval by the Senate establishes the creation of a mixed individual account for unemployment, housing and pension purposes, using part of the contributions to the housing sub-account of private-sector workers, managed by the National Housing Fund Institute for Workers (INFONAVIT). Under the proposal, the current 5% employer contribution to INFONAVIT would be divided into two parts: i) a housing account which would continue to function as under the present system, but with the amount of contribution reduced from 5% to 2% of earnings; and ii) a new mixed account, in which the remaining 3% of the employer contribution would be placed.

This mixed account could be used for three purposes: unemployment benefits, mortgage payments or retirement income. As is already the case today, accumulated balances in both accounts could be used for housing finance, while future contributions to both accounts would be used for making mortgage payments. Similarly, any balances remaining in either account would be added to the individual retirement account at the time the worker becomes eligible for retirement. The main change would be that, at the same time, workers would be able to use the balance in the mixed account for unemployment insurance. Eligible individuals may collect unemployment benefits for up to six months, once every five years.[27] In addition, in contrast with the present situation, where INFONAVIT retains the funds in the housing sub-account even if the worker does not request a housing loan, under the current law proposal, the worker would be free to transfer the mixed account to the AFORE of his/her choice after July 2017. Therefore, workers willing to increase their future retirement income could either leave the funds in their mixed account with INFONAVIT or transfer it to an AFORE.

The main limitation of this proposal with respect to the objective of increasing the future retirement income of private-sector workers is that the resources in the mixed account are not earmarked for retirement. There is the risk that all the assets in the mixed account would be depleted at retirement, with workers drawing as many unemployment benefits as possible or using the fund for housing finance. There is therefore no guarantee that the creation of the mixed account would eventually increase replacement rates for private-sector workers.

Expanding on the reform proposal, one could go one step further and consider diverting part of the contributions to INFONAVIT directly to the DC individual retirement accounts. Earmarking part of INFONAVIT contributions for retirement would increase mandatory pension contributions, without increasing workers' and employers' total social security contributions.

Most pension stakeholders in Mexico seem to be in favour of diverting part of the housing fund contributions to the DC individual retirement accounts. They argue that the housing fund could perform its basic function of providing housing to low-income individuals with lower contribution rates. There is the question of why INFONAVIT needs captive funds from workers to finance loans to buy housing, when the banking sector could provide this without contributions. Moreover, affordable housing is provided in many other OECD countries without the recourse to contributions from workers into a housing fund. Finally, the rate of return on contributions to the housing fund has been disappointing (OECD, 2015a). It used to be paid by the operating profits of the institution, but seems in practice to have followed the growth rate of the minimum wage.

Currently, INFONAVIT follows a self-defined investment regime that resembles that of basic SIEFORE 2.

However, the unions and workers representatives seem to dislike the idea of shifting part of INFONAVIT contributions to the individual retirement accounts because then the money becomes earmarked for retirement and workers cannot have access to it to finance housing if needed.

Introduce automatic voluntary contributions with an opt-out option

Another option to increase overall contribution rates is to increase voluntary savings by nudging people in an automatic manner. This automatic voluntary contribution scheme would be accompanied by an opt-out option, giving workers the option not to contribute if they decide so.

Automatic enrolment has gained popularity in recent years to increase coverage in voluntary pension systems. It involves signing-up people automatically to private pension plans but giving them the option to opt-out within specified timeframes. Automatic enrolment aims to harness individuals' inertia in thinking about retirement and pension saving, while preserving individual choice and responsibility for the decision about whether to save in a private pension arrangement.

This mechanism could be implemented as follows. Starting from a given date, employers could deduct part of the workers' salary and pay workers' contributions to the voluntary sub-accounts of the DC system (preferably one of those having a long-term perspective where contributions cannot be withdrawn before retirement). Workers would have a specified timeframe (called opting-out window) to decide to opt out of the scheme, or do nothing and continue contributing. Chapter 4 of OECD (2014) identifies elements of the design of automatic enrolment schemes that may influence coverage and contribution outcomes, looking at the experience of implementing automatic enrolment in six OECD countries (Canada, Chile, Italy, New Zealand, the United Kingdom and the United States). In particular, it assesses the potential impact of the target population, the opting-out window, contribution rates, financial and non-financial incentives, and other pension plan characteristics, including default options.

In the case of Mexico, matching contributions from the employer and/or from the state could also be envisaged for those who do not opt-out, as a way to encourage workers to contribute.[28] The next sub-section explores in greater details how incentives could be improved in Mexico to encourage further voluntary pension savings.

Improve incentives for voluntary pension savings

As long as they have a long-term perspective, voluntary pension savings enjoy tax advantages in Mexico in order to promote additional savings for retirement. Workers can deduct from their income tax base contributions up to four times the minimum annual wage or 10% of the taxpayer's total gross income, whichever is the lowest.[29] However, tax deductions give the greatest incentive to save for retirement to those with the highest level of income, as they are subject to the highest marginal tax rates. This is illustrated in Figure 4.17 with contribution rates of 5% and 10%. The deduction limit reduces the incentive, measured as a reduction in the effective tax rate, only for the very high-income workers. In addition, only workers with income above MXP 400 000 per year (18 times the minimum wage) are legally required to file an income tax return. Workers with an income below that threshold can ask the employer to withhold the tax due. This is however uncommon. Therefore, in practice, the fiscal incentive is not an enticement for the majority of the population.

Figure 4.17. **Incentives of tax deductions for different contribution rates, by income**

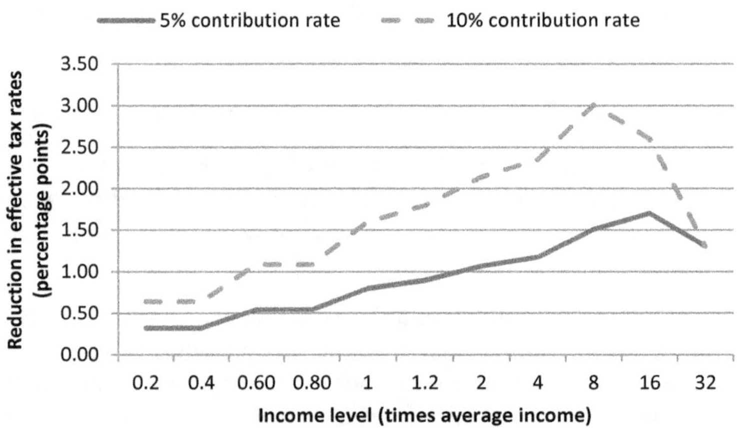

Source: Authors' calculations using current tax brackets in Mexico.

An alternative way of introducing tax incentives that changes the incentive inversely with income is to use a tax credit (OECD, 2012). Tax credits entail that after calculating taxable income and applying the tax rates relative to the income brackets to determine the tax due, one can apply a deduction to the tax due. This deduction can be a fixed amount equal for all income levels or a percentage of contributions with a cap. In both cases the incentive of tax credits is lower for higher income individuals (see Figure 4.18). Replacing tax deductions with tax credits may therefore help increasing the incentive to make additional voluntary contributions among middle-to-low income individuals.

Figure 4.18. **Incentives of tax credits, by income**

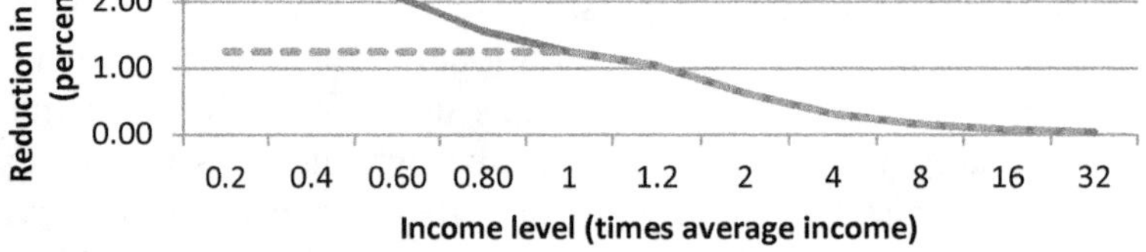

Notes: The calculations assume a 5% contribution rate. The credit is equal to 25% of the amount contributed and the cap is equal to the credit for the average income.

Source: Authors' calculations using current tax brackets in Mexico.

International evidence shows that, besides tax incentives, other types of financial incentives, in particular flat subsidies and matching contributions, have a positive impact on coverage and contribution levels in voluntary private pension arrangements. Moreover, flat subsidies and matching contributions seem to reduce the disparity in coverage rates by income level in voluntary systems. The Australian, German and New Zealand experiences (Chapter 4, OECD, 2012) highlight the strong impact that subsidies and matching contributions can have on coverage and contribution rates in voluntary private pension arrangements. The German experience suggests that flat subsidies have a positive effect on the coverage rate for low-income individuals, while the Australian case shows that matching contributions encourage higher contributions but are not necessarily effective in raising coverage among low-income groups. New Zealand, which combines both subsidies and matching contributions, achieves a similar income distribution of KiwiSaver members and the eligible population.[30]

There is already a matching contribution in the Mexican pension system for public-sector workers affiliated to the ISSSTE (the Solidarity Savings programme). People can contribute between 1% and 2% of their income voluntarily and the government matches each peso with 3.25 pesos. Since its introduction, the amount of voluntary contributions has increased (see Figure 4.12 above). However, this programme may prove very costly for the federal government, which effectively pays 76% of all the contributions to solidarity savings accounts.

There is a proposal to introduce matching contributions for private-sector workers affiliated to the IMSS.[31] Under the current proposal, voluntary savings would be complemented by an automatic contribution from the federal government equal to a fraction of workers' savings, up to a pre-defined limit. The government would contribute MXN 0.20 for each peso contributed, up to a maximum of MXN 60 per year (for MXN 300 of contributions from the worker).

However, the match may not be sufficient to entice private-sector workers to make additional voluntary contributions. Indeed Figure 4.19 shows this match in the dotted line, assuming that people contribute the maximum MXN 300. When comparing it to a typical fixed match contribution of 1 to 5 (solid line), less than the match for public-sector employees but more than for private-sector employees, it is clear that the proposed match for private-sector employees may be low as the reduction in the effective tax rate would be very limited. The figure also shows that establishing a cap after a certain income level (here the average income), dashed line, can have the expected results in encouraging voluntary retirement savings, while reducing its costs as the incentive falls for higher income.[32]

Figure 4.19. **Incentives of government matching contribution, by income**

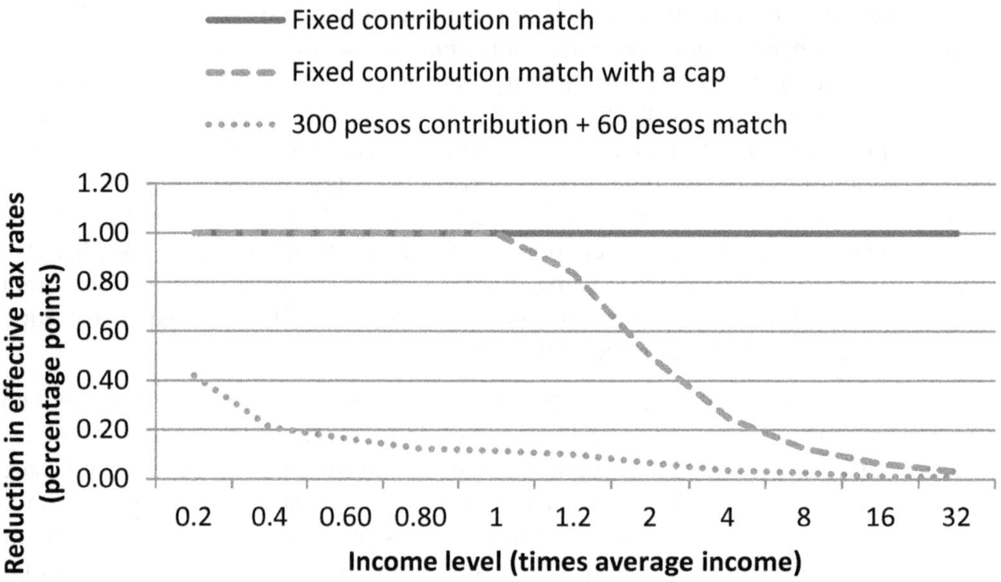

Notes: The calculations assume a 5% contribution rate and a 1% matching contribution. The cap is equal to the match for the average income. The "dot" line represents the incentive provided by a MXN 60 matching contribution from the government for MXN 300 of contributions by the worker.

Source: Authors' calculations using current tax brackets in Mexico.

Mexico may consider applying other match rates, looking at international experience. As shown in Table 4.9, match rates in OECD countries (excluding Mexico) vary from 4.25% in Austria to 50% in Australia, Iceland and New Zealand. On the one hand, the Solidarity Savings programme, with a match rate of 325%, stands out as very generous and costly for the federal government. On the other hand, the proposal for private-sector workers, with a match rate of 20% up to an annual limit of MXN 60, may not be a sufficient incentive to encourage workers making additional voluntary contributions.

Finally, as regard matching, tax deductions combined with capped matching contributions can make tax incentives more neutral with respect to income. Figure 4.20 shows the overall incentive in terms of reduction in effective tax rates of having tax deductions of contributions and adding a matching contribution of 1 percentage point, given a contribution rate of 5%. The tax deduction increases incentives with income: adding the incentive of a 1 percentage point match just shifts the curve upwards, increasing the incentive but without changing the income structure of the incentive (solid line). However, adding a matching contribution of 1 percentage point with a cap on the match (e.g. a cap equal to the match for the average income) changes the tax incentive relationship with income by making it more flat (dashed line).

Table 4.9. **Matching contribution programmes in OECD countries**

Country	Description of the matching contribution programme
Australia	The super co-contribution is a government matching contribution for eligible individuals. The match rate is 50% since 2012-13. Individuals with an income below the lower income threshold (AUD 34 488 for 2014-15) can get 50 cents for each dollar contributed, up to the full maximum entitlement (AUD 500 for 2014-15). For every dollar that the individual earns above the lower income threshold, the maximum entitlement is reduced by 3.333 cents.
Austria	Personal contributions to a state-sponsored retirement provision plan can attract state matching contributions. The matching contribution rate corresponds to a fixed flat rate of 2.75% plus a variable rate depending on the annual general level of interest rate. For 2014, the variable rate is 1.5% (thus the total matching rate is 4.25%). As of 1 January 2014, the maximum personal contributions considered to calculate the state contribution is EUR 2 495.12 (thus the maximum state matching contribution for 2014 is EUR 106.04).
Chile	Workers making voluntary contributions and assigning those savings to increase or bring forward their pension are entitled to a state matching contribution, corresponding to 15% of the amount saved annually, subject to a limit. These funds are added to the individual capitalisation account each year. For each calendar year this contribution is limited to 6 UTM (*Unidad Tributaria Mensual* in Spanish, or Monthly Tax Unit).
Czech Republic	Employee contributions made into supplementary pension insurance plans are matched each month by the government according to the following scale: - CZK 230 if the individual contributes at least CZK 1 000 the same month. - CZK 210 if the individual contributes between CZK 900 and CZK 999 the same month. - CZK 190 if the individual contributes between CZK 800 and CZK 899 the same month. - CZK 170 if the individual contributes between CZK 700 and CZK 799 the same month. - CZK 150 if the individual contributes between CZK 600 and CZK 699 the same month. - CZK 130 if the individual contributes between CZK 500 and CZK 599 the same month. - CZK 110 if the individual contributes between CZK 400 and CZK 499 the same month. - CZK 90 if the individual contributes between CZK 300 and CZK 399 the same month. - CZK 0 if the individual contributes less than CZK 300 the same month.
Iceland	According to collective agreements, employers contribute minimum 2% to voluntary personal pension plans if the employee matches the amount with a least the same percentage. The most common contribution rate (employee and employer) is therefore 6% of the employee's salary when employees contribute their maximum percentage (4%).
Mexico	Solidarity Savings are a federal government matching mechanism to motivate public-sector workers affiliated to the pension system to make voluntary contributions. For each peso that the worker contributes voluntarily for retirement purposes, the federal government in its capacity as employer contributes 3.25 pesos. Workers can contribute either 1% or 2% of their salary.
New Zealand	The government makes an annual contribution towards KiwiSaver accounts as long as members contribute and are aged 18 and over (and satisfy some additional criteria). The government pays 50 cents for every dollar of member contribution annually up to a maximum payment of NZD 521.43.

Figure 4.20. **Incentives of adding matching contributions to tax deductions, by income**

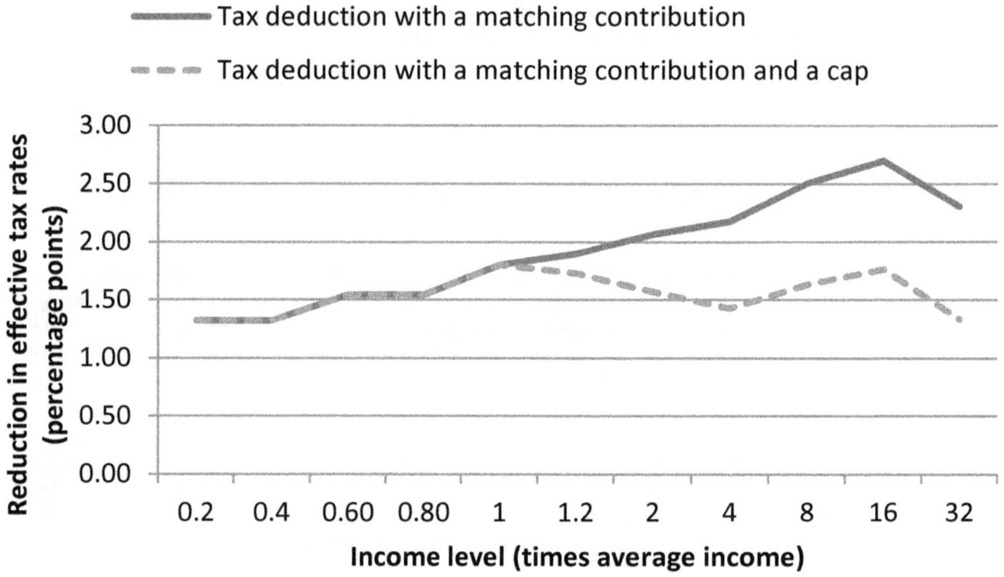

Note: The calculations assume a 5% contribution rate and a 1% matching contribution. The cap is equal to the match for the average income.

Source: Authors' calculations using current tax brackets in Mexico.

The international evidence also suggested that having subsidies may encourage voluntary contributions, especially for mid-to-low income people. The German experience suggests that flat subsidies have a positive effect on the coverage rate for low-income individuals.

Germany experienced an important increase in coverage, especially for low earners, thanks to the introduction of "Riester" pensions in 2001. Riester products can be purchased by anyone covered by the social insurance system and who is subject to full tax liability. Participants qualify for subsidies and tax relief from the state, the level of which depends on the respective contribution rate and number of children. To receive the full state subsidy, pension participants must invest at least 4% of their previous year's income in a Riester plan.[33] Since 2008, the basic annual state subsidy is EUR 154 for single persons, EUR 308 for married couples (when each partner has his/her own plan) and EUR 185 for every child (EUR 300 for children born in 2008 or after). Only very low-income households can get the full subsidy without investing 4% of their income if they contribute at least EUR 60 annually. This exception holds for people receiving minimum social benefits, low-income workers (earnings less than EUR 800 per month) and non-retired inactive people without income. The coverage rate of Riester pension plans was 29.3% of the working-age population at the end of 2013 (see Figure 4.21) and seems to have reached a plateau since 2011.

Figure 4.21. **Coverage over time of Riester pension plans**

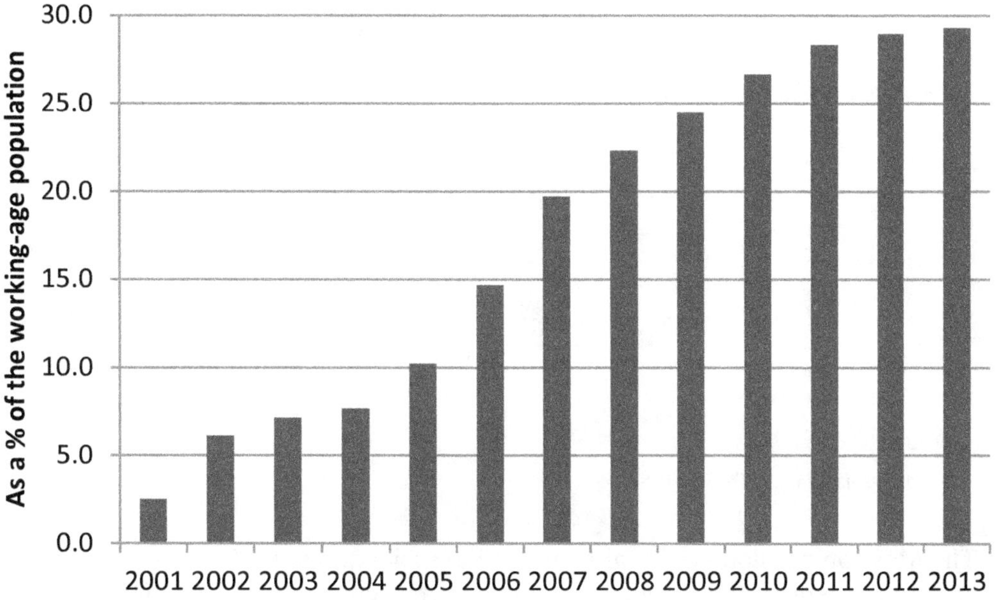

Source: German Ministry of Labour and Social Affairs.

Unlike occupational and other personal pensions in Germany, Riester pensions generally achieve a better distribution of coverage across income groups. Figure 4.22 shows the percentage of households where at least one of the partners is enrolled in a private pension plan other than a Riester plan (right panel) or in a Riester plan (left panel). When Riester plans are excluded, the higher the income of the household, the higher is the coverage rate of private pension plans. Coverage rates for Riester pensions are on the other hand more homogeneous across income groups and actually peak for individuals in the medium-income groups (4th and 7th deciles). The distribution of coverage rates by income is also more concentrated for Riester plans than for other private pension plans. In particular, Riester plans achieve higher coverage rates for low-income households (e.g. 13.6% of the labour force in the 1st decile) than other private pension plans (4.5%), even though the average coverage rate of Riester plans is lower. As Riester plans have been primarily designed so as to be accessible to low earners (through the minimum annual contribution of EUR 60 for people receiving minimum social benefits for instance), it is actually easier for them to get the full state subsidy. This is most probably the prime factor behind the comparatively high coverage rates among low earners.

Figure 4.22. **Coverage rate of private pension plans in Germany according to the income of the household and the type of plan, December 2008**

As a percentage of the labour force

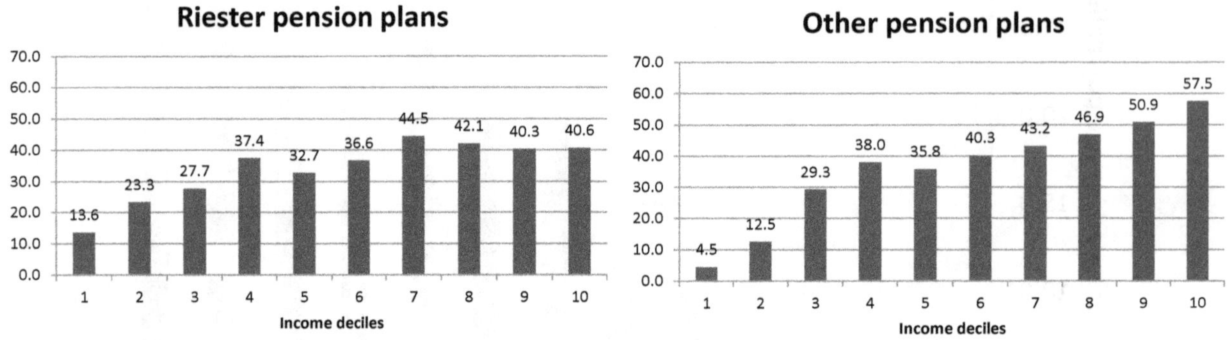

Source: OECD calculations using the 2009 SAVE Survey.

The Mexican pension system already has the social quota that is a subsidy paid by the federal government in the mandatory individual retirement account. However, it is not used to promote additional voluntary pension savings.[34]

The Mexican authorities may want to consider introducing flat subsidies on the voluntary saving component of their pension system to promote higher voluntary savings, especially for mid-to-low income individuals. However, as the social quota on mandatory contribution does not seem to increase coverage much for private-sector workers, policy makers may need to consider that matching contributions may work better.

4.6.2. Introduce a pro-rata system for transitional workers

To smooth out the steep change in retirement income and replacement rates that would occur when the transition period ends, one needs to combine an increase in contribution rates with a pro-rata system for transitional public and private-sector workers. The increase in contribution rates that would be needed to completely offset the drop in pension income for public and private-sector workers when the transition period ends may be quite high, especially for private-sector workers. Figure 4.23 illustrates for reasonable increases in contribution rates (see dashed black line in Figure 4.23) that, although the sharp step would be attenuated, there would still be a marked difference between people retiring under the old DB system and those under the DC rules.[35] The steep change could be smoothed out further by applying a pro-rata system from today onwards for all transitional workers (see dotted black line in Figure 4.23).

The pro-rata system is for all transitional workers, public and private-sector. All the pension rights earned under the old DB formula would be kept, but from today onwards, workers would only earn pension benefits under the DC rules, so their retirement pension benefits would comprise two components, DB and DC:

- DB component: The corresponding pension payment would be calculated based on the old DB formula and the number of years spent in the DB system up to today. Assets accumulated up to today in the individual retirement accounts of private-sector workers (plus the returns on investment until retirement) would partially finance the DB component. When this balance is depleted, the DB component would be then financed from the federal budget. For public-sector workers that chose to stay in the old DB system, as they do not have assets accumulated, the DB component would be fully financed from the federal budget.

- DC component: New accumulation in the individual retirement accounts from today until retirement would be used to pay for the DC component. The corresponding pension payment would depend on returns on investment and the number of years to retirement.

Figure 4.23. **Illustration of the smoothing-out of the transition period**

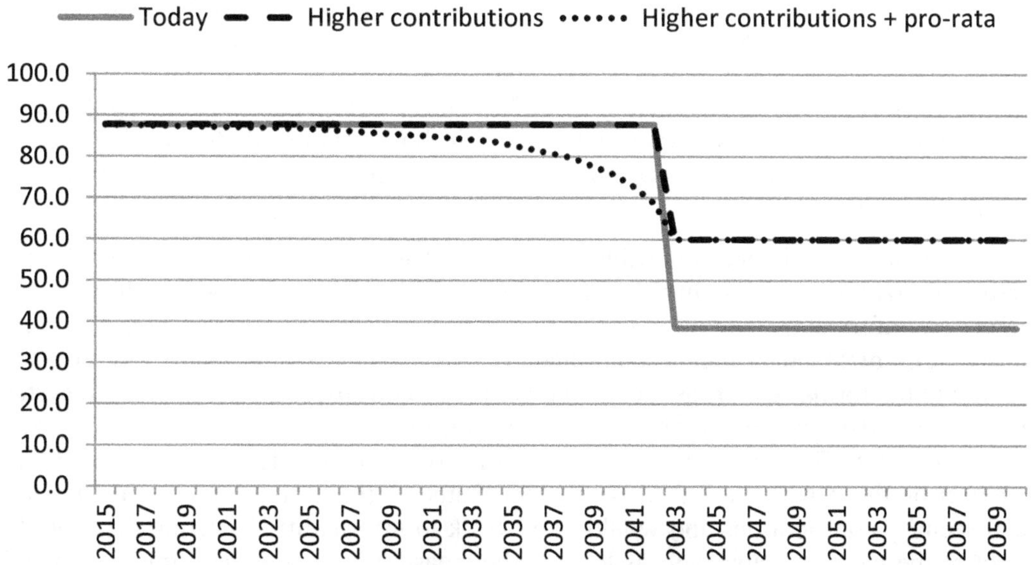

This proposal would improve the new DC system. Firstly, it would make the new DC system look less unfair for workers that entered the labour market after the reforms where implemented (1997 for private-sector workers and 2007 for public-sector workers). However, transitional workers would see their potential pension benefits reduced, but those benefits were not fully backed by the current level of contributions, as discussed previously. Secondly, the sense of ownership for workers, especially transitional workers, of their individual retirement accounts would increase, thereby increasing financial discipline by both contributors and pension funds, and probably eventually limiting inefficient public spending.

The pro-rata proposal would also have an impact on government finances. Substantial savings would arise from lowering potential DB liabilities when applying the pro-rata system to private-sector workers. Currently, DB pensions for transitional private-sector workers choosing the old system at retirement are paid from the assets accumulated in their individual retirement accounts, which are transferred to the federal government. However, the contributions that built those assets are not enough to cover the benefits promised under the old DB formula. The government therefore needs to provide complementary finance. The introduction of the pro-rata system would limit the government payments and therefore its potential liabilities, as only DB rights acquired up to today would need to be covered. For public-sector workers that chose to stay in the old DB system, the government would experience an increase of expenses in the short-term as today's contributions would not pay any longer for today's pension benefits.

Contributions would instead accumulate in workers' individual retirement accounts. However, the pro-rata system applied to public-sector workers would reduce future government expenses because from today onwards their future pension benefits would be based on the assets accumulated in their individual retirement accounts.

4.6.3. Increase coverage and densities of contributions

The main reason why coverage and contribution densities are relatively low in Mexico, despite the mandatory affiliation of employees, pertains to the importance of the informal sector.[36] At the end of 2014, as much as 58.1% of workers were in the informal sector, therefore not contributing to the pension system. In addition, according to the National Survey of Labour Paths, many workers switch between formal and informal sectors several times during their career, leading to low contribution densities in the pension system.[37] Between January 2007 and July 2012, 17.1% of the workers had switched from formality to informality and 17.6% from informality to formality. Over the 5-year period, 24% of the workers had worked in both sectors. Reducing the informal sector is therefore a key policy objective in order to increase coverage and contribution densities in the pension system.

Introducing mandatory contributions for self-employed workers would help increasing coverage and contribution densities. By definition, most self-employed workers are informal as they do not have to contribute to the pension system. At the end of 2014, self-employed workers represented 22.5% of workers in Mexico. Only 11.6% of them are in the formal sector, as they make voluntary contributions to the pension system (see Figure 4.10). Implementing compulsory pension contributions for self-employed workers may not affect those already contributing voluntarily (11.6%) but it would have an impact on those who are informal (88.4%). Some of them may not be willing to pay social security contributions and would move back to informality, lowering therefore the impact of the measure. However, as long as the measure increases the number of people previously informal contributing to the system, it would have a positive impact.

Chile has introduced mandatory contributions for self-employed workers in a gradual manner. The pension reform of 2008 establishes the obligation for self-employed workers in a certain tax category to contribute to the private pension system starting from 1 January 2012.[38] Their participation was voluntary before that date. The law stipulates a gradual process of pension system affiliation and mandatory contributions between 2012 and 2015. During this period, pension contribution will be paid from the tax rebates owed to the workers unless the latter explicitly state that they do not wish to pay contributions. In addition, the share of covered earnings taken into account for contributions is gradually increasing, from 40% in 2012 to 70% in 2013 and 100% in 2014. From 2015, all eligible self-employed workers will have to contribute based on their full covered earnings with no possibility to opt-out. According to the Chilean Superintendence of Pensions, 304 011 self-employed individuals, representing 32% of those affected by the policy, automatically contributed to the pension system in 2013 based on their self-employment earnings of 2012. Only 11% of them did not have a DC account before and became new members of the pension system (all the others were already members of the pension system). In addition, 60% had already contributed to the pension system as employees during the year, so their contributions as self-employed came to fill the gap of contributions for the total income earned (as employee and self-employed). In 2014, 254 055 self-employed individuals contributed for their self-employment earnings of 2013, representing 27% of the targeted population that year.

The success of this policy has however been limited so far, as Chilean self-employed workers have largely used the temporary opt-out option. Indeed, 68% of self-employed individuals have decided not to contribute for the year 2012 and 73% for the year 2013. These high rates were observed despite the fact that only part of covered earnings were taken into account for contributions. One of the reasons for refusing to contribute may be the lack of willingness to lower net earnings due to the contributions to the pension system. This and other related factors explaining why only around 4% of self-employed workers were covered by the Chilean pension system before 2012 are likely relevant explanations for the high opt-out rates. Indeed, both income and employment of self-employed workers are unstable, which prevents them from contributing on a monthly basis. In addition, there is a lack of information regarding the benefits of contributing to the pension system and of a "pension culture", as well as preference for liquidity.[39]

4.6.4. Improve public understanding and confidence in the pension system

Find a better alignment between public and private-sector pensions

The fragmentation of the pension system (with special pension regimes for local governments, state universities and some state-owned companies) and the existence of different rules for public and private-sector workers in the SAR limits labour mobility and could undermine public confidence in the pension system. In particular, while new generations of public and private-sector workers all participate in the SAR, contributing into DC individual retirement accounts, the two groups of workers are subject to different rules and can expect quite different replacement rates. The main contrasting parameter is the contribution rate, which is much lower for private-sector workers (at 6.5% of the basic salary) than for public-sector workers (11.3% of the basic salary), and leads to significant differences in replacement rates.[40] For example, CONSAR estimates a replacement rate of 42.1% for a full-career private-sector worker earning four times the minimum wage, as opposed to 65.6% for a public-sector worker at the same earnings level.[41] In addition, public-sector workers benefit from advantageous conditions to make voluntary contributions through the solidarity savings programme, with a state matching contribution of 3.25 pesos for each peso that the worker contributes voluntarily for retirement purposes. There is no equivalent programme yet for private-sector workers and the current reform proposal envisages a much lower match rate of MXN 0.20 for each peso contributed.

There is a need to find a better alignment between public and private-sector pensions. As mentioned earlier, the OECD considers that contribution rates should increase in Mexico. Any reform affecting the contribution rate could be the occasion to make the two systems gradually converge on (i) the total contribution rate; (ii) the split between employer, employee and state contributions; and (iii) the social quota. Special regimes should also converge gradually in a view to harmonise the rules for all workers. Such convergence could increase public support in the pension system and improve labour mobility. In addition, the caps on earnings when calculating pension contributions (25 times the minimum wage for private-sector workers and 10 times the minimum wage for public-sector workers) could be removed for both types of workers. This would allow high-income earners to contribute on their full salary and increase their replacement rate.

Improve the information provided in pension statements

As Mexico is gradually moving to a DC pension system, the role of workers to build their own retirement income is increasing. Future pensions from DC pension plans depend on workers' choices regarding which AFORE is managing their resources, how much to contribute (on top of mandatory contributions), when to retire and how to allocate assets accumulated at retirement. Therefore, in order to take these decisions, workers must understand the nature of their pension plan and the risks they face.

Pension benefits from DC pension plans are inherently uncertain. Future pension benefits from these plans depend on a number of factors such as returns on investment, discount rates, inflation, wages and employment, as well as life expectancy, all of which are uncertain. The difficulty in making decisions is that the changes in these factors are unknown at the time the decisions are made.

One important tool in helping workers manage this task is the pension statement. The OECD (2014) argues that the statement should provide clear and simple information about key facts. Moreover, the pension statement should be more than a passive document that delivers information, it should aim to engage workers and encourage them to take active steps to improve retirement income adequacy by, for example, increasing contributions and/or postponing retirement. Pension statements can also help in conveying the uncertainty about future pension benefits and provide projections about future benefits, although those projected pension benefits are never certain and workers need projections they can readily comprehend.

Another item that could be included in the pension statement is the total number of contribution weeks. This information would be very useful for those workers getting near retirement age to review whether the total number of weeks computed at the IMSS or the ISSSTE matches their labour history. If not, they could check this information with the corresponding institute and ask for a revision.

Statement organisers in Mexico should set clear and measurable objectives and introduce thorough evaluation processes. In the absence of robust evaluation, pension statements are unlikely to perform an optimal role in the communication of key information; they will not encourage members to take appropriate actions; nor will they support broader national DC communication programmes, for example in relation to pension reform and national financial literacy campaigns.

In 2014, the Mexican authorities organised the sending to all IMSS and ISSSTE affiliates of a document providing an estimation of their future monthly pension, assuming different rates of additional voluntary contributions. The objectives were to warn people about the low level of contributions in the pension system, stimulate higher voluntary savings and increase financial literacy. Using the actual current account balance in the worker's retirement account, the document estimates the likely monthly pension amount in case the worker starts contributing voluntarily 1%, 3% or 5% of his/her wage until retirement. An asterisk warns the individual that this estimation exercise has only an informative role and does not guarantee the ultimate amount of the future pension. Unfortunately, there has not been any evaluation of the impact of this document on workers' behaviour regarding voluntary contributions so far.

This simulation exercise could be generalised and added to the pension statement sent by AFORE. Starting in 2014, CONSAR requires AFORE to send an annual pension report which contains an estimate of the future pension level, as well as voluntary savings scenarios. However, including this report directly in the pension statement could have a bigger impact. It would help workers realise about the (low) level of their expected pension income. Providing different scenarios with different levels of voluntary contributions could prompt workers to react and take actions by starting making voluntary contributions or increasing them. Different scenarios regarding the retirement age could also help people understand the positive impact of postponing retirement on pension income, as doing so increases assets accumulated to finance retirement and reduces the retirement period that those assets need to finance.

If one of the goals of the pension statement is to increase competition between AFORE, pension statements could also include a simulation of future pension income with different scenarios regarding investment returns and fees. The objective would be to make workers aware of the magnitude of the impact of the performance of their AFORE and of the fees they charge on future pension income.

Organise well-designed National Pension Communication Campaigns to better promote pension savings and increase financial literacy

In 2014, CONSAR launched a communication campaign to promote voluntary pension savings in 7-Eleven convenience stores. The objective of the campaign was to explain to workers that they can save easily in any of the 1 780 7-Eleven stores around the country, from MXN 50 and as often as they wish, with the possibility to withdraw their money. The campaign consisted of advertising the new savings programme in newspapers and TV spots both in Mexico City and in the different states.

Unfortunately, there is no evaluation of the impact of the campaign. Since the programme runs, there is no data on the number of people who have actually deposited money in their AFORE through 7-Eleven stores. In addition, feedback from individuals would be helpful to monitor the impact of the programme.

As future campaigns will probably take place to better promote pension savings and increase financial literacy, the Mexican authorities could learn from the experience in other countries regarding the design of National Pension Communication Campaigns (NPCCs). The OECD has carried out an analysis of NPCCs in different countries, covering all aspects of NPCCs, from design to implementation and evaluation. The main policy guidelines or lessons that emerge from that analysis are contained in Chapter 5 of the OECD Pensions Outlook 2014. The thrust of those recommendations is that NPCCs should be part of an overall national strategy; major events (e.g. pension reforms) call for specific NPCCs; successful NPCC are driven by clear, realistic, and well-targeted objectives that produce outcomes that can be measured, evaluated and monitored against their goals and processes; robust evaluation processes are essential; and NPCCs should avoid having many messages and focus on less accessible groups.

Notes

1. The OECD pension model additionally assumes 2% inflation, 1.25% real earnings growth and a 2% discount rate. Individual earnings (including the minimum wage) are assumed to grow in line with the economy-wide average. The OECD pension model in the case of DC plans, like in Mexico, uses the annuity formula to convert the amount of assets accumulated at retirement into a retirement income stream, and applies a 15% discount for charges and fees.

2. Estimations from CONSAR lead to higher replacement rates due to a different set of assumptions. Assuming a 40-year career with flat salaries, a real rate of return of 5.19% and administrative charges of 1.19%, they find replacement rates of 42.1% for

a worker earning four times the minimum wage (average) and 64.4% for a worker earning two times the minimum wage (median).

3. As of December 2014, 14 382 transitional workers have chosen to retire under the DC rules because they were entitled to the minimum guaranteed pension, which is higher than the minimum pension under the DB formula (respectively MXN 2 600.96 and MXN 2 046.74 in December 2014).

4. Active accounts are defined as those that received at least one contribution during the last three years.

5. These calculations assume a real rate of return of 5.19% and administrative charges of 1.19%.

6. A public-sector worker earning four times the minimum wage and contributing respectively 1% and 2% of his/her salary voluntarily can expect a replacement rate of 86.2% and 107.8% respectively thanks to the generous state matching programme.

7. The new DC pension system was introduced for public-sector workers 10 years after the one for private-sector workers.

8. The reduction in replacement rates may be partially offset for public-sector workers making additional voluntary contributions as part of the Solidarity Savings programme (see section 4.3).

9. The number of accounts held by private-sector workers affiliated to the IMSS are those which are registered with an AFORE as well as assigned accounts for workers who have not chosen an AFORE. It does not mean that 60% of working-age individuals are actually contributing to their accounts.

10. Formal sector workers are defined here as workers paying social security contributions.

11. As described in Chapter 2, Solidarity Savings is the state matching contribution programme for public-sector workers affiliated to the ISSSTE.

12. In the case of DC schemes, if an employee has been contributing to the plan, he/she can withdraw the resources when leaving the company.

13. The same tax treatment applies to contributions by public-sector workers who decided to stay in the old DB system.

14. The regulation to the Income Tax Law, from 2006, has not been updated to match the recent Income Tax Law amendments from 2015. This creates confusion as to the extent to which the tax deduction of contributions to occupational pension plans apply to DC and hybrid plans.

15. The general deduction limit also applies to other expenses such as hospital and medical expenses, funeral expenses and mortgage real interests.

16. The geographic area "A" covers Mexico City (Federal District) and its metropolitan area; the states of Baja California, Baja California Sur; the cities of Acapulco, Guerrero, Ciudad Juarez, Chihuahua, Guadalajara, Jalisco and its suburbs, Monterrey, Nuevo León and its metropolitan area, Hermosillo, Sonora, Matamoros and Reynosa, Tamaulipas and Coatzacoalcos, and Veracruz.

17. Individuals whose only taxable income is composed of interest income can consider the withholding tax as their final tax payment as long as these interests do not exceed MXN 100 000 per year.

18. Workers can also get the balances accumulated between 1992 and 1997 in the individual retirement account as a lump sum upon retirement. Those are also exempted from tax up to 90 times the minimum wage annually.

19. Explained versions of the four pension statements can be found on CONSAR website: www.consar.gob.mx/principal/nuevo_estado_cuenta_afores.aspx.

20. The resources that the worker will be able to withdraw as a lump sum are the resources left in the housing sub-account (only if he/she chooses the DB system), balances accumulated in the individual retirement account between 1992 and 1997, the amount corresponding to the retirement insurance contribution in the retirement sub-account (2% of the base salary paid by the employer) accumulated since 1997, and the voluntary savings.

21. The contributions for retirement insurance, severance at old-age and old-age do not accumulate in the individual retirement account but are paid directly to the ISSSTE to finance the old PAYG system.

22. According to the 2013 National Survey on the knowledge and perception of the Retirement Savings System, 58.7% of private-sector workers affiliated to the IMSS receive their pension statement less often than three or four times a year.

23. Ultimately, depending on the bargaining power of employees, increasing contributions may affect negatively workers' incomes.

24. In the case of the United Kingdom, contributions to the automatic enrolment scheme are voluntary and come as a complement to the mandatory pension contributions to the public PAYG system. For more details on the automatic enrolment scheme, see Chapter 4 of OECD (2014).

25. See OECD, 2012a.

26. The figure presents the contribution rates needed to achieve different target replacement rates with a 95% probability based on different career lengths, a portfolio composed of 60% long-term government bonds and 40% equities, and a stochastic model with uncertainty about returns, interest rates, inflation, life expectancy, employment prospects and career real wage growth paths (see Antolin and Payet, 2011).

27. For more details, see Chapter 5 of OECD (2015a).

28. An analysis of the fiscal cost of this proposal is out of the scope of this report.

29. This deduction limit applies to the sum of all tax-deductible contributions, see Section 4.4.

30. New Zealand removed the state "kick-start" contribution of NZD 1 000 as of May 2015 because it was considered too costly for the government.

31. This is part of the reform proposal currently pending approval in the Senate.

32. As a way of comparison, a 2% contribution rate under the Solidarity Savings programme for ISSSTE affiliates reduces the effective tax rates between 6.6 and 7.2 percentage points depending on income (between 3.3 and 3.6 percentage points with

a 1% contribution rate) due to the very generous matching from the federal government.

33. Both own contributions and state subsidies are taken into account to calculate this rate.

34. The social quota for private-sector employees is progressive and decreases with income, while for public-sector employees it is a flat subsidy equal for all workers with less than ten minimum wages.

35. The illustration in Figure 4.23 is the same for private and public-sector workers, although the parameters would be different.

36. There are different types of informal workers, (i) the self-employed or independent workers, who are not obliged to participate in the mandatory individual retirement account system, and (ii) other workers who, despite having to participate and contribute, somehow fail to make contributions.. For a "legalistic" or "social protection" definition of informality, see Gasparini and Tornarolli (2007).

37. The National Survey of Labour Paths was a special module of the National Survey of Occupation and Employment conducted in 2012.

38. The policy targets self-employed workers who personally carry out an activity by which they obtain work income taxed under Article 42 No.2 of the Income Tax Law. All male workers who are at least 55 years of age, and female workers who are at least 50 years of age, as of 1 January 2012, are exempt, as well as self-employed workers who have an early retirement benefit or who are members of a pension institution of the old PAYG system, of the Social Security Department of the Chilean Police Force or of the National Defence Social Security Fund. Self-employed workers for whom it is difficult to determine their income and oversee their contributions, such as agricultural and fishery workers and micro entrepreneurs, are not covered by the automatic enrolment programme. Participation in the pension system remains voluntary for them.

39. It is also argued that separating pension contributions from other social contributions (e.g. health care) for self-employed workers could make more tolerable for the self-employed to accept introducing mandatory pension contributions, and it could increase their participation in the pension system.

40. The cap applied to the basic salary to calculate pension contributions is lower for public-sector workers (10 times the minimum wage) than for private-sector workers (25 times the minimum wage). This reduces the effective contribution rate for high-income earners more heavily for public-sector workers. However, less than 10% of paid workers receive an income higher than 5 times the minimum wage. The cap is therefore not binding for most workers.

41. The calculations assume a 40-year career with flat salaries, a real rate of return of 5.19% and administrative charges of 1.19%.

References

Pablo Antolin and Stéphanie Payet (2011), "Assessing the Labour, Financial and Demographic Risks to Retirement Income from Defined-Contribution Pensions", *OECD Journal: Financial Market Trends*, Vol. 2010/2. DOI: *http://dx.doi.org/10.1787/fmt-2010-5kggc0z23fr5.*

Bosch, M., A. Melguizo and C. Pagés (2013), *Better Pensions, Better Jobs: Towards Universal Coverage in Latin America and the Caribbean*, Inter-American Development Bank, Washington, DC.

CONSAR (2012), "Resultados de la primera Encuesta Nacional de Trayectorias Laborales", Press Release, No. 21/201, 21 November, Comisión Nacional del Sistema de Ahorro para el Retiro, Mexico City, available at: *www.consar.gob.mx/sala_prensa/pdf/boletines/2012/BP_21_2012.pdf;* results summarised in: "Encuesta de Trayectorias Laborales", available at: *www.consar.gob.mx/sala_prensa/pdf/presentaciones/2012/encuesta_trayectorias_laborales.pdf.*

Gasparini, L. and L. Tornarolli (2007), "Labour Informality in Latin America and the Caribbean: Patterns and Trends from Household Survey Microdata", Working Document n°46, Center for Distributional, Labor and Social Studies at Universidad Nacional de La Plata (Argentina).

Inland Revenue (2011), *KiwiSaver Annual Report 4, July 2010-June 2011.*

Instituto Mexicano del Seguro Social (IMSS) (1996), *Aportaciones al debate*, Mexico D.F.

OECD (2015b), *OECD Urban Policy Reviews: Mexico 2015: Transforming Urban Policy and Housing Finance*, OECD Publishing, Paris. DOI: *http://dx.doi.org/10.1787/9789264227293-en.*

OECD (2015b), *Pensions at a Glance 2015.* Forthcoming.

OECD (2014), *OECD Pensions Outlook 2014*, OECD Publishing, Paris. DOI: *http://dx.doi.org/10.1787/9789264222687-en.*

OECD (2013), *Pensions at a Glance 2013: OECD and G20 Indicators*, OECD Publishing, Paris. DOI: *http://dx.doi.org/10.1787/pension_glance-2013-en*

OECD (2012a), *OECD Pensions Outlook 2012*, OECD Publishing, Paris. DOI: *http://dx.doi.org/10.1787/9789264169401-en*

OECD (2012b), *The OECD Roadmap for the Good Design of Defined Contribution Pension Plans. www.oecd.org/finance/private-pensions/50582753.pdf.*

OECD (2008), "Declaring Work or Staying Underground: Informal Employment in Seven OECD Countries", in OECD, *OECD Employment Outlook 2008*, OECD Publishing, Paris. DOI: *http://dx.doi.org/10.1787/empl_outlook-2008-4-en.*

OECD (2005), *Recommendation on Principles and Good Practices for Financial Education and Awareness. www.oecd.org/finance/financial-education/35108560.pdf.*

OECD/IDB/The World Bank (2014a), *Pensions at a Glance: Latin America and the Caribbean*, OECD Publishing, Paris. DOI: *http://dx.doi.org/10.1787/pension_glance-2014-en.*

Chapter 5

Improving the design of the accumulation phase in the Mexican pension system

This chapter focuses on the accumulation phase of the funded defined contribution part of the Mexican pension system. It looks at the different investment strategies adopted by pension plans (SIEFORE) within the framework of the multi-funds age-related scheme. It also discusses the impact of existing investment restrictions, issues related to fees charged to members and the different approaches implemented to increase competition and reduce fees, risk-based supervision, governance and regulation. The chapter concludes with some recommendations that allow more choice on investment strategies, address high charges and increase competition among pension funds (AFORE).

* The statistical data for Israel are supplied by and under the responsibility of the relevant Israeli authorities. The use of such data by the OECD is without prejudice to the status of the Golan Heights, East Jerusalem and Israeli settlements in the West Bank under the terms of international law.

This chapter focuses on the accumulation phase of the Mexican fully funded defined contribution (DC) system and argues that there is room to improve its design. The accumulation phase is organised around specialised private asset managers (*Administradoras de Fondos para el Retiro*) known as AFORE that manage workers' individual retirement accounts where IMSS and ISSSTE workers deposit their contributions.[1] AFORE place contributions in investment funds called SIEFORE (*Sociedades de Inversión Especializadas en Fondos para el Retiro*). AFORE manage individual retirement accounts and SIEFORE invest the assets accumulated in those accounts.

This chapter looks at the different investment strategies adopted by SIEFORE within the framework of the multi-funds age-related scheme. It also discusses the different investment restrictions and their impact on investment strategies. The chapter then addresses issues related to fees charged to members and the different approaches implemented to increase competition among AFORE and thus reduce fees. Other issues related to the accumulation phase include risk-based supervision (RBS), governance and regulation in general. The chapter ends with some recommendations based on the OECD Roadmap for the Good Design of Defined Contribution Pension Plans, the OECD Core Principles for Pension Fund Regulation, and the IOPS Principles for Supervision.

5.1. The current investment regime of SIEFORE may not be optimal

AFORE manage individual retirement accounts placing contributions in SIEFORE that invest the assets accumulated in those accounts. At the end of 2014, the net asset of SIEFORE was MXN 2 373 381 million, representing 14.1% of GDP (see Figure 5.1), which puts Mexico in the middle range of OECD countries after only 17 years of existence of the funded pension system. Over those 17 years, the assets managed by SIEFORE have grown on average by 41.9% annually (Figure 5.2). In addition, the Retirement Savings System (SAR) has yielded on average a nominal annual rate of return of 12.53% and a real annual rate of return of 6.20% since 1997.

According to the Mexican pension regulation, each AFORE must have four SIEFORE for investing the compulsory savings, called basic SIEFORE (SB), and they may have additional SIEFORE for voluntary contributions and occupational pension plans. Each basic SIEFORE has a specific investment regime that depends on the age of the worker. The basic SIEFORE are classified by the following employee's age brackets:

- SB4: up to 36 years old;
- SB3: between 37 and 45 years-old;
- SB2: between 46 and 59 years-old;
- SB1: 60 years-old or older.

Figure 5.1. **Mexico's pension fund assets in an international context, 2014**

As a % of GDP

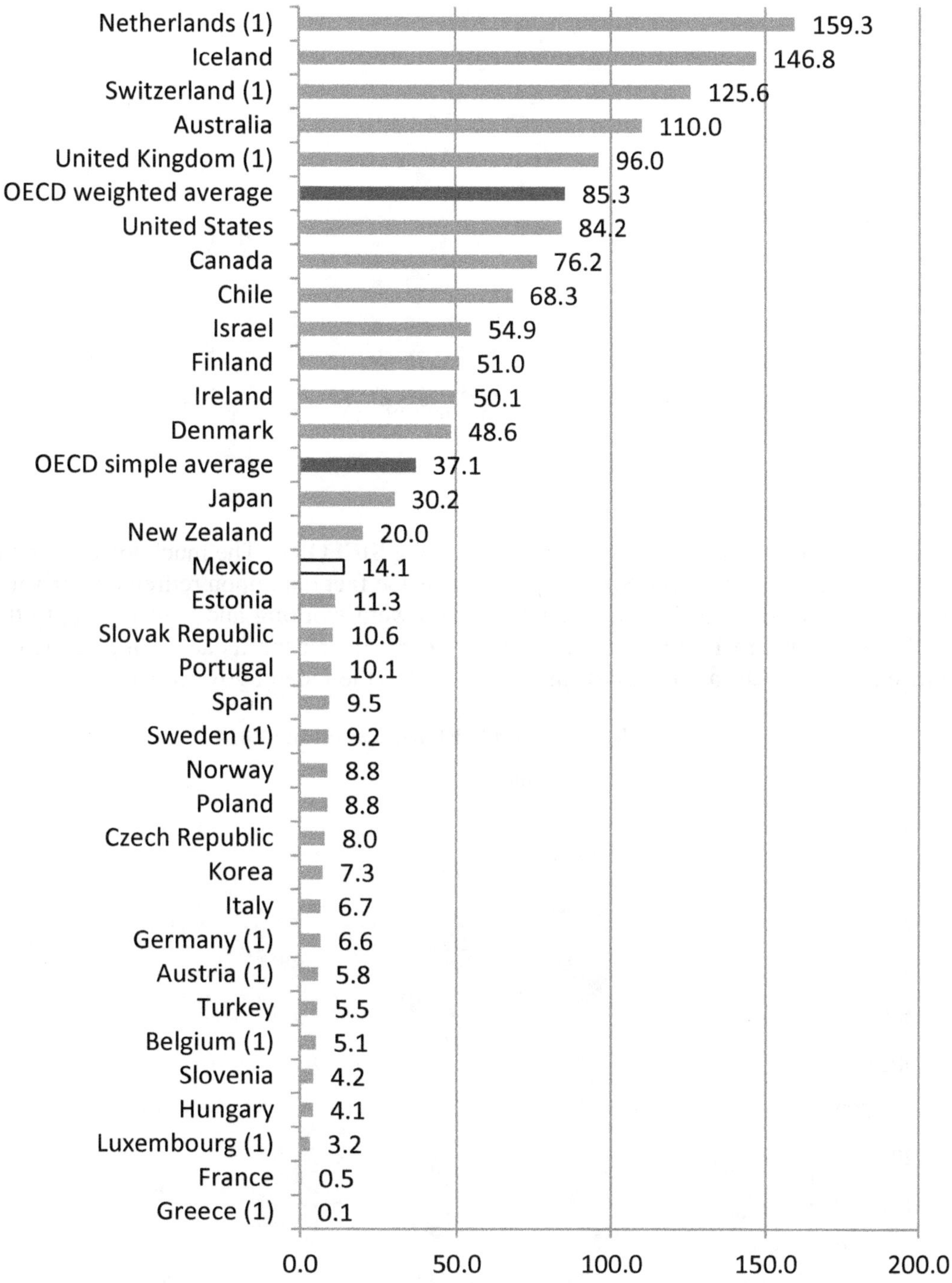

1. Preliminary data.

Source: OECD Global Pension Statistics.

Figure 5.2. **Net assets managed by SIEFORE**

In millions of pesos

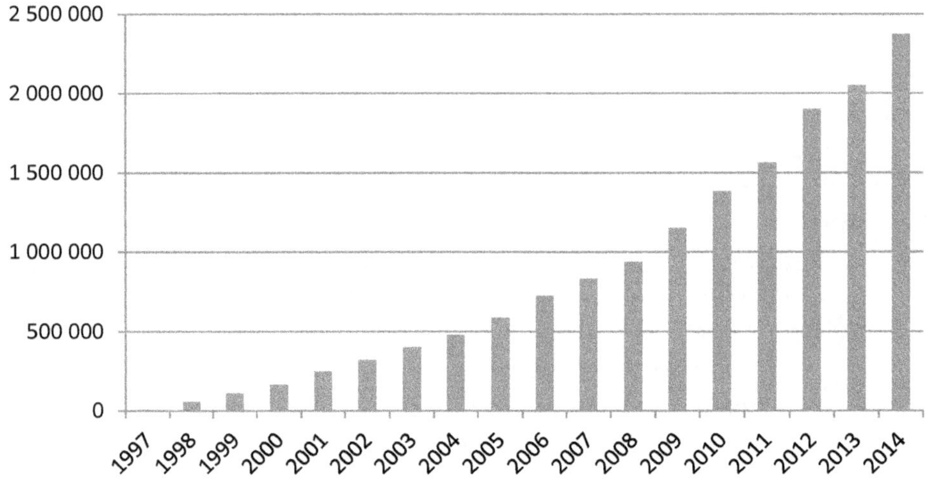

Source: CONSAR.

Figure 5.3 shows the distribution of assets among SIEFORE. The much lower amount of assets managed by the basic SIEFORE 1 reflects the fact that, upon retirement, private-sector workers of the transitional generation (who were working and contributing to the old DB system before 1 July 1997) can choose to get their benefits according to the old DB formula, in which case the assets are transferred to the federal government.

Figure 5.3. **Net assets of SIEFORE, December 2014**

In millions of pesos

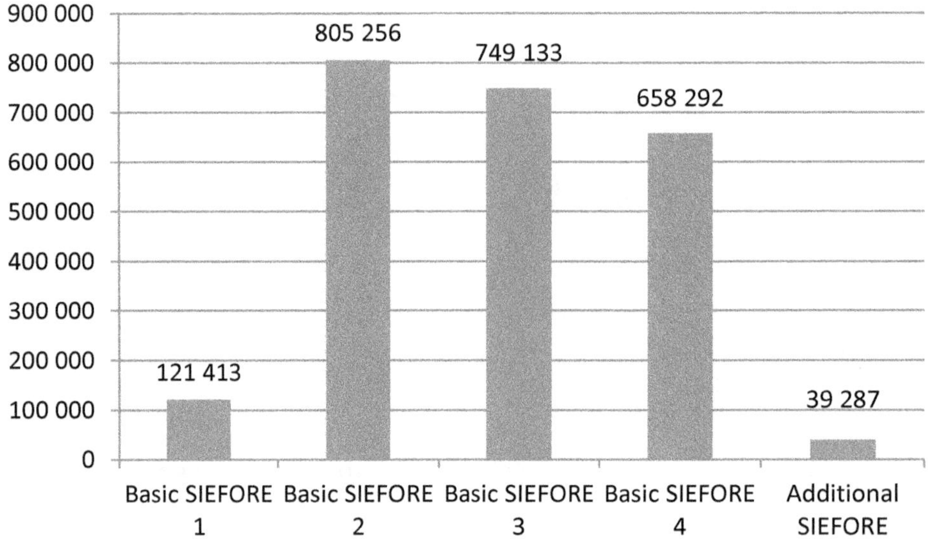

Note: The additional SIEFORE invest the voluntary savings of workers, as well as the social provision funds of public and private entities administered by AFORE.

Source: CONSAR.

Net returns in SIEFORE compare well with returns in other OECD countries. Table 5.1 shows net returns by AFORE and basic SIEFORE over the last five years, while Table 5.2 shows the average nominal and real returns of the SAR over the same period in an international context.

Table 5.1. **Net nominal returns, by type of basic SIEFORE and by AFORE**

As of December 2014

Basic SIEFORE 1	Net return 58 months
PensionISSSTE	8.05%
Invercap	7.77%
SURA	7.38%
Profuturo GNP	7.27%
Banamex	7.03%
XXI-Banorte	6.64%
MetLife	6.56%
Principal	6.36%
Azteca	5.94%
Coppel	5.43%
Inbursa	4.87%
Simple average	6.66%
Weighted average (1)	7.01%

Basic SIEFORE 2	Net return 60 months
SURA	9.58%
PensionISSSTE	9.54%
Banamex	8.94%
Profuturo GNP	8.80%
XXI-Banorte	8.46%
Invercap	8.26%
MetLife	8.26%
Principal	7.80%
Azteca	7.18%
Coppel	6.98%
Inbursa	5.04%
Simple average	8.08%
Weighted average (1)	8.49%

Basic SIEFORE 3	Net return 62 months
SURA	10.91%
PensionISSSTE	10.73%
Banamex	9.90%
Profuturo GNP	9.69%
Invercap	9.50%
MetLife	9.44%
XXI-Banorte	9.29%
Principal	8.76%
Azteca	8.15%
Coppel	7.59%
Inbursa	5.72%
Simple average	9.06%
Weighted average (1)	9.51%

Basic SIEFORE 4	Net return 62 months
SURA	12.19%
Banamex	11.22%
Profuturo GNP	11.06%
PensionISSSTE	10.90%
MetLife	10.47%
Invercap	10.47%
XXI-Banorte	10.11%
Principal	9.71%
Azteca	8.51%
Coppel	7.85%
Inbursa	6.20%
Simple average	9.88%
Weighted average (1)	10.38%

Notes: The net return indicator represents the long-term historical performance of SIEFORE, net of fees.
(1) Weighted by assets under management.

Source: CONSAR.

Table 5.2. **Nominal and real 5-year average net returns of SIEFORE in an international context**

As of December 2014

	5 year-average	
	Real	**Nominal**
Netherlands	7.8	9.8
Denmark	7.1	8.9
Canada	6.9	8.7
New Zealand (1)	6.3	8.6
Australia (2)	6.0	8.8
Norway	4.9	6.6
Israel (3)	4.8	6.5
Iceland	4.5	8.0
United States	4.5	6.2
Mexico (4)	4.1	8.2
Chile	3.7	7.1
Spain	2.9	4.4
Slovenia	2.7	4.2
Austria	2.5	4.7
Italy	2.4	4.0
Korea	2.1	4.2
Japan	1.8	2.5
Portugal	1.3	2.9
Estonia	0.9	3.6
Czech Republic	0.6	2.3
Slovak Republic	0.3	2.1

Notes: The average net returns have been calculated following a common methodology for all countries.

1. The 5-year average returns have been calculated over the period March 2009 - March 2014.
2. The 5-year average returns have been calculated over the period June 2009 - June 2014.
3. Data refer to new pension plans only.
4. Data refer to the Retirement Savings System only (occupational plans are not included).

Source: OECD Global Pension Statistics.

The investment regime of Mexico is in accordance with the OECD guidelines. The OECD Roadmap encourages establishing default life-cycle investment strategies as a default option to protect people close to retirement against extreme negative outcomes. In this regard, each basic SIEFORE has a specific investment regime that depends on the age of the worker. For instance, the SB4 (for young workers) has the most aggressive investment regime and SB1 (for workers near to retirement) has the most conservative one. As members get older, their pension assets are invested in a more conservative investment regime, with lower exposure to equity and a greater proportion of fixed-income instruments, to reduce the volatility of their returns. Thus, a young affiliate will gradually move from basic SIEFORE 4 (SB4) to SB3, SB2 and finally SB1. Nonetheless, any affiliate may opt to invest his/her resources in a more conservative fund than the default option. The glide-path of risky investments along a worker's career is illustrated in Figure 5.4, according to the maximum limits allowed by regulation for each basic SIEFORE (see Table 5.3).

However, the Mexican investment regime does not fully follow the OECD guidelines as it does not provide choice between investment options with different risk profiles and investment horizons. Indeed, workers have very limited choices in this multi-funds system. They cannot have resources invested in more than one basic SIEFORE and have no say on the investment strategy of their resources within that fund. The investment strategy of each basic SIEFORE is decided by the AFORE, within the limits established by regulation (see Table 5.3). Despite those limits, there is a great heterogeneity of investment strategies implemented by AFORE for each basic SIEFORE. For example, at the end of December 2014, equity investment of basic SIEFORE 4 varied from less than 20% for PensionISSSTE (15.6%) and Inbursa (16.9%) to more than 34% for XXI Banorte (34.3%) and Invercap (36.3%), with a regulatory limit of 40%. This heterogeneity in investment strategies is reflected in the net returns in Table 5.1. The only options given to workers are to select the AFORE of their choice, based on returns and investment strategies information provided in their pension statement and in CONSAR's website, and to invest their resources in a more conservative fund than the default option.

Figure 5.4. **Multi-funds schemes by age**

Investment limits as a % of total investment

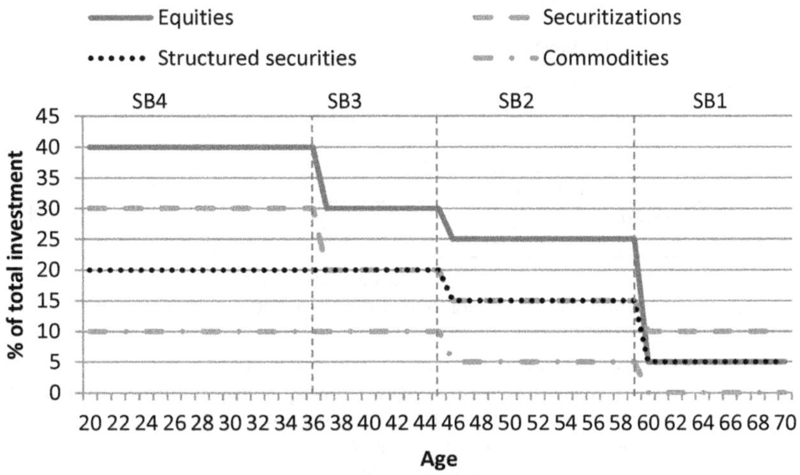

Source: CONSAR.

When workers reach the age limit between two SIEFORE, the regulation allows AFORE to carry out the transfer of the assets in cash or by transferring a proportion of the portfolio from the ceding SIEFORE to the receiving SIEFORE. The second option allows the AFORE to send assets from one SIEFORE to another without the need to sale financial assets. This aims at preventing any distortion in prices in the financial markets as well as eliminating the brokerage and market costs for the worker. CONSAR establishes the date of the transfer of the assets. The valuation of funds is done in the usual way, i.e. using the official prices vectors provided by the authorised rate providers. The prices used to value the assets leaving the ceding SIEFORE are the same as those used to value the assets of the receiving SIEFORE.

The Mexican pension system establishes strict investment requirements.[2] The investment regime of the basic SIEFORE is characterised by its differentiated quantitative limits and qualitative requirements. The quantitative limits are established depending on the permitted asset class (equity, currency, securitizations, inflation protected securities, commodities), the nationality of the issuer, the credit rating of the issuer, holdings in a single issuance and conflicts of interest limits and provisions. The investment and risk management limits are summarised in Table 5.3.

Table 5.3. **Limits contained in the investment regime applicable to SIEFORE (1)**

			SB1	SB2	SB3	SB4
Market and liquidity risks		Value at Risk (2)	0.70%	1.10%	1.40%	2.10%
		Difference of the Conditional Value at Risk (2)	0.30%	0.45%	0.70%	1.00%
		Liquidity coverage ratio (3)	80%	80%	80%	80%
Risk by issuer and/or counterparty (4)	Local (5)	Debt from mxBBB to mxAAA or int'l currencies BB to AAA	5%	5%	5%	5%
		Subordinated debt mxBB+ to mxBBB- or int'l currencies B+ to BB-	1%	1%	1%	1%
	Int'l	Foreign securities from BBB- to AAA from one issuer or counterparty (6)	5%	5%	5%	5%
		Holding of a single issuance (7)	Maximum {35%; $300mdp}			
Asset class limits		Foreign securities (4)	20%	20%	20%	20%
		Equity (4,8)	5%	25%	30%	40%
		Foreign currency (4)	30%	30%	30%	30%
		Securitizations (9)	10%	15%	20%	30%
		Structured securities (4,10)	5%	15%	20%	20%
		Infrastructure or housing	NA	10%	13%	13%
		Others	NA	5%	7%	7%
		Inflation protected securities (11)	Yes	No	No	No
		Commodities (4)	0%	5%	10%	10%
Conflict of interest (4)		Securities by related entities	15%	15%	15%	15%
		Securities by entities with patrimonial affiliation with the AFORE (12)	5%	5%	5%	5%
Vehicles and derivatives		Investment mandates	Yes	Yes	Yes	Yes
		Derivatives	Yes	Yes	Yes	Yes

Notes: This is a summary table of the Basic SIEFORE's current regulation. Additional SIEFORE (e.g. voluntary savings) can determine different parameters according to their objective and in compliance with the SAR Law. NA = not applicable; Int'l = international.

1. All the limits are maximum percentages, except the inflation protection limit.
2. As a percentage of the Assets Under Management (AUM) directly managed by the SIEFORE. The Value at Risk will no longer be a regulatory limit once the AFORE satisfies the criteria set up in the Financial Provisions (CUF). The limits of the Difference of the Conditional Value at Risk were determined by the Risk Analysis Committee (CAR), which may be stricter than the limits set up in the Investment Regime Provisions.
3. As a percentage of the High Liquid Assets of the SIEFORE. It is defined as the ratio between the Value of the SIEFORE's reserves for derivatives exposure and the Value of High Liquid Assets.
4. As a percentage of the Total AUM of the SIEFORE, including the assets managed by the Specialised Investment Manager ("Mandatario").
5. Rating of the medium- and long-term issuances, as well as the issuer and/or endorser, in the corresponding proportion. Repos and derivatives are computed in these limits as well.
6. The regulation permits investments in foreign securities with a credit rating below A- and equal to or greater than BBB-, nevertheless the AFORE must abide by the Investment Regime Provisions and the Financial Provisions (CUF).
7. Applies to the asset holdings of all the pension funds by the same fund manager (AFORE), and for debt and structured securities. A CKD may exceed this limit if the issuance meets certain conditions.
8. Includes individual stocks, IPOs, domestic and international equity indexes listed in the Index Lists, and mandatory convertible debt into share from Mexican issuers.
9. Securitizations fulfilling the Eighth Transitory Provision of the Investment Regime Provisions are computed in this limit and are considered as being issued by an independent issuer.
10. Includes CKDs, REITs, Mexican REITs (FIBRAS) and Debt in which the income source comes from real assets. The regulation prohibits the investment in CKDs for the Basic SIEFORE 1.
11. Minimum investment limit in securities that ensures a return equal to or greater than the inflation rate in Mexico. The minimum is 51% for the basic SIEFORE 1.
12. The limits is written down in the SAR Law, Art 48, paragraph X. In exceptional cases it could be increased up to 10%. The limit is 0% for financial entities with patrimonial affiliations.

Source: CONSAR.

The pension regulator, CONSAR, has relaxed gradually restrictions on certain asset classes over time. Table 5.4 shows the changes in investment restrictions since 1997. For example, SIEFORE are allowed to invest in equities (with restrictions on the level) since 2005, and swaptions and REITs are only allowed since 2013.

Table 5.4. **Adjustments to the investment regime of SIEFORE since 1997**

	1997	1998	1999	2000	2001	2002	2003	2004	2005	2006	2007	2008	2009	2010	2011	2012	2013	2014
Debt	√	√	√	√	√	√	√	√	√	√	√	√	√	√	√	√	√	√
Currencies	√	√	√	√	√	√	√	√	√	√	√	√	√	√	√	√	√	√
Equity	x	x	x	x	x	x	x	x	√	√	√	√	√	√	√	√	√	√
CKDs & FIBRAS	x	x	x	x	x	x	x	x	x	x	√	√	√	√	√	√	√	√
Structured assets	x	x	x	x	x	x	x	x	x	x	√	√	√	√	√	√	√	√
Commodities	x	x	x	x	x	x	x	x	x	x	x	x	x	x	√	√	√	√
Swaptions	x	x	x	x	x	x	x	x	x	x	x	x	x	x	x	x	√	√
REITs	x	x	x	x	x	x	x	x	x	x	x	x	x	x	x	x	√	√

Notes: CKDs and FIBRAS are Mexican private equity funds and real estate funds respectively.
REITs = Real Estate Investment Trusts.
Source: CONSAR.

The main effect of relaxing investment restrictions has been an increase in the diversification of SIEFORE's portfolios. Figure 5.5 shows that SIEFORE have reduced their concentration in government securities, from 82.8% in 2005 to 49.4% in 2014. Investment in domestic equity has increased from 0.9% to 7.4% over the period and foreign investment (equity and fixed income) represented 18.3% of total investment at the end of December 2014.

Figure 5.5. **Asset allocation of SIEFORE in September 2005 and December 2014**

As a % of total investment

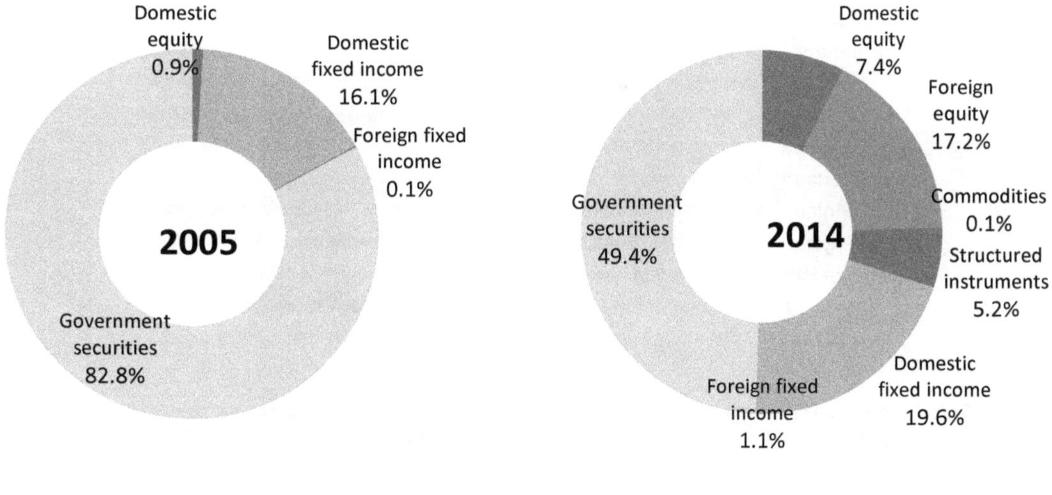

Source: CONSAR.

Despite the increased diversification, Mexico's pension funds are still significantly concentrated in debt relatively to other OECD countries. At the end of 2013, SIEFORE had 75.1% of their portfolio invested in bills and bonds (public and private). Only four of the 31 OECD countries with available data in Figure 5.6 had a larger exposition to bills and bonds: Sweden (75.2%), Slovenia (78.1%), Hungary (83.1%) and the Czech Republic (86.5%).

Figure 5.6. **Pension funds' asset allocation for selected investment categories in selected OECD countries, 2013**

As a % of total investment

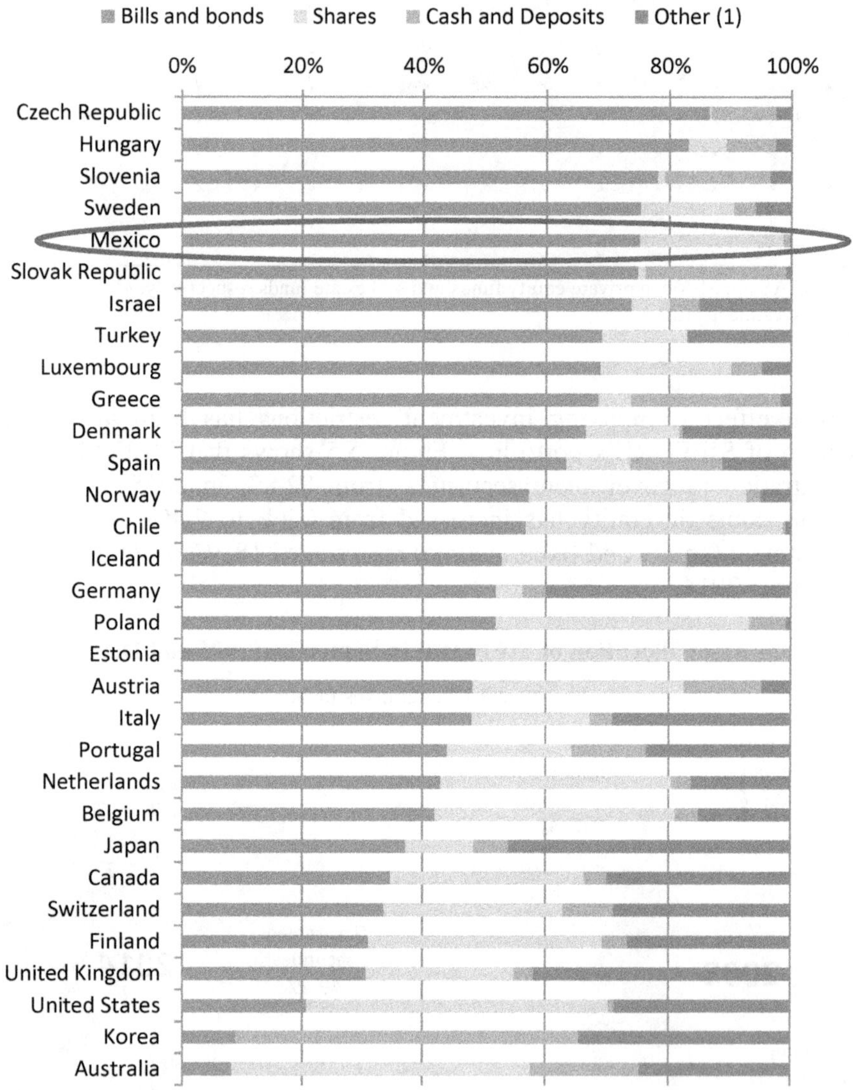

1. The "Other" category includes loans, land and buildings, unallocated insurance contracts, hedge funds, private equity funds, structured products, other mutual funds (i.e. not invested in cash, bills and bonds, or shares) and other investments.

Source: OECD Global Pension Statistics.

In addition, Mexico is still among the OECD countries with the stricter investment limits on equities and foreign securities. At the end of 2014, 19 OECD countries had no quantitative limit on the equity investment of pension funds (see Table 5.5). Among the 15 other OECD countries, Mexico is at the bottom of the ranking, with limits between 5%

and 40% depending on which of the basic SIEFORE is considered. Chile, the Czech Republic and the Slovak Republic, like Mexico, have different limits for different types of funds. However, in the three countries, the most dynamic funds are allowed to invest up to 80% of the assets in equities, as compared to 40% in basic SIEFORE 4. With respect to foreign securities, only Chile and Mexico have specific limits applying to the overall foreign investment of pension funds. Limits for Chile vary from 35% for the most conservative fund to no limit for the most dynamic fund, all Chilean limits being higher than the 20% limit applying to all basic SIEFORE in Mexico.

Table 5.5. **Limits on equity investment in OECD countries at the end of 2014**

As a % of total investment

Countries with no limit on equity investment	Australia, Belgium, Canada, Finland*, Hungary, Ireland, Israel, Italy, Japan, Korea, Luxembourg, Netherlands, New Zealand, Norway, Spain, Sweden, Turkey, United Kingdom, United States	
Countries with limit on equity investment	Chile (Fund A)	80%
	Czech Republic (dynamic fund)	80%
	Slovak Republic* (non-guaranteed fund)	80%
	Estonia*	75%
	Austria	70%
	Denmark	70%
	Greece	70%
	France	65%
	Chile (Fund B)	60%
	Iceland	60%
	Portugal	55%
	Switzerland	50%
	Poland	47.5%
	Chile (Fund C)	40%
	Czech Republic (balanced fund)	40%
	Mexico (SB4)	**40%**
	Germany (Pensionskassen)	35%
	Mexico (SB3)	**30%**
	Slovenia	30%
	Mexico (SB2)	**25%**
	Chile (Fund D)	20%
	Chile (Fund E)	5%
	Mexico (SB1)	**5%**
	Czech Republic (conservative fund)	0%
	Slovak Republic* (guaranteed fund)	**0%**

Note: * Data refer to mandatory pension funds.

Source: OECD Survey of Investment Regulation of Pension Funds.

The investment limits for equities and foreign securities are binding for most basic SIEFORE. As shown in Figure 5.7, equity investment is near its regulatory limits for all basic SIEFORE. It is not necessary to have current investment exactly at the limit to consider the limit as binding. Indeed, pension funds need room below the limit to allow for market upswings and avoid being in a situation to be forced to sell equities when markets are going up. Except for basic SIEFORE 1, the 20% limit on foreign securities can also be considered as binding.

Figure 5.7. **Investment in equity, foreign securities, structured securities and securitizations versus limits, December 2014**

As a % of total investment

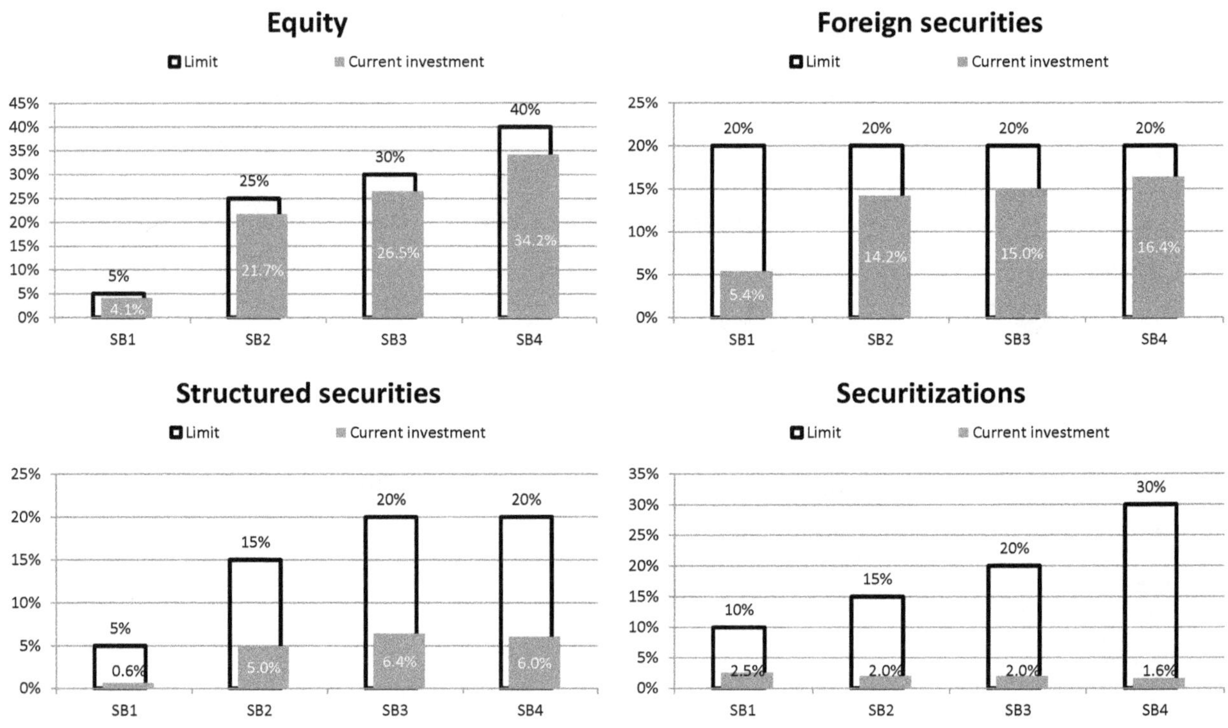

Note: The current investment of SIEFORE includes derivative exposures, while the regulatory limits exclude them.

Source: CONSAR.

Finally, Figure 5.7 also shows that SIEFORE do not use the whole range of financial instruments allowed by regulation at their full potential. Indeed, investments in structured securities and securitizations are far from the respective regulatory limits for each basic SIEFORE. In addition, while commodities are allowed by regulation since 2001, only the basic SIEFORE of one AFORE (Banamex) invest in commodities at levels between 0.2% and 0.4% of total investment (far below the limits allowed). There is therefore room for even more diversification in SIEFORE's portfolios if AFORE build appropriate investment teams with the skills to invest in non-traditional asset classes.

5.2. Fees charged by AFORE are still high when comparing with other countries despite current mechanisms to foster competition

The Mexican regulatory system uses different mechanisms to foster competition among AFORE in order to reduce fees charged to members and thus increase net retirement income. There are three main mechanisms implemented by CONSAR aiming at fostering competition among AFORE: (i) the diffusion of comparative information to members about net returns through the pension statement; (ii) the approval process of fees charged by AFORE by the Governing Board of CONSAR; and (iii) the incentives embedded in the registration, assignment and transfer processes.

As already shown in Chapter 4 (Section 4.5), the pension statement is the document that should help workers select the AFORE that best suits their needs. However, not all workers receive their pension statement regularly. In addition, low financial literacy leads to a lack of interest in the pension statement, which fails at engaging members and encouraging them to take active steps to increase their retirement savings. As a result, members do not always choose the pension fund with the highest net return as shown below.

Since 2008, every year in December, the Governing Board of CONSAR must approve the fees proposed by the AFORE, that they will charge during the following year. The Governing Board of CONSAR has the power to refuse permission for fees, considering the following factors: (i) the revenues of the AFORE given the assets under management; (ii) the use of economies of scale by the AFORE; (iii) the financial profitability; (iv) the competition scheme; (v) the ability to attract new accounts; (vi) the operating results; (vii) the performance; and (viii) the efforts from the AFORE to improve its future operative and financial performance. If the proposal is rejected, the AFORE has to charge a fee equivalent to the average of the market authorised for that year. AFORE not submitting a proposal have to charge the minimum fee authorised for the following year. The authorised fees for 2014 and 2015 are as follows.

Table 5.6. **Fees for Basic SIEFORE, 2014 and 2015**

As a % of assets under management

AFORE	2014	2015
PensionISSSTE	0.99	0.92
XXI Banorte	1.07	1.04
Banamex	1.09	1.05
Inbursa	1.14	1.08
Profuturo GNP	1.17	1.11
SURA	1.15	1.11
Principal	1.24	1.17
Invercap	1.32	1.18
Metlife	1.25	1.18
Azteca	1.31	1.19
Coppel	1.34	1.20
Simple average	1.19	1.11
Weighted average	1.15	1.09

Source: CONSAR.

This mechanism has favoured a reduction in fees, as shown in Figure 5.8. Between 2008 and 2015, the simple average fee has declined from 1.81% of assets under management to 1.11%.

Figure 5.8. **Average fees charged as a percentage of assets under management, 2008-2015**

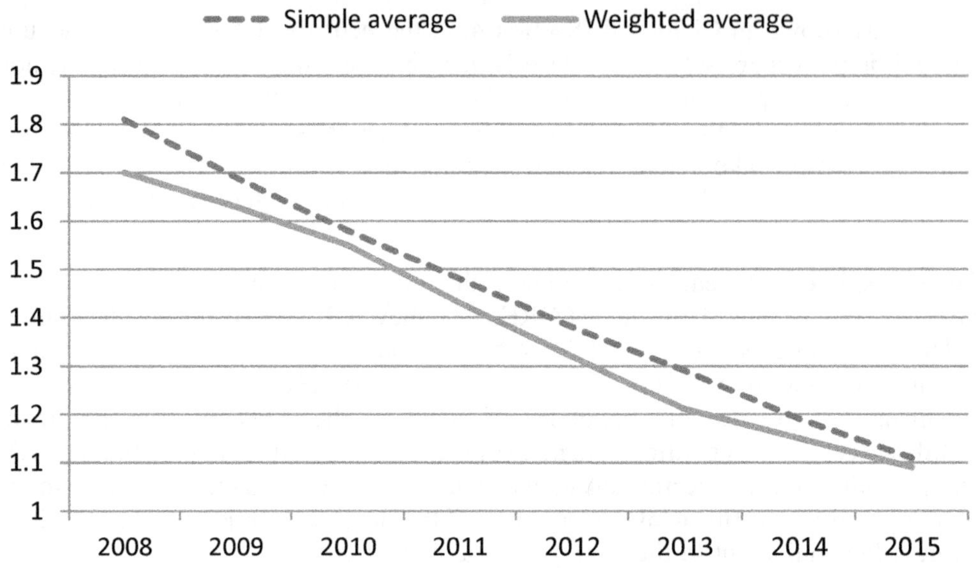

Source: CONSAR.

However, fees charged by AFORE in Mexico are still high in international comparison. With fees paid in 2013 worth 1.17% of the total assets under management at the end of 2013, Mexico ranks in the first half of Figure 5.9, in which countries with available information are sorted by descending fees. Among the countries listed, fees range from 0.45% of assets under management for Hungary to 2.59% for Turkey.

Figure 5.9. **Total fees charged in 2013 as a percentage of assets under management at the end of 2013, in selected OECD and IOPS countries**

As a % of assets under management

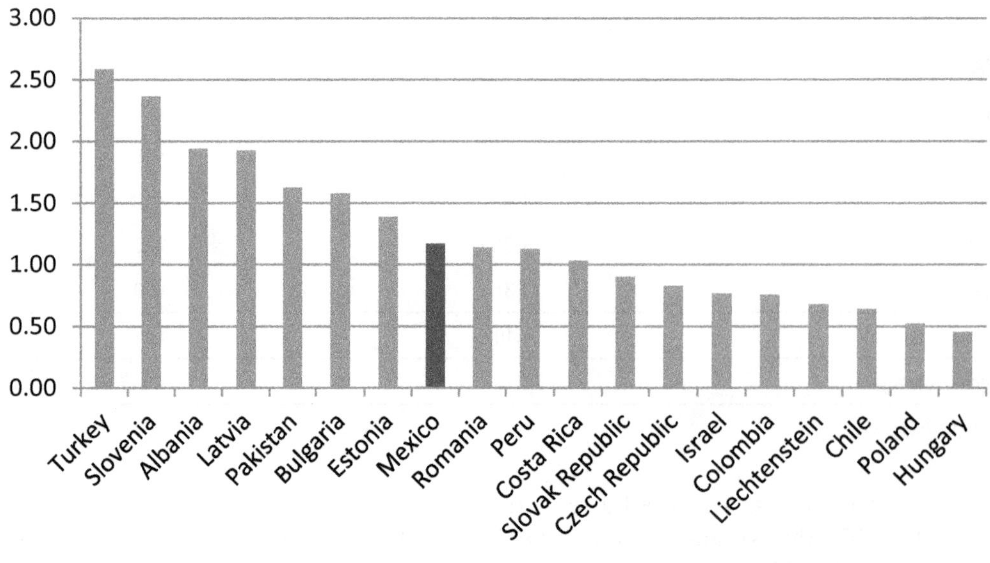

Source: OECD Global Pension Statistics.

The maturity of the funded pension system may partially explain the still relatively high fees in Mexico. Figure 5.10 compares fees charged by pension administrators in Chile and Mexico according to the number of years passed since the inception of each system. It shows that Mexico follows a similar pattern to Chile so far. Eighteen years after the inception of the system, fees represent 1.07% of total assets under management in Mexico, which is actually lower than in Chile, where fees represented 1.43% of total assets under management after the same number of years.

Figure 5.10. **Evolution of fees charged in Chile and Mexico since the inception of each system**

As a % of assets under management

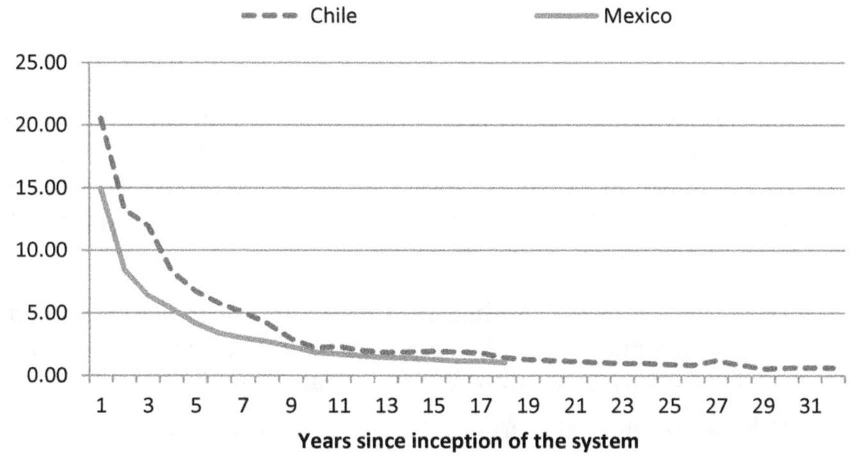

Source: Chile: Superintendence of Pensions; Mexico: CONSAR.

However, the current approval process of fees provides little incentive to further lower fees for AFORE with charges already below the average. For example, between 2014 and 2015, AFORE over the average have reduced fees by 11 basis points on average, as opposed to a reduction of only 5 basis points for AFORE below the average (see Table 5.7).

Table 5.7. **Fees' reduction between 2014 and 2015**

	AFORE	Fees 2014 (%)	Fees 2015 (%)	Reduction (percentage points)	
AFORE above the average	Coppel	1.34	1.20	0.14	Average decrease of 11 basis points
	Azteca	1.31	1.19	0.12	
	Invercap	1.32	1.18	0.14	
	Metlife	1.25	1.18	0.07	
	Principal	1.24	1.17	0.07	
AFORE below the average	Profuturo GNP	1.17	1.11	0.06	Average decrease of 5 basis points
	SURA	1.15	1.11	0.04	
	Inbursa	1.14	1.08	0.06	
	Banamex	1.09	1.05	0.04	
	XXI Banorte	1.07	1.04	0.03	
	PensionISSSTE	0.99	0.92	0.07	

Source: CONSAR.

Finally, the incentives embedded in the registration, assignment and transfer processes are not enough to foster competition. The account registration is a way to secure the right of workers of getting benefits from the pension system. Through the registration process, the worker selects the AFORE that best suits his/her own interest and designates beneficiaries. This is the primary vehicle to access to information about the account (for example, reception of the pension statement).

When the worker does not register his/her individual account with an AFORE, there is an assignment process following two modalities:

- Assigned workers with money deposited in the Bank of Mexico: This refers to inactive accounts. In that case, there is only one services provider (*Prestadora de Servicios*) that keeps track of and control the accounts, the AFORE XXI Banorte. It charges a commission of 0.10% of the balance since July 2014 for assigned accounts. The resources are deposited in the Bank of Mexico in a pooled account and are invested in securities or loans issued by the federal government, or if applicable by the states. The performance is determined by the Ministry of Finance. Inactive accounts include accounts initially assigned to an AFORE (see following point) but that were returned to the Bank of Mexico because the condition of receiving contributions during at least six consecutive two-month periods is not fulfilled.
- Assigned workers with money deposited in a SIEFORE: The active accounts of the services provider are assigned to the AFORE with the highest net return indicator. The assignment is realised once a year, according to a calendar set by CONSAR.

The AFORE have the obligation to provide the same services to registered workers and to assigned workers with money deposited in a SIEFORE. However, assigned workers may not be able to make use of these services because they do not necessarily know which AFORE is managing their account. For example, they may not receive their pension statement because the AFORE has no information on their domicile. In any case, the worker can decide at any moment to register his/her account.

To increase the level of registration of assigned accounts and foster competition, only AFORE with net returns in the last three deciles of the distribution can receive assigned accounts. In turn, those with the largest amount of registration of assigned accounts get the largest proportion of assigned accounts. In addition, if an assigned account with active contributions is not registered after two years, it gets re-assigned to a new AFORE.

At the end of 2014, there were 52 728 388 individual retirement accounts, of which 36 028 527 (or 68%) were registered, 10 492 588 (20%) were assigned accounts with money deposited in a SIEFORE and 6 207 273 (12%) were assigned accounts with money deposited in the Bank of Mexico. Figure 5.11 shows the evolution of the number of individual retirement accounts since 1997.

Figure 5.11. **Evolution of the number of individual accounts, by type of account**

In millions

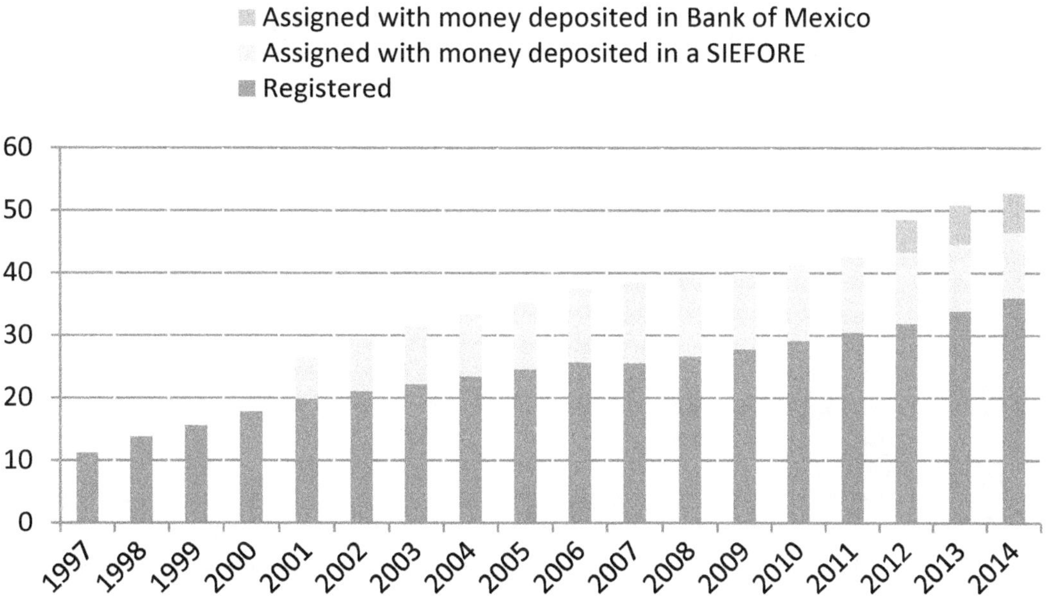

Note: The services provider started operating in January 2010. However, CONSAR only began to collect information on assigned accounts with money deposited in the Bank of Mexico in 2012.

Source: CONSAR.

In order to further promote competition and to allow workers to choose the AFORE that best suits them, it is possible to switch between AFORE. Transfers are allowed once a year and even within a shorter timespan when changing to an AFORE providing a higher net return indicator. The transfer is free for the worker. However, according to Calderón-Colín et al. (2008), account transfers among AFORE in Mexico barely respond to price or return considerations and in general have not improved the workers' pension balance. Using 2006 data, they show that, instead of strengthening competition through lower fees and higher returns for the workers, AFORE switching had resulted in lower pensions for more than half of workers. Figure 5.12 shows that during the last four years, more than half of the workers who switched AFORE did so to an AFORE providing a lower net return (negative transfer). In addition, the number of transfers has increased, from 1 788 883 in 2012 to 2 128 947 in 2013 and 2 436 697 in 2014. Fund managers actually increase their market share through a larger commercial cost and a greater number of sales agents that try to convince workers to switch. This is illustrated in Figure 5.13.

Figure 5.12. **Quality of account transfers**

As a % of all transfers

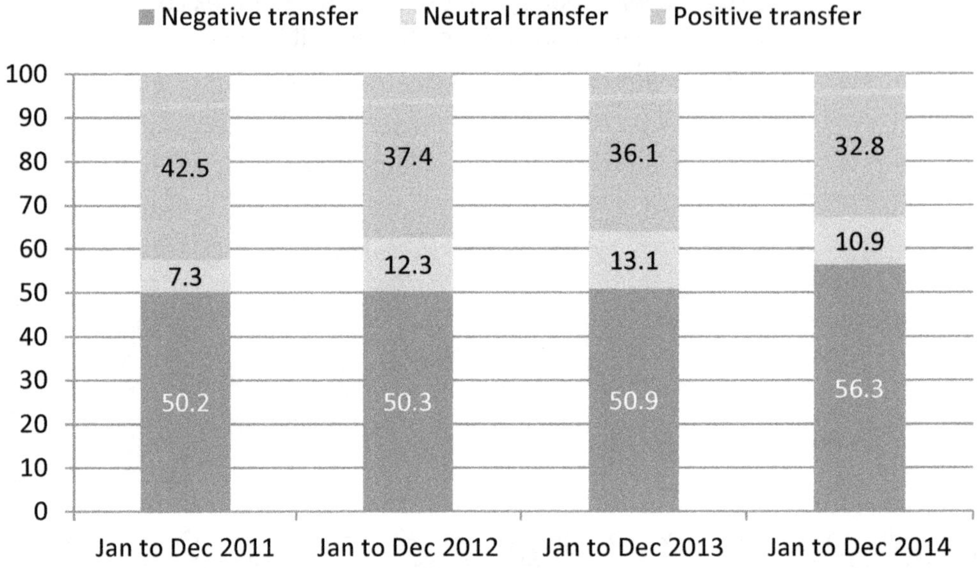

Notes: A negative transfer is one to an AFORE offering a lower net return. A neutral transfer is one to an AFORE offering the same net return or a net return less than 5% higher than the one offered by the previous AFORE. A positive transfer is one to an AFORE offering a net return at least 5% higher than the one offered by the previous AFORE.

Source: CONSAR.

Figure 5.13. **Evolution of AFORE's commercial cost and number of sales agents between 2010 and 2014**

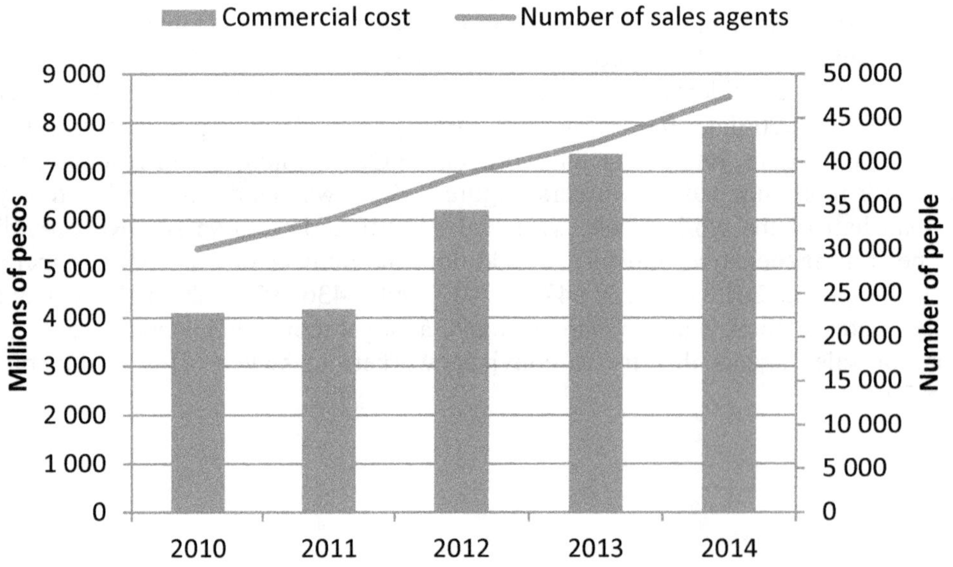

Source: CONSAR.

Besides AFORE's marketing methods, the proportion of negative transfers may also come from the lack of incentives for transitional private-sector workers to choose the best AFORE in terms of higher performance and lower fees. Indeed, these workers retain the right to choose at retirement the higher of the acquired benefits under the old PAYG DB system and the accumulated balances in their individual retirement accounts under the new funded DC system. As the old DB system is generally more generous (see Chapter 4) and provides benefits independently of the resources accumulated in the individual retirement account, most transitional workers have little incentives to maximise the resources accumulated at retirement in their individual account. The federal government is therefore the one suffering most from bad management and high fees as it receives a potentially lower amount from the accumulated balances to finance the promised benefits of the PAYG system.

Since 2 March 2015, new rules are in place to limit negative transfers. There is a stricter control of sales agents through the creation of a new electronic database and periodic examinations. Sales agents will also be subject to a new remuneration scheme in which transfers of accounts with less than 30 months in the current AFORE will only be remunerated 20% of the normal fee. In addition, AFORE are now allowed to retain a worker for more than one year by offering better services. Finally, workers have to sign a form when asking for a transfer of their account which highlights the consequences of the transfer. Therefore, in the case of a negative transfer, the form makes clear to the worker the fact that this means a transfer from an AFORE with a better net return to an AFORE with a lower net return. These changes are however too recent to see a positive impact on the number and quality of transfers.

5.3. Robust risk-based supervision but AFORE's corporate governance could be improved

Mexico introduced a risk-based supervision approach in 2004, based on the management of operational and financial risks. Both quantitative and qualitative risk controls are in place.

The primary quantitative financial risk supervision tool is the historical Value at Risk (VaR) of the portfolio. The VaR determines the maximum expected loss of an instrument or portfolio over a given time horizon and confidence level. To calculate the VaR, CONSAR uses the historical methodology, which consists in using the most recent information on the various risk factors, in this case the last 1 000 days given a 95% confidence level, in order to examine the possible values that a portfolio can reach, with the losses, with respect to the current value, assuming that what happened in the recent past can repeat itself. Therefore, information on risk factors for each day that passes is incorporated in the estimation of the VaR for the next 1 000 days, which gives a certain memory to this risk measure. Each SIEFORE has a different maximum VaR limit: 0.7% for SB1, 1.1% for SB2, 1.4% for SB3 and 2.1% for SB4, increasing with the risk profile of each SIEFORE (Table 5.3 above).

Losses caused by violations of VaR limits or any other breach to regulation by the AFORE must be compensated with special reserves kept by AFORE in each operating SIEFORE, equivalent to 0.8% of the assets under management. Furthermore, financial regulation imposes the re-composition of the portfolio when any quantitative limit is exceeded, including the limit on historical VaR.

AFORE must calculate and meet the VaR limit on a daily basis, as well as calculate the parametric VaR and the Monte Carlo VaR, in order to monitor risks and take investment decisions.

In 2010, as a result of the financial crisis, the governing bodies of CONSAR approved adjustments to the calculation of the VaR with the aim to incorporate exogenous volatility inherent in financial markets and to prevent pro-cyclicality. For each group of SIEFORE, CONSAR has set up a benchmark portfolio that replicates the investment conditions in the investment regime. When these benchmarks exceed regulatory VaR limits, the confidence level decreases, so that AFORE do not need to sell some of their positions because of the volatility in the market. When market conditions improve, the confidence level goes back to its original level. This allows the re-composition of portfolios to happen only under favourable market conditions. Such adjustment creates conditions to allow pension funds to be a fundamental element to stabilise domestic markets.

In October 2012, in order to limit the leverage generated by financial operations with greater sensitivity, the governing bodies of CONSAR approved the "difference of the Conditional Value at Risk" measure (ΔCVaR), which is the difference between the Conditional VaR of the portfolio of a SIEFORE and the Conditional VaR of the same portfolio excluding derivatives. The implementation of the ΔCVaR has been gradual and has encouraged a management approach based on stronger corporate governance. Each SIEFORE has a different maximum ΔCVaR limit, as shown in Table 5.3. At the same time, the regulatory VaR has been removed, subject to compliance with investment and risk rules.

In addition to the aforementioned quantitative limits, qualitative measures are in place. The AFORE must show that it has a robust corporate governance and internal investment/risks procedures in order to have the permission, granted by CONSAR, to operate with all different types of financial instruments and asset classes. It is worth mentioning that the corporate governance soundness and compliance with the investment regime is reviewed periodically by CONSAR through on-site inspections, focusing on the performance of the Investment and Risk Committees, the independent advisors, the compliance officer, and the involvement of the AFORE's board. For instance, if an AFORE wants to gain exposure to a specific asset class, it should show that the AFORE's Investment and Financial Risk Committees approved the investment, that it has performed an appropriate investment and risk analysis, and that it has an appropriate infrastructure to coordinate the operation. For instance, in the latter, if the investment is done through derivatives, the AFORE should have CONSAR's non objection to operate derivatives. CONSAR evaluates if the AFORE has the proper systems and human capital to manage them.

In order to ensure best corporate governance practices, CONSAR requires AFORE to manage investment and financial risks through different bodies: a Comprehensive Risk Management Unit (*Unidad para la Administración Integral de Riesgos*, UAIR), a Financial Risk Committee and an Investment Committee. Each AFORE is required to have the UAIR headed by a Chief Risk Officer who reports to the board of directors. This unit provides support to the Financial Risk Committee. It identifies, measures, monitors and informs the AFORE's board of directors of the risks faced by the AFORE and SIEFORE. The UAIR reports on a quarterly basis about the economic, financial and other consequences that the AFORE would face if risks should materialize.

The Financial Risk Committee must include one independent member of the board, one non-independent member and the person responsible for the UAIR. The General

Director of the AFORE chairs this committee. Those in charge of financial risk and the compliance office also attend the committee meetings. The Financial Risk Committee is responsible for determining risk tolerance levels and risk limits, for approving and reviewing models and measurement methods, ensuring policy and procedure manuals are up to date, checking compliance with risk policies and reviewing limit breaches and the corrective action taken. This committee is also responsible for the Financial Risk Management Policies and Procedures Manuals. The board must approve these policies, which must be sent to CONSAR for endorsement.

The Investment Committee must be composed by at least five members, among them should be considered an independent member, the AFORE's General Director and other members or officers appointed by the board of the pension fund. The Investment Committee is responsible for determining the investment policy and strategy within the limits proposed by the Financial Risk Committee.

Each AFORE is required to have a board of directors of at least five members appointed by shareholders, of which at least two members must be independent experts. The board has specific legal responsibilities and an important role in managing and controlling investment risks. It is responsible for the constitution of the Financial Risk Committee for the SIEFORE. The board also sets the level of financial risk tolerance for the AFORE within the limits allowed by regulation.

Risk officers, investment officers, independent board members, the compliance officer and the person responsible for the back office have to be certified to master general financial knowledge and have at least 5 years of relevant experience. This certification is performed by independent agencies, and has to be validated every 3 years. The General Director of an AFORE should reside in Mexican territory, have at least 5 years of experience in top finance positions, and not have worked in a regulatory agency or political institution for the last 2 years. An external auditor evaluates risk management on an annual basis.

Despite quite comprehensive risk management rules, following the OECD Core Principles of Occupational Pension Regulation (OECD, 2010), improvements could be achieved in AFORE's corporate governance, especially with reference to accountability, suitability and risk-based internal controls. The OECD Core Principles establish that the governing body of a pension fund should be accountable to the pension plan members and beneficiaries, calling for safe harbour rules that clarify the responsibilities and liabilities of the governing body. According to the SAR Law, the main objective of AFORE is to dedicate themselves to manage individual accounts and channel the resources of the sub-accounts in a regular and professional way, as well as to manage SIEFORE. However, the Law does not mention that the activities of the AFORE must be carried out in the best interest of plan members. Adding this broad objective into the Law may help addressing issues related to high fees, low returns and low services.

According to the OECD Core Principles, membership in the governing body of a pension fund should be subject to minimum suitability standards (such as "fit and proper" criteria) in order to ensure a high level of integrity, competence, experience and professionalism in the governance of the pension fund. The SAR Law defines minimum standards for risk officers, investment officers, independent board members, the compliance officer, the person responsible for the back office, the General Director of the AFORE and the external auditor. However, no specific qualifications and experience are required for non-independent board members.

Finally, it is important to identify and deal with conflicts of interest situations in a suitable manner. In certain cases, banning the concentration of functions in a single person or entity that would otherwise lead to conflicts of interest may be the preferred solution. In other cases, disclosure of the conflicts of interest to the governing body may suffice, who should be required to monitor these cases closely. It may be the fund's best interest to adopt policies which prevent even the appearance of a conflict of interest. In the case of Mexico, the independence and autonomy of independent board members and the compliance officer could be reinforced with respect to regulatory agencies, political institutions and different players in the Retirement Savings System.

5.4 Proposals to improve the design of the accumulation phase

5.4.1. Provide choice between different investment strategies while keeping default life-cycle investment strategies

The OECD Roadmap for the Good Design of Defined Contribution Pension Plans argues for the establishment of appropriate default investment strategies, while also providing choice between investment options with different risk profile and investment horizon. It also argues for establishing default life-cycle investment strategies as a default option to protect people close to retirement against extreme negative outcomes. The Mexican pension system as discussed previously already provides default life-cycle investment strategies. However, people can only choose the AFORE but do not have any choice as regard investment strategies.

The investment strategy is determined by the investment regulation applying to SIEFORE. Therefore, people willing and able to select other investment strategy may end-up with suboptimal choices given the current multi-funds scheme structure. The Roadmap argues that, if they wish, people should be allowed to choose the investment strategy best suited for them according to their risk profile and their level of risk tolerance, as well as their different overall pension arrangements.

Investment choice needs to go hand-in-hand with appropriate default investment strategies. Behavioural economics and the financial literacy research show that some people are either unwilling or unable to choose, let alone to actively manage their own portfolio investments. Given the low level of financial literacy in Mexico, a large proportion of workers may end-up in that category. Therefore, default investment strategies are necessary, as they incorporate the lessons learned from behavioural economics on the importance of inertia and passive decision making, to make sure that those people are assigned to appropriate investment strategies.

As argued in OECD (2012), default investment strategies should concentrate on reducing the risk of extreme negative outcomes on retirement income. Life-cycle investment strategies are appropriate defaults in this respect. The Mexican multi-funds system enters in that category, as pension assets are invested in a more conservative investment regime as members get older, by moving automatically from one basic SIEFORE to the next at specific ages.

There are two ways to adapt the current multi-funds system in Mexico to a system with investment choice and default investment strategies. The first consists in keeping the structure with basic SIEFORE and add lower and upper limits for risky assets, as is done in the case of Chile. This would allow individuals to choose their preferred allocation within the limits of each basic fund. The middle of the bracket between the lower and the upper limits could be used to define the default option.

The second way consists in allowing AFORE to provide different investment strategies as well as a life-cycle default investment strategy. The default life-cycle strategy should be common to everyone, especially in a mandatory system where low income and low education individuals also participate.

Finally, regulatory limits for equities and foreign securities could be gradually relaxed to further encourage portfolio diversification. The current law proposal also puts forward the expansion of alternative investments for SIEFORE by allowing investment in private securities registered in the National Securities Registry and including new types of instruments, such as lending and repurchase securities, different from those issued by the federal government, the Bank of Mexico and the banking institutions. However, AFORE do not use the whole range of financial instruments already allowed by regulation at their full potential. Increasing skills in AFORE's investment teams will therefore be essential to allow for appropriate diversification in SIEFORE's portfolios.

5.4.2. Address high charges and increase competition

The amount of fees that pension providers charge can have an important negative impact on pension benefits. Pension providers charge fees for the services they offer, such as account administration and investment management. Fees may be charged on contributions or assets under management or paid separately by the plan member (switching fees for example). They affect the benefits that plan members receive, as the higher the charge, the lower will be the benefits that members receive for a given contribution, or the higher will be the total contribution required to achieve the same level of benefits. Table 5.8 below shows the impact of different levels of asset management charges in terms of reductions in pension benefits, assuming a 40-year contribution period. Halving the management fees from a level of 1% of assets under management to 0.5% can raise pension benefits by about 10%. High fees may sometimes be worth paying for a better quality service or for higher risk-adjusted returns. However, more often, they are symptomatic of a seller-dominated pension industry, in which individual plan members have a clear informational and financial disadvantage compared to pension providers.

Table 5.8. **Fee levels and impact on pension benefits**

Fee as % of assets	Reduction of pension (%)
0.05	1.2
0.15	3.6
0.25	5.9
0.50	11.4
0.75	16.5
1.00	21.3
1.50	29.9

Source: OECD (2012).

Policy makers need to ensure that there are incentives in place to improve efficiency and reduce costs and fees in the pensions industry. Various policy solutions have been considered in OECD countries to address this issue, which can be divided into three main groups: disclosure-based initiatives, pricing regulations and structural solutions.

Disclosure-based solutions include ensuring that members receive timely information on the fees they pay, including comparisons between providers. This solution is already implemented in Mexico. Pension statements include information on commissions paid by the worker. Although they do not allow comparing fee levels across AFORE directly, comparisons are done between net returns, which represent the long-term historical performance of SIEFORE, net of fees. The main limitation of such initiatives, especially in countries that target lower income employees, is that pension statements do not always succeed in prompting members' action regarding their retirement savings.

Pricing regulations include allowing a single charge structure (only contribution-based or only asset-management charges) and setting ceilings on the fees that pension providers can apply. Such solutions can be effective in avoiding high fees, but they are not necessarily conducive to cost-reductions and efficiency improvements in the industry. Poland has successfully used price caps to lower fees. In 2004, Poland capped the management fee at 7% of contributions. In 2010, a new legal limit of 3.5% was introduced. Under the 2014 pension reform law, the maximum fee fell again to 1.75%. The United Kingdom has also recently introduced successfully caps on fees and charges.

Mexico has pricing regulation as AFORE charge only fees on assets under management, but there is not a cap on fees charged. The main measure to control fees and charges is the power that the Governing Board of CONSAR has to reject fee proposals by AFORE and force them to apply the average of the industry. This may implicitly put a cap on fees and charges but it does not provide any incentive for AFORE that already charge fees below the average to lower them further. In addition, AFORE charge the same level of fees for all workers, whether they are registered or assigned, even though assigned workers get fewer services from the AFORE.

There are currently three reform proposals aimed at reducing fees and charges:

- Impose to AFORE for which the Governing Board of CONSAR has rejected the fee proposal for the following year to charge fees at 75% of the average of the market.
- Charge lower fees for assigned accounts. Only AFORE differentiating assigned accounts with lower fees would be potential candidates to get assigned workers. This proposal would encourage AFORE to register these assigned accounts (today, assigned accounts are maintained like this).
- Keep the current scheme of charging fees only on assets accumulated, but structure it into two components, one calculated as a percentage of the value of assets under management, and the other one calculated as a percentage of the performance of the fund. The second component could represent up to 0.3% of assets under management. This proposal aims at increasing competition in the system and aligning the interest of AFORE with the goal of generating higher returns in the long-term for the benefit of workers. In any case, the two-component fee would not exceed the current one-component fee (see illustration in Figure 5.14).

Figure 5.14. **Illustration of the proposal for a new fees' structure**

Millions of pesos

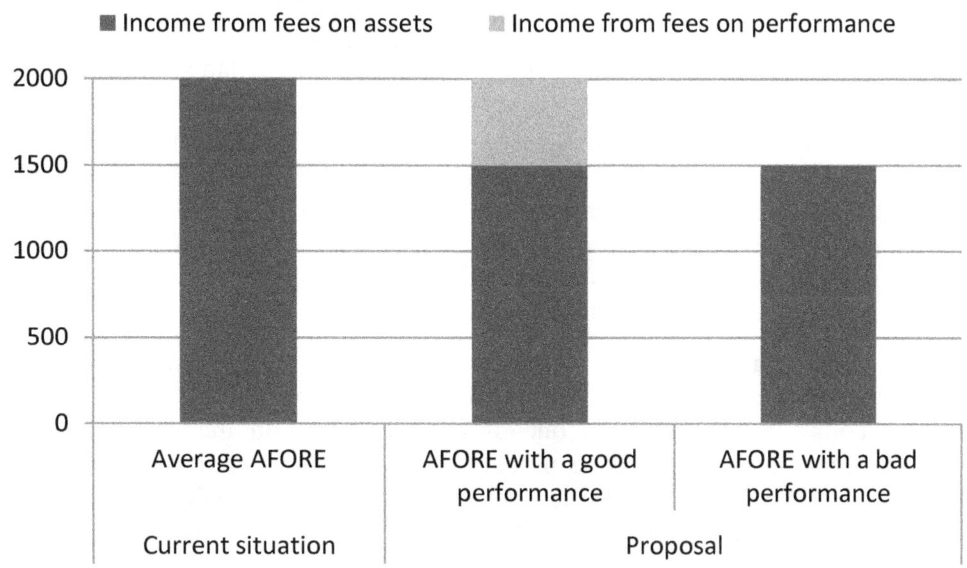

These proposals may have some traction in reducing fees and charges but they may not bring them down to the most cost-efficient level. The first one, by increasing the penalty for AFORE that have their fee proposal rejected, may increase the quality of their proposal but not necessarily bring down the fees charged because the level of fees is not a direct criterion to reject the proposal. Moreover, AFORE with fees on the average or lower may not have any incentive to reduce them further even if they could. The second proposal is fair, different services, different costs, and then different charges. Finally, it is positive to introduce performance-based fees because it may force AFORE to improve their performance to be able to keep current fees. However, it will not reduce fees, let alone bring fees down to those determined by a competitive market.

The third type of policy solutions implemented in some OECD countries to reduce fees is structural in the sense that it involves a specific industrial organisation set-up. In personal plans, a structural solution may involve the establishment of a centralised institution that is in charge of either delivering the various pension services, directly or via an outsourcing arrangement, or of negotiating better terms (lower fees) on behalf of individual plan members (e.g. the Swedish PPM system or NEST in the United Kingdom). This policy solution can be very effective in achieving low fees as it ensures economies of scale and can avoid the marketing expenses of the retail model. However, it may be difficult to implement once a DC industry of competing providers is established, at least in a mandatory system. A centralised institution can also raise governance challenges that call for effective and independent oversight.

There are other structural solutions which can also be conducive to lower fees that may work better when a DC industry of competing providers is already established. This includes establishing a tender process, for example by the regulator, for assigning new or undecided workers to a single pension provider (e.g. Chile and New Zealand). For example in Chile, an auction mechanism was introduced in 2008 for new members who enrol into the system. The auction applies to the fees charged for the management of the individual accounts for new members. New members are automatically enrolled in the pension fund which charges the lowest fees and they are required to remain in this pension fund for 24 months. After that, members can freely transfer their accounts to another pension fund. There have been three auctions since the reform was enacted. The first auction took place in 2010 and it allowed a new pension fund to enter the market starting from August of that year, offering the minimum fee of the system equal to 1.14% of salary. The same pension fund won the second auction in January 2012, decreasing the fee offered to 0.77% of salary. As a result, another pension fund decided to lower its fees from June 2012, the first reduction by any of the incumbents since 2009. During the third auction, carried out in January 2014, the pension fund previously with the highest fee won the auction by lowering it to 0.47% of salary. Again, such a solution calls for strong public-sector governance and institutional capability.

The Mexican authorities could consider extending the assignment process to new entrants using a tender mechanism. In Mexico, there is no tender process, but non-registered accounts are assigned to one of the AFORE with the highest net return indicator. A tender process could be used to allocate all new entrants in the pension system to the AFORE with the best offer, not just members with non-registered accounts. In addition, using the net return (net of fees) as a criterion to select the AFORE that would receive all new entrants may be more appropriate than using the fees only, as long as providers do not increase the risk-return profile of their investment portfolio to obtain large returns. The possibility of creating a tender mechanism that uses fees and historical net return (net of fees) as the decision parameters in the auction process should also be explored, in order to incentivise not just the performance of the AFORE but the fee competition among them.

The assignment process does not seem to foster competition among AFORE. As of December 2014, there were 16.7 million accounts held without being registered. AFORE do not have enough incentives to register these accounts, even though the re-assignment process means that they can lose these members after two years. Of those 16.7 million accounts, 6.2 million were inactive (contributions have not been paid to the account during six consecutive two-month periods) and managed by the services provider. These accounts only get a minimum return, usually much lower than returns provided by SIEFORE to registered accounts and active assigned accounts.

The reform proposal would help increasing incentives to register assigned accounts. It suggests giving more powers to CONSAR to determine the characteristics and requirements to assign accounts. For example, it could be decided that accounts with some activity (to be defined by CONSAR) would be assigned to the AFORE that offers the best conditions, such as returns, services and registration efforts. The management of totally inactive accounts would still continue with the services provider. Assigned workers for whom an AFORE would register their account would have to stay at least three years with that AFORE. However, workers would still be able to transfer their account after one year to another AFORE with better returns, lower fees and better services. In addition, AFORE would be forced to charge lower fees for assigned accounts, thus reinforcing the incentive to register those accounts.

The bill also proposes initiatives to ensure that transfers of accounts between AFORE are done in an informed manner and are not only the results of commercial strategies from AFORE:

- Extend the period during which workers cannot transfer their account from one to three years, with the possibility of transferring the account after one year only if the AFORE receiving the account offers better returns and better services;
- Perform operational and regulatory reforms to ensure that workers gain more awareness of the importance of the choice of the AFORE, with information on returns and services delivered by each AFORE;
- Oblige AFORE to send workers an annual pension forecast report, giving information about their current retirement savings situation and the outlook for the pension income under various scenarios;[3]
- Introduce the concept of "re-certification" through which workers would receive a visit or a call from their AFORE annually to confirm their registration with it. This would be the occasion for the AFORE to improve the services provided to the worker. This process intends to avoid transfers for reasons like unifying accounts, correcting information, making withdrawals for unemployment or wedding, without considering the net return.
- Keep a record of sales agents through a comprehensive database. To be certified, agents would have to comply with the requirements established by CONSAR, which would have the ability to suspend or cancel the certification of sales agents.

Lengthening the period during which people cannot switch between AFORE from one to three years should help both to decrease the number of negative switches and to lower commercial costs, as less sales agents would be needed to contact a reduced number of potential clients. In addition, the new form that workers have to sign when asking for a transfer of their account should make clear the consequences of a negative switch and maybe discourage them. Unfortunately, transitional workers would have another incentive structure. Their pension benefits do not depend on fees charged or the performance of pension funds (i.e., returns) because they can choose to receive their pension according to the old DB formula which is not linked to the amount of assets accumulated in their DC account. The pro-rata system proposed in chapter 4 would help making all workers concerned about how their assets are invested.

The COFECE (*Comisión Federal de Competencia Económica*) recently proposed to limit marketing costs by imposing a maximum limit, either in absolute or relative terms (COFECE, 2014). Indeed, in 2013 nearly half of AFORE's spending was in marketing costs (affiliation and transfers), while only 4% was used for investment activities. In addition, those marketing costs have not translated so far in clear benefits for members, as illustrated by the fact that more than half of transfers over the last four years took place towards AFORE offering lower returns. Imposing a maximum limit on such costs should be considered. Some OECD countries, such as Sweden and Poland, have gone all the way to outlaw advertising in their mandatory pension system.

5.4.3. Improve AFORE's corporate governance

The OECD Core Principles of Occupational Pension Regulation (OECD, 2010) establish governance as a key element in maintaining sound, effective and compliant pension plans. Strong governance is essential as regulation alone cannot achieve the good practice necessary for integrity and effectiveness. Weak governance in pension funds is a serious problem with potentially major and damaging consequences for pension entities and plan members.

To achieve good governance, members of the governing body should have suitable knowledge, experience and training which allow them to understand and challenge advice they receive from outside experts. Additionally, conflicts of interest within boards and in relation to independent officers must be addressed, and there is a strong need to strengthen the fiduciary responsibility of pension plan providers in DC systems in order to ensure that plans are managed with the interest of the members in mind.

The current reform proposals pending in the Senate seek to align the corporate governance systems of the AFORE with best domestic and international practices. It would help addressing issues related to conflicts of interest. Regulations of CONSAR would define with greater precision the responsibilities and functions of the governing bodies, including directors, the administrators and key executives. The AFORE will be required to have an Audit Committee and a Corporate Practice Committee as well as adequate internal safeguards. The responsibilities of independent board members and the compliance function would be strengthened. In particular, independent board members and compliance officers may not have, simultaneously to their function, a position, a financial link or labour link with the AFORE to which they provide services, with any other financial intermediary (independently of whether the intermediary belongs to the financial or business group of the AFORE or not), with commercial entities controlled or subsidiaries of the corporate group of the AFORE, and with any other participant in the Retirement Savings System. In addition, it is proposed to establish a temporary four-year initial period, renewable once for an equal duration, for independent board members and the compliance officers in order to strengthen their autonomy. CONSAR would also co-operate with other supervisors in scrutinising the activities of financial groups when AFORE are part of such a group, in order to detect possible conflicts of interest and risks of contagion.

The fiduciary duty of AFORE would also be strengthened, as the new law would require AFORE to carry out all the steps necessary for obtaining adequate performance and secure investments in the SIEFORE they manage. In accordance with their functions, they should exclusively look after the interests of workers and ensure that all operations are carried out with this objective in mind.

The suitability of all members of the board of directors of AFORE may however still need to be improved, especially for non-independent members. Minimum suitability standards as the ones required for independent board members may be required, as well as regular training to ensure they can understand the decisions of the professionals that operate the fund.

Notes

1. Self-employed workers can also voluntarily choose to save in an AFORE.
2. See the OECD Survey of Investment Regulation of Pension Funds (*www.oecd.org/finance/private-pensions/annualsurveyofinvestmentregulationofpensionfunds.htm*) for international comparisons.
3. CONSAR actually requires AFORE to send an annual pension report which contains an estimate of the future pension level, as well as voluntary savings scenarios since 2014.

References

Calderón-Colín, R., E.E. Domínguez and M.J. Schwartz (2008), "Consumer confusion: The choice of AFORE in MEXICO", *IMF Working Paper* 08/177, International Monetary Fund.

COFECE (2014), *Trabajo de investigación y recomendaciones sobre las condiciones de competencia del sector financiero*, Comisión Federal de Competencia Económica.

OECD (2012), *OECD Pensions Outlook 2012*, OECD Publishing, Paris. DOI: *http://dx.doi.org/10.1787/9789264169401-en.*

OECD (2010), *OECD Principles of Occupational Pension Regulation: Methodology for Assessment and Implementation*, OECD Publishing, Paris. DOI: *http://dx.doi.org/10.1787/9789264087095-en.*

Chapter 6

Improving the design of the pay-out phase in the Mexican pension system

This chapter discusses the current structure of the pay-out phase of the Mexican funded defined contribution pension system and proposes approaches to improve it. The chapter first introduces the main modalities that exist in Mexico to allocate assets accumulated in individual retirement accounts and thus finance retirement income. Individuals can generally choose between programmed withdrawals and life annuities. Only one type of life annuity is allowed. The chapter also discusses the problems with annuity markets and the management of longevity risk by insurance companies and occupational defined benefit pension plans. It concludes with recommendations regarding the management of longevity risk, the operation of the annuity market and the regulatory framework.

The statistical data for Israel are supplied under the responsibility of the relevant Israeli authorities. The use of such data by the OECD is without prejudice to the status of the Golan Heights, East Jerusalem and Israeli settlements in the West Bank under the terms of international law.

6.1. Modalities of allocating assets accumulated

6.1.1. Transitional workers choosing the old DB formula also receive lump sums from their DC account

Private-sector workers who were contributing to the PAYG system in place before 1 July 1997 have the right, upon retirement, to choose to get their pension benefits according to the old DB formula or according to the new DC rule. When choosing the old DB formula, private-sector workers must be 65 or older and only need 500 weeks of contributions to be entitled to a pension. Upon retirement, they receive as a lump sum any resources left in the housing sub-account, balances accumulated in the individual retirement account between 1992 and 1997, and the amount corresponding to the retirement insurance contribution in the retirement sub-account (2% of the base salary paid by the employer) accumulated since 1997. The remaining balances in the retirement sub-account (coming from the severance at old-age and old-age contributions) accumulated since 1997 are transferred to the federal government to pay the DB benefits (see Box 6.1).

Of the 2 072 518 public-sector workers affiliated to the ISSSTE in April 2007, only 294 736 (14.2%) chose the new DC system and received recognition bonds in their DC account. All the others (85.8%) decided to keep the old DB formula to calculate their pension benefits, with new rules regarding the minimum age of retirement and the contribution rate. Upon retirement, they receive as a lump sum any resources left in the housing sub-account, balances accumulated in the individual retirement account between 1992 and 2007, and the amount corresponding to the retirement insurance contribution in the retirement sub-account (2% of the base salary paid by the employer) accumulated since 2007. The federal government pays the DB benefits from the federal budget (severance at old-age and old-age contributions are not deposited in an individual retirement account for these workers, but are paid directly to the ISSSTE to finance the PAYG system).

In both cases, part of the resources accumulated in the individual retirement account is reverted to the worker upon retirement as a lump sum, because part of the accumulation took place before the implementation of the new Social Security Laws. This amount, originated from pension contributions, is eventually not used to finance pension benefits. Although such rule may be seen as an incentive for workers to participate in the pension system, diverting too much money that was initially intended to finance retirement may affect negatively retirement income adequacy.

6.1.2. Options available when retiring at 65 years old under the new DC scheme

To get an old-age pension under the new DC scheme, workers must be 65 or older and have contributed at least 1 250 weeks in the case of private-sector workers, or 25 years in the case of public-sector workers. When those requirements are met, the worker can choose to allocate all resources accumulated in the retirement sub-account, in the housing sub-account (in case there is money left) and in the voluntary savings sub-account (if the worker has made voluntary savings during his/her career) according to the following options:

- Programmed withdrawals: In this option, the AFORE pays a monthly pension using the resources left in the individual account (after deducting the amount needed to buy an immediate survivor annuity in favour of the member's beneficiaries if applicable) and taking into account investment income and remaining life expectancy. The pension amount is variable and depends on the annuity factor (URV) by age and gender.[1] It is recalculated every year and paid until the balance in the account is depleted. In case the remaining assets are close to be inadequate to pay a pension equal to the guaranteed minimum pension, the member is informed and can opt for a guaranteed minimum pension using his/her remaining balance. In case of death, the remaining balance is distributed to the member's beneficiaries. This pay-out option is not indexed to consumer price inflation.

- Annuity: The member purchases an annuity from an insurance company with the amount saved in the AFORE. The annuity also covers the member's beneficiaries in case of death. The pension is updated with inflation every year in February.[2]
- Guaranteed minimum pension (PMG): If the resources accumulated in the individual account are not enough to buy a life annuity or to receive a pension in the form of programmed withdrawals of a minimum level, the worker is entitled to a guaranteed minimum pension granted by the federal government. The AFORE initially makes the payments of the PMG from the accumulated assets. Once these are depleted, the federal government pays the pension until the member passes away. At the pensioner's death, the federal government must purchase through the IMSS or the ISSSTE an immediate annuity granting the PMG for the member's beneficiaries.

When the worker does not meet the requirements for obtaining a pension, the IMSS or the ISSSTE gives a negative statement (*negativa de pensión*). In this case, at age 65 the member can withdraw the total accumulated balance in the individual account all at once.

Not all resources accumulated are used to finance retirement. Balances potentially accumulated between 1992 and the date of the reforms (respectively 1997 for private-sector workers and 2007 for public-sector workers) in the housing sub-account and in the individual retirement account are always surrendered to workers upon retirement in the form of a lump sum. For public-sector workers, even the potential resources left in the housing sub-account, accumulated since 2008, are surrendered to the worker as a lump sum and are not used as a complement to buy an annuity or to get programmed withdrawals.

Box 6.1. **Destination of money deposited in individual retirement accounts for IMSS and ISSSTE affiliates depending on the pension scheme chosen**

Type of account	IMSS workers – DB scheme	IMSS workers – DC scheme (3)	ISSSTE workers – DB scheme	ISSSTE workers – DC scheme (3)
SAR 92 (1)	Paid to the worker as a lump sum			
Housing sub-account 92 (2)	Paid to the worker as a lump sum			
Retirement insurance contribution (2%) in the retirement sub-account	Paid to the worker as a lump sum	Used to get an annuity, programmed withdrawal or PMG	Paid to the worker as a lump sum	Used to get an annuity, programmed withdrawal or PMG
Severance at old-age and old-age contributions in the retirement sub-account	Transferred to the federal government	Used to get an annuity, programmed withdrawal or PMG	Not accumulated in an individual account	Used to get an annuity, programmed withdrawal or PMG
Housing sub-account	Paid to the worker as a lump sum	Used to get an annuity, programmed withdrawal or PMG	Paid to the worker as a lump sum	Paid to the worker as a lump sum

Notes: (1) "SAR 92" represents the balances accumulated in the retirement sub-account before the respective reforms (1997 and 2007). (2) "Housing sub-account 92" represents the balances left in the housing sub-account from contributions made before the respective reforms. (3) Annuity is the only option available in case of disability or survivor pensions.

6.1.3. Early retirement is possible from age 60

Early retirement from age 60 is allowed both under the old DB system and the new DC system, provided that the worker is not employed and fulfils the minimum contribution period (respectively 500 weeks and 1 250 weeks). In the old DB system, workers suffer a 5-percentage points penalty in their pension benefit for each year of anticipation. In the new DC system, pension benefits depend on assets accumulated and are defined according to the same modalities as when people retire at 65.

The incentive to retire early is strong for low-income workers. Indeed, for those who are entitled to the PMG because the resources accumulated in the individual account are not enough to get a pension above that minimum, working beyond age 60 does not translate into higher pension benefits as long as the minimum contribution period criterion is already fulfilled at 60 years old. According to official statistics (*Sistema de Información Delegacional sobre las Prestaciones Económicas, Coordinación de Prestaciones Económicas del IMSS*), many workers opt for early retirement. Of the 162 308 new pensions in payment in 2014 for former private-sector workers (both under the old DB and the new DC systems), 79.0% corresponded to early retirement pensions.

Early retirement increases public pension liabilities related to the payment of the PMG. The PMG is indeed first paid by AFORE from the assets accumulated in the individual retirement account and then by the federal government. Therefore, early retirement for PMG-entitled workers implies that the individual retirement account gets depleted more rapidly and that the cost of the PMG for the federal government increases because it needs to pay for it for a longer period.

In addition, as there is no plan so far to link the retirement age to life expectancy, public pension liabilities may increase further in the future. As showed in Chapter 3, large increases in life expectancy are expected to take place in Mexico. If the eligibility age to get the PMG stays constant, the number of years of retirement to be financed will increase. The cost of the PMG is therefore likely to increase for the federal government as it bears the tail risk.

6.1.4. Partial early withdrawals for unemployment and marriage

In a view to help workers dealing with special circumstances, partial early withdrawals from the individual retirement account are allowed in case of unemployment and marriage. Table 6.1 summarises the requirements and details for such withdrawals.

Private-sector workers are entitled to make partial withdrawals from the balance in their individual retirement account in two cases: unemployment and marriage. Affiliates, who at the moment they marry for the first-time have complied with a minimum of 150 weeks of contribution payments, are entitled to a partial withdrawal of funds for an amount equivalent to 30 days of the current general minimum wage in Mexico City. This right can only be exercised once and cannot be requested for subsequent marriages. Exercising this benefit reduces the balance in the individual account as well as the number of weeks of contributions paid into the IMSS. In order to subsequently cover the number of lost weeks of contributions, the employee who exercised this right must deposit the amount withdrawn.

Affiliates who have been paying contributions into the IMSS, but are unemployed, are entitled to a partial withdrawal of funds as of the 46th calendar day of unemployment once every five years. The amount that can be withdrawn depends on how long the account has been opened:

- If the account has been open for at least three years, and the worker has paid contributions into the account for at least two years, the affiliate can receive the equivalent of 30 days of his/her last registered wage, with a limit of 10 times the current general minimum wage in Mexico City.
- If the account has been open for at least five years, the affiliate may withdraw the lower amount between the equivalent of 90 days of his/her wage and 11.5% of the retirement sub-account.

Like private-sector workers, public-sector workers are entitled to make partial withdrawals from the balance in their individual account in case of unemployment, but not for marriage. However, the benefit formula is slightly different. ISSSTE affiliates may withdraw the lower amount between the equivalent of 75 days of their wage and 10% of their account balance, as of the 46th calendar day of unemployment. Affiliates are entitled to this partial withdrawal once every five years.

Table 6.1. **Characteristics of partial early withdrawals**

	Unemployment	Marriage
Membership duration	IMSS: The account has been open at least 3 years before and at least 2 years of contribution ISSSTE: The account has been open for at least 5 years before	IMSS: 150 weeks of contributions to the RCV account
Amount withdrawn	IMSS: With 3 years of membership duration, 30 days of the last base salary up to 10 times the minimum wage. With 5 years of membership duration, the minimum between 90 days of the base salary and 11.5% of the accumulated balance. ISSSTE: The minimum between 75 days of the base salary and 10% of the accumulated balance.	IMSS: 30 days of minimum salary
Requirements	IMSS: Be certified as unemployed by IMSS (certification given from the 46th day of unemployment) ISSSTE: Certificate issued by the institute, given from the 46th day of unemployment	IMSS: Resolution from IMSS to help with marriage costs
Are weeks of contributions lost?	IMSS: Yes, however, these contributions can be recovered ISSSTE: Yes	IMSS: No
How often can this benefit be claimed?	IMSS: Every 5 years ISSSTE: Every 5 years	IMSS: Only once in life

6.1.5. Withdrawals of voluntary savings

Workers who made voluntary contributions may withdraw these resources as follows:

- Short-term voluntary contributions can be withdrawn from 2 to 6 months after the deposit;
- Complementary contributions to individual retirement accounts and long-term voluntary contributions can be withdrawn from the age of 65 only or when the worker receives a pension resolution.

6.2. A sluggish annuity market

6.2.1. A low demand for annuity products and a few market players

The potential demand for annuity products comes from the following individuals and cases:

- Disability and survivor insurance: The IMSS or the ISSSTE has to buy an annuity from a private insurance sector specialised annuity provider to cover the related benefits. However, the worker chooses the annuity provider.
- Severance at old-age and old-age pension insurance: Workers in the DC pension system[3] can choose upon retirement between a programmed withdrawal[4] offered by an AFORE or an annuity offered by a specialised annuity provider (provided they are

entitled to a pension and have accumulated enough in their individual retirement account).

Due to the difference in generosity between the old and new old-age benefits, it is expected that most transitional workers will elect the old DB formula. In other words, the short- to medium-term prospects for development of the annuity market in Mexico very much depend on the accumulated funds in the disability and survivorship lines of benefits only.

None of the transitional private-sector workers chose so far to retire under the DC system with either a programmed withdrawal or an annuity. Only 14 382 transitional private-sector workers have chosen to retire under the DC system because they were entitled to the minimum guaranteed pension. However, looking at public-sector workers, the vast majority (99.4%) of those who chose the DC system back in 2007 bought an annuity at retirement, as shown in Table 6.2.

Table 6.2. **Choice at retirement of public-sector workers affiliated to the ISSSTE who chose the DC system**

	Programmed withdrawal	Annuity	Total
2009	35	601	636
2010	8	1 513	1 521
2011	2	1 311	1 313
2012	1	1 261	1 262
2013	2	1 705	1 707
2014	6	2 247	2 253
Total	54	8 638	8 692

Source: CNSF.

Therefore, the annuity market is small and will remain so because there is no demand for annuities. Demand will increase as the transition period reaches its end in around 2035. In the meantime, the lack of demand drives the market and it is difficult to assess whether it is competitive or not. Nevertheless, it is important to assess the structure of the market to determine if there is room for improvements.

Annuity providers for the mandatory DC pension system are ring-fenced subsidiaries of insurance companies. Insurance companies can set up a separate entity to provide annuities to IMSS and ISSSTE. These annuity providers are ring-fenced from the other business of their parent insurance company (life and non-life business). They can only provide annuities to the DC pension system and not to individuals outside the pension system. The life business of insurance companies can provide annuities to individuals outside the DC pension system, but not to the DC pension system. Consequently, annuity companies cannot diversify risks (e.g. mortality) with other products as normal insurance companies offering annuities would do. These annuity companies are subjected to a more restrictive investment regime than insurance companies. This may remove incentives for insurance companies to create annuity providers. It also increases the cost of annuities (and thus reduces the amount of the pension payment) compared with what a life insurance would offer.

Ring-fencing these annuity providers from the general insurance business of the parent company may increase the security that they will fulfil their payment promises.

This greater security comes at a cost: lower annuity payments and lower diversification. However, the costs and benefits need to be carefully evaluated.

Annuity providers in the market today in Mexico are a small number. There were 14 companies operating during the period 1997 to 2001. This number dropped from 12 to 3 between 2002 and July 2009. Today there are only four active insurance companies in the annuity market and there are six other companies managing their annuities portfolio. Initially the market for annuities grew driven by a surge in demand as all disability and survival pensions granted by IMSS were issued as insurance contracts. However, following the amendment of the Social Security Law on 20 December 2001 providing IMSS with more power to select annuity providers, most IMSS affiliates retiring the years following this reform chose to get their benefits following the old PAYG DB rule, paid by the government. Therefore, the annuity market is now driven by the almost inexistent demand coming from transitional workers.

Insurers' lack of interest in participating in the annuity market can also be due to other reasons. First, the absence of financial instruments to hedge longevity risk; second, the regulator imposed a minimum discount rate from 1997 to 2008 of 3.5%. Insurers that left the market pointed to the increasing difficulty to obtain similar returns on investment for reserves. However, 10-year government bonds yielded much more during that period. Finally, high administration costs generated by small pensions (descent and orphans) may have led to unattractive profit margins. Figure 6.1 and Figure 6.2 show respectively the annuity premiums paid and the number of annuity contracts since 1997 under the DC system and illustrate the drop in the annuity market after 2001. In 2014, written premiums were MXN 19 736 million for 21 027 annuitants.

Figure 6.1. **Annuity premiums paid, 1997-2014**

In millions of December 2014 pesos

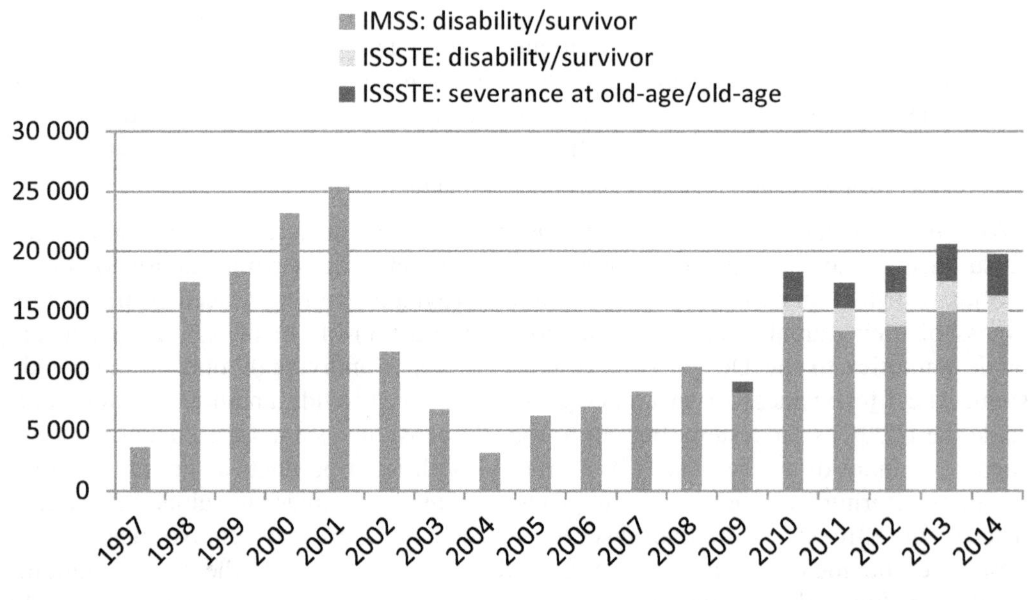

Notes: "IMSS: disability/survivor" refers to premiums for disability and survivor pensions for IMSS affiliates; "ISSSTE: disability/survivor" refers to premiums for disability and survivor pensions for ISSSTE affiliates; "ISSSTE: severance at old-age/old-age" refers to premiums for severance at old-age and old-age pensions for ISSSTE affiliates.

Source: CNSF.

Figure 6.2. **Number of annuity contracts, 1997-2014**

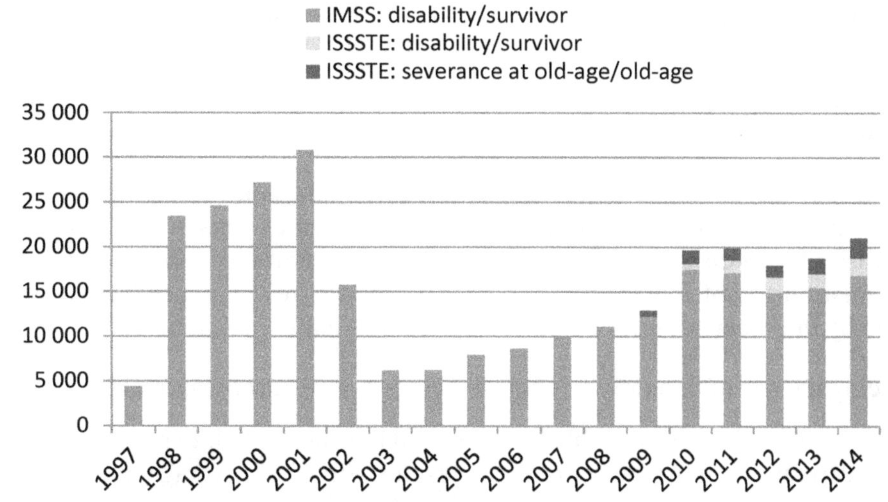

Notes: "IMSS: disability/survivor" refers to annuity contracts for disability and survivor pensions for IMSS affiliates; "ISSSTE: disability/survivor" refers to annuity contracts for disability and survivor pensions for ISSSTE affiliates; "ISSSTE: severance at old-age/old-age" refers to annuity contracts for severance at old-age and old-age pensions for ISSSTE affiliates.

Source: CNSF.

Finally there is a severe product restriction. By law, annuity providers can only offer one annuity product to workers retiring from the IMSS or the ISSSTE: a single premium annuity that provides pensioners a flow of payments throughout their lifetime, indexed to inflation.

6.2.2. Pricing of annuities: towards more competition in the market

A committee composed of officials from the Ministry of Finance and Public Credit, the IMSS, the ISSSTE, CONSAR and the National Insurance and Surety Commission (*Comisión Nacional de Seguros y Fianzas*, CNSF), named *Comité del Artículo 81 de la Ley del SAR*, agreed on the implementation of a new operative scheme for the annuity market in 2009. One of the main aspects was the establishment of a market mechanism in order to determine the price of annuities, by which annuity providers could compete through discount rates estimations that would reflect financial market conditions. The market mechanism intends to:

- Capture market fluctuations of real rate long-term risk-free bonds so that annuity providers could offer a discount interest rate in line with the financial conditions at the moment of the underwriting of annuity contracts;
- Switch from a fixed price scheme where discount interest rates and biometric assumptions (mortality tables) were pre-defined to a scheme in which the premium depends on parameters offered by each annuity provider such as discount interest rates and mortality tables;
- Define an homogenous methodology for the determination of the annuity price; and

- Try to align incentives so that pensioners elect the annuity provider that bid the bigger discount interest rate, and therefore a lower amount of assets are needed to pay the DB promises.

Additionally, in order to mitigate longevity risk, prudential regulation applicable to annuities was strengthened by:

- Updating the mortality tables for disabled, injured and non-disabled pensioners with "ad-hoc" data (transition from population mortality data to pensioners' mortality data). In the case of non-disabled pensioners, generational mortality tables were introduced and all mortality tables are subject to a periodically revision mechanism with data provided by the social security institutes as well as annuity providers.
- Introducing the use of derivatives, exclusively for hedge purposes, in order to:
  - Enhance asset-liability matching to reduce the insurers' risk exposure. Transactions with derivatives must be carried out exclusively for coverage purposes. In this respect, all the transactions performed with derivatives have to be associated to financial securities assigned, to technical provisions or to the solvency capital requirement;
  - Get senior officers and committee members elected by the Board of Directors to be involved in the oversee of market's risks administration, liquidity and other relevant risks;
  - Assure that financial operators of annuity providers have the necessary background for operating derivatives, as they must be certified by an independent third-party determined by the CNSF. Similarly, the responsible area of comprehensive risk management must be certified by an independent third-party.

In the first stage of the implementation of this market mechanism, annuity providers were able to (i) make their pricing and bid using the discount interest rate that they were able to offer looking at the prevailing conditions of the long-term financial market, and (ii) offer their own biometric assumptions on the survival of pensioners.

However, the bidding scheme had two restrictions. First, the discount interest rate offered by insurers could not be lower than a reference interest rate.[5] And second, mortality tables that insurers used for pricing purposes could be neither more conservative than the mortality tables used for the calculation of the solvency capital requirement, nor less conservative than the mortality tables used for the valuation of technical provisions. As shown in Table 6.3, between 2011 and 2013, the deviation of the rates offered by insurers with respect to the reference interest rate was negligible (0 or 1 basis point). There was no incentive for insurers to offer a better rate.

Table 6.3. **Reference interest rate and average difference with observed rates in the annuity market**

In per cent and difference in basis points

	IMSS		ISSSTE	
	Reference rate (%)	Market rate – Reference rate (bp)	Reference rate (%)	Market rate – Reference rate (bp)
2009	3.51	8	3.58	15
2010	2.83	17	2.88	22
2011	3.41	0	3.41	0
2012	2.48	0	2.48	0
2013	2.34	0	2.35	1

Source: CNSF.

In November 2012, the committee approved adjustments for the annuity market, with the introduction of a fully market mechanism for DC severance at old-age and old-age pensions. Since January 2014, this market mechanism expanded to disability and survivor pensions. As a result of the strategy adopted, there is an evident competition between the market participants that has generated savings for the social security system explained by the spread between the discount interest rate offered by market participants and the reference rate used previously (see Figure 6.3).

Figure 6.3. **Discount interest rate offered by annuity providers in 2014 and former reference rate**

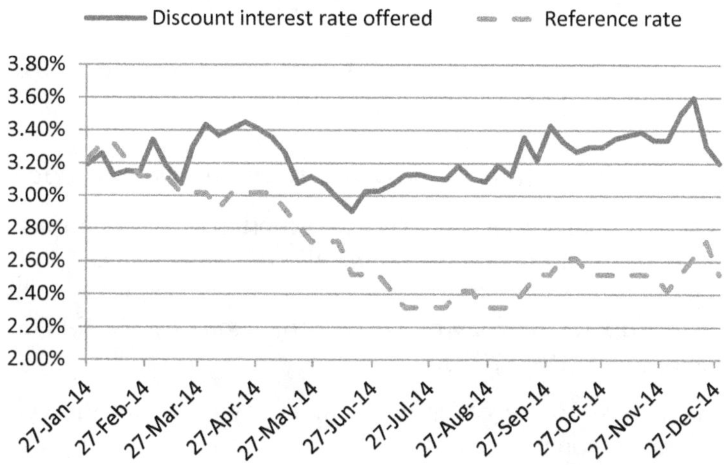

Source: CNSF.

In December 2013, the CNSF also approved the introduction of a mechanism of repeated auction to guarantee price competition. The process is described below:

- Annuity providers receive electronically on a weekly basis information about pension applicants and their beneficiaries, without personal identification data but with elements that allow them to bid the amount of pension.
- They bid pension payments for each pension applicant, disclosing the discount interest rate that they are able to offer and the biometric assumptions that reflect the estimation

of survival for each individual into a webpage that hosts the Offers and Resolution Management System (*Sistema Administrador de Ofertas y Resoluciones*, SAOR).

- The SAOR processes under a homogeneous basis the bidding of the annuity providers and gathers them in a single offer document so that pension applicants can compare all the different pension offers (the old DB formula and the new DC rule for transitional private-sector workers, programmed withdrawals,[6] survivor benefits, disability benefits) and select the one that best suits them. For DB pensions, the offer document displays the pension paid by the social security institute (either IMSS or ISSSTE) and the lump sum that the pension applicant can receive. For DC pensions, the offer document displays the amount of pension derived from the annuity or programmed withdrawal.
- The offer document includes a clear and visible legend highlighting the "optimal choice". In the case of disability and survivor pensions, the optimal choice is the one offering the promised benefit for the lowest lump sum possible. In the case of severance at old-age and old-age pensions, the optimal choice is the one offering the larger pension.

There is a financial incentive for workers to select the optimal choice in the case of disability and survivor pensions. Indeed, these pensions are funded by social security institutes (i.e. IMSS and ISSSTE), but the choice of the annuity provider is done by the worker, who will receive the same pension payment, independently of this choice. The IMSS and the ISSSTE therefore pay a lump sum of up to MXN 9 000 to workers choosing the optimal choice, i.e. the cheapest choice.[7] The offer document also includes a section that must be filled in and signed by the pensioner in case of not selecting the optimal choice, to make sure he/she is fully aware of his/her decision.

6.3. Assessment of the potential longevity risk in standard mortality tables used by pension funds and annuity providers

6.3.1. Mortality tables, regulatory requirements and market practice

There are no minimum requirements for mortality assumptions imposed on occupational plan sponsors in Mexico, who typically rely on the EMSSA 97 table.[8,9] This table is based on population mortality experience and in practice is typically improved to 2011 for males and 2013 for females based on projections by CONAPO (the National Council of Population) from 1990-2030.

Annuity providers have to use generational mortality tables for the valuation of their liabilities. The insurance company must perform the valuation of its reserves for non-disabled pensioners with the EMSSAH-Rva-09 (for men) and EMSSAM-Rva-09 (for women) tables. However, if they apply any other more conservative assumption, they must use the EMSSAH-CMG-09 (for men) and EMSSAM-CMG-09 (for women) tables.[10] These tables were updated in 2009 based on data provided by IMSS and ISSSTE rather than population data. Future mortality improvements in these tables are specified by age and gender. Given that the market has adopted the more conservative tables for pricing (EMSSAH-CMG-09 and EMSSAM-CMG-09), they must use these mortality tables for the purpose of valuing liabilities. The same tables are used by AFORE offering programmed withdrawals.

Insurers generally price their annuity products using their own set of assumptions, though they have been free to do so only since August 2009. The insurers frequently use the generational 2009 tables listed above for non-disabled pensioners. These tables are updated from time to time in an effort to ensure that they appropriately reflect up-to-date experience of mortality rates.

The Mexican regulatory framework includes an additional level of provision for improvements in longevity above and beyond those already included in the standard tables in their financial reporting or in their embedded value metrics, and are required to hold an additional reserve of 2% of the mathematical reserve to cover the possibility of unexpected demographic experience. However, an additional reserve would not typically be applied for pricing or solvency purposes.

To provide additional protection to policyholders, regulation has also set up a special fund to assist insurers in the case that an external event, such as a variation in the financial markets that impedes insurance institutions to obtain the financial products covering the technical reserves and to guarantee the appropriate resources to fulfil their obligations regarding the policyholders, or in the case of demographic experience deviations, threatens the ability of the insurer to meet its obligations to the policyholder. This special fund can only be used if the insurance company has already used the special mathematical reserve and the contingency reserve.

Table 6.4. **Mortality tables and improvements required by regulation and used in practice in Mexico**

		Required
Minimum table required by regulation	Annuity providers	Yes
	Occupational pension plans	No
Mortality improvements required by regulation	Annuity providers	Yes
	Occupational pension plans	No
Mortality improvements used in practice	Annuity providers	Yes
	Occupational pension plans	No

Source: OECD (2014).

6.3.2. Recent trends in life expectancy and mortality improvements

Mexico has relatively low life expectancy for both men and women. Moreover, projected improvements are also relatively low. Nevertheless, there is room for life expectancy to catch up with that of other countries and mortality improvements to accelerate in the near future. If this were to happen, the longevity risk that annuity providers and occupational pensions would be exposed to will be much higher that the one assessed below.

Figure 6.4 and Figure 6.5 show the evolution in population life expectancy at age 65 for males and females for fifteen selected countries, including Mexico, demonstrating the increase in period life expectancy from 2000 to 2010 as well as average additional life expectancy taking into account future mortality improvements as predicted by projection models (i.e. cohort life expectancy for 2010).[11]

Figure 6.4. **Male population life expectancy at age 65**

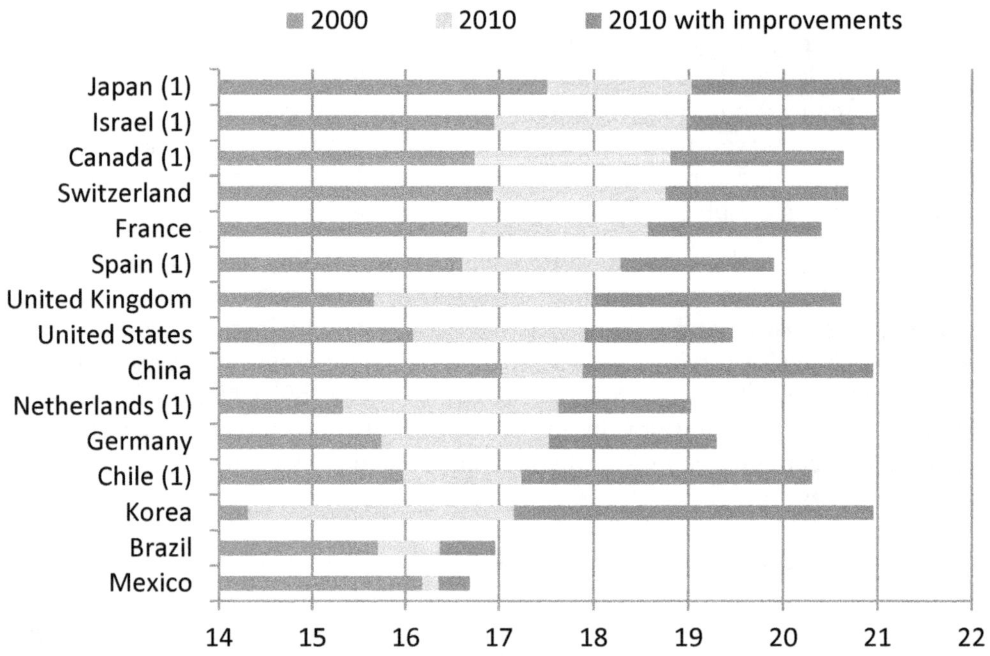

1. Period life expectancy 2010 estimated based on the average increase of the last five years available data.

Source: OECD (2014).

Figure 6.5. **Female population life expectancy at age 65**

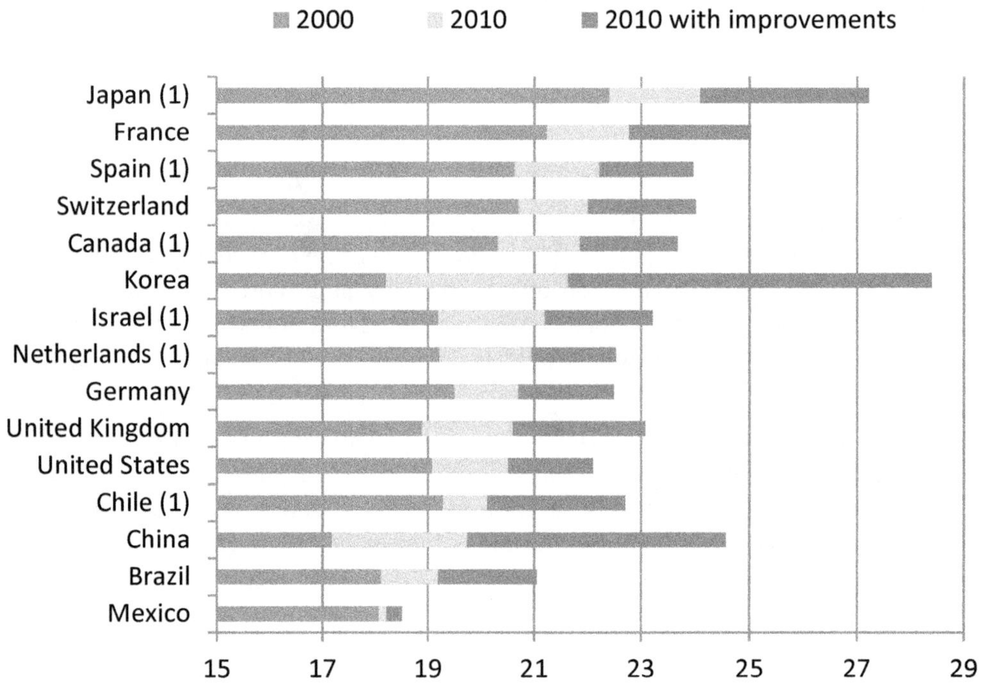

1. Period life expectancy 2010 estimated based on the average increase of the last five years available data.

Source: OECD (2014).

The difference between the period life expectancy and the cohort life expectancy of 2010 shows the impact that future improvements are expected to have on life expectancy. On average, the projected mortality improvements add two years of life expectancy for males and 2.5 years for females. Chile, China, Japan, Korea and the United Kingdom are expected overall to have the highest increase in life expectancy for both genders. Of these countries, Chile, China and Korea have relatively low life expectancies compared to that in other countries, and the high improvements projected by the models likely reflect the fact that life expectancy in these countries is catching up with the other countries, particularly for Korea for whom projected improvements have the largest impact on life expectancy. Once life expectancy is more in line with the other countries, it could be expected that the mortality improvement beyond that point will also align with average levels, thus the analysis presented here may overstate somewhat the longevity risk in these countries.

Figure 6.6 and Figure 6.7 show that life expectancy has been increasing in Mexico, for both men and women, albeit at a rather slower pace over the last two decades than other selected OECD countries. For example, male life expectancy at 65 increased by 0.5 years between 1990 and 2009 in Mexico, by 3.1 years in Canada, 1.8 years in Chile (between 1992 and 2005), 2.9 years in France, 3.2 years in Germany, 2.7 years in Japan, 3 years in the Netherlands, 3.4 years in Switzerland and 2.7 years in the United States. The gap in life expectancy between the two genders in Mexico has decreased slightly but has been overall stable at just under two years.[12]

Figure 6.6. **Life expectancy at age 65, males, selected OECD countries, 1990-2009**

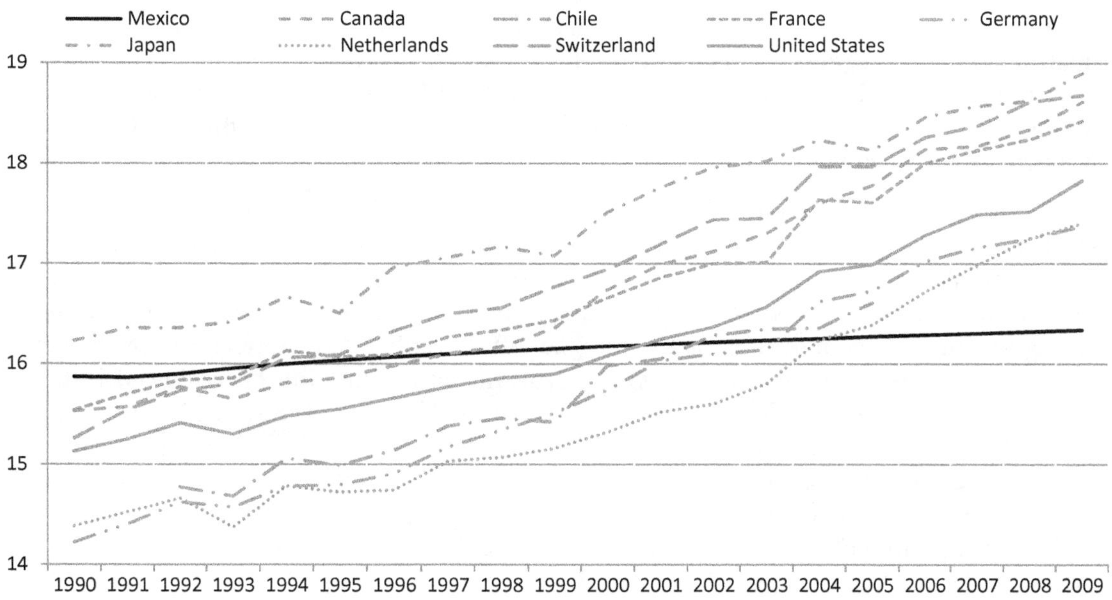

Source: OECD (2014).

Figure 6.7. **Life expectancy at age 65, females, selected OECD countries, 1990-2009**

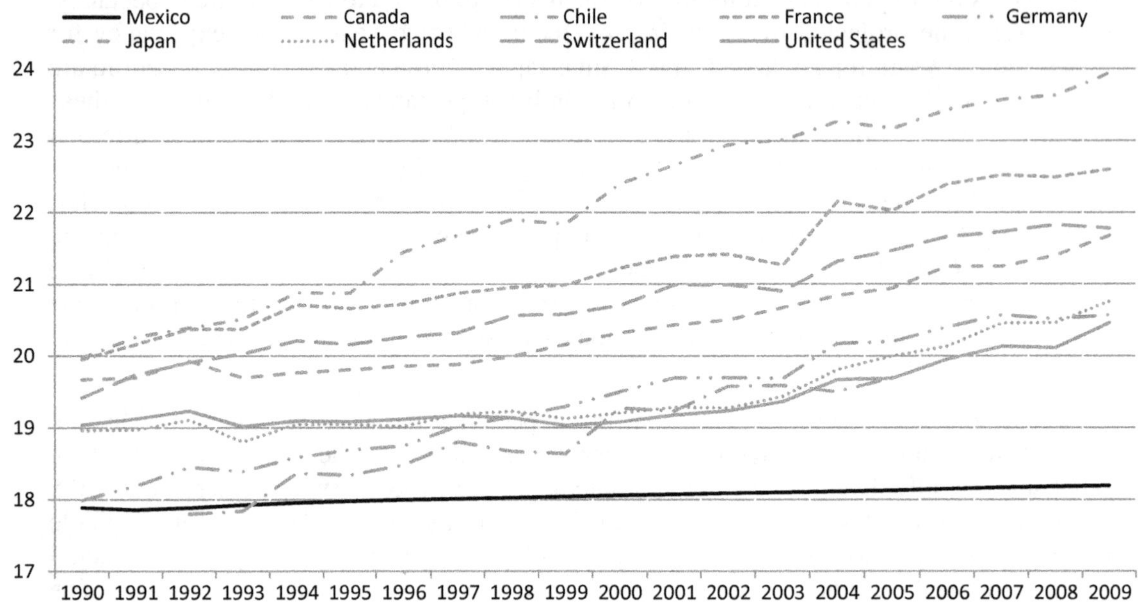

Source: OECD (2014).

6.3.3. Assessment of the potential longevity risk in the standard mortality tables

OECD (2014) examines the mortality tables commonly used by pension funds and annuity providers against several well-known mortality projection models (the Lee-Carter, the Cairns-Blake-Dowd, P-splines and the CMI models) with the purpose of assessing the potential shortfall in provisions. The main results of this analysis for Mexico are provided below.

Table 6.5 shows the annualised improvement to mortality rates in Mexico for age groups of five years. The evolution of mortality improvement from one decade to the next shows the shift of mortality improvement across age groups over time.[13] This aids not only in judging the appropriateness of assumptions given in existing tables, but also the appropriateness of the model outputs. From the left of Table 6.5, historical improvements in the population's mortality are shown. Improvements in mortality have slowed in the last decade for both genders, with the assumptions in the EMSSA-CMG-09 being optimistic compared to recent experience. The stochastic models (Lee-Carter and Cairns-Blake-Dowd) project forward a pattern in line with the overall average improvements, while the P-splines model continues the low improvements of the recent decade, and the CMI converges to the 1% long-term improvement which has been assumed for Mexico in the longer term.

Table 6.5. **Historical and future mortality improvements predicted by tables and projection models**

	Population		EMSSA09		LC		CBD		PS		CMI	
Males	*1990-2000*	*2000-2009*	*2010-2020*	*2020-2030*	*2010-2020*	*2020-2030*	*2010-2020*	*2020-2030*	*2010-2020*	*2020-2030*	*2010-2020*	*2020-2030*
55-59	1.5%	0.5%	1.3%	1.3%	1.0%	1.0%	1.0%	1.0%	0.5%	0.5%	0.8%	1.0%
60-64	1.2%	0.4%	1.1%	1.1%	0.8%	0.8%	0.8%	0.8%	0.4%	0.4%	0.6%	0.9%
65-69	0.9%	0.3%	0.9%	0.9%	0.6%	0.6%	0.6%	0.6%	0.3%	0.3%	0.5%	0.9%
70-74	0.6%	0.3%	0.8%	0.8%	0.4%	0.4%	0.4%	0.4%	0.3%	0.3%	0.4%	0.8%
75-79	0.3%	0.2%	0.6%	0.6%	0.3%	0.3%	0.3%	0.3%	0.2%	0.2%	0.5%	0.9%
80-84	0.0%	0.2%	0.6%	0.6%	0.1%	0.1%	0.1%	0.1%	0.1%	0.2%	0.6%	1.0%
85-89	-0.2%	0.0%	0.6%	0.6%	0.0%	0.0%	-0.1%	-0.1%	0.2%	0.2%	0.8%	1.0%
90-94	-0.5%	0.0%	0.5%	0.5%	-0.2%	-0.2%	-0.2%	-0.2%	-0.1%	-0.1%	0.9%	1.0%
95-99	-0.6%	0.0%	0.4%	0.4%	-0.3%	-0.3%	-0.3%	-0.3%	-0.1%	-0.1%	0.8%	0.8%
100-104	-0.7%	-0.1%	0.0%	0.0%	-0.3%	-0.3%	-0.4%	-0.4%	-0.2%	-0.2%	0.6%	0.6%
105-110	-0.8%	-0.1%	0.0%	0.0%	-0.4%	-0.4%	-0.5%	-0.5%	-0.4%	-0.3%	0.4%	0.4%

	Population		EMSSA09		LC		CBD		PS		CMI	
Female	*1990-2000*	*2000-2009*	*2010-2020*	*2020-2030*	*2010-2020*	*2020-2030*	*2010-2020*	*2020-2030*	*2010-2020*	*2020-2030*	*2010-2020*	*2020-2030*
55-59	1.3%	0.5%	1.8%	1.8%	0.9%	0.9%	0.9%	0.9%	0.5%	0.5%	0.8%	1.0%
60-64	1.0%	0.4%	1.5%	1.5%	0.8%	0.8%	0.7%	0.7%	0.4%	0.4%	0.6%	0.9%
65-69	0.7%	0.3%	1.3%	1.3%	0.6%	0.6%	0.5%	0.5%	0.3%	0.3%	0.5%	0.9%
70-74	0.5%	0.3%	1.0%	1.0%	0.4%	0.4%	0.4%	0.4%	0.3%	0.2%	0.5%	0.9%
75-79	0.2%	0.2%	0.9%	0.9%	0.2%	0.2%	0.2%	0.2%	0.2%	0.2%	0.4%	0.9%
80-84	0.0%	0.2%	0.7%	0.7%	0.0%	0.0%	0.0%	0.0%	0.1%	0.1%	0.5%	1.0%
85-89	0.0%	0.0%	0.6%	0.6%	0.1%	0.1%	-0.1%	-0.1%	0.1%	0.1%	0.8%	1.0%
90-94	-0.6%	0.0%	0.5%	0.5%	-0.2%	-0.2%	-0.2%	-0.2%	-0.1%	0.0%	0.9%	1.0%
95-99	-0.7%	-0.1%	0.3%	0.3%	-0.3%	-0.3%	-0.4%	-0.4%	0.0%	-0.1%	0.8%	0.8%
100-104	-0.8%	-0.1%	0.0%	0.0%	-0.4%	-0.4%	-0.4%	-0.4%	-0.1%	-0.1%	0.6%	0.6%
105-110	-0.8%	-0.1%	0.0%	0.0%	-0.4%	-0.4%	-0.5%	-0.5%	-0.3%	-0.3%	0.4%	0.4%

Notes: Darker shades indicate higher improvements.
LC = Lee-Carter model;
CBD = Cairns-Blake-Dowd model;
PS = P-splines model;
CMI = CMI model.

Source: OECD (2014).

The Tables 6.6 and 6.7 show the values for the cohort life expectancy, the annuity value based on a 4.5% nominal discount rate, and the annuity payment as a per cent of the initial investment (net of margins and fees).[14] Life expectancy and annuity values are key indicators of pension and annuity liabilities. The two are closely related, with the latter taking into account the time value of money. The figures given for each of the projection models applied are shown for the general population as well as adjusted to the level of insured and pensioner mortality (see OECD, 2014 for details on the methodology).

Table 6.6. **Cohort life expectancy, annuity values and payments at age 55, 65 and 75 – males**

Mortality tables		Life expectancy 2010			Annuity factors			Annuity payment		
		55	65	75	55	65	75	55	65	75
EMSSA97		25.3	17.1	10.3	7.0	11.8	8.3	14.4%	8.5%	12.1%
EMSSA09		29.6	21.7	14.8	7.9	13.5	10.6	12.6%	7.4%	9.4%
Modelled Mortality										
Population	LC	23.8	16.5	10.6	6.4	11.3	8.3	15.7%	8.8%	12.0%
	CBD	23.8	16.5	10.8	6.4	11.3	8.5	15.7%	8.8%	11.8%
	P-Spline	23.8	16.5	10.7	6.3	11.3	8.4	15.8%	8.8%	11.9%
	CMI	25.0	17.2	11.1	6.6	11.5	8.6	15.1%	8.7%	11.7%
Adjusted										
EMSSA97: 1997	LC	25.0	16.8	10.1	6.9	11.6	8.1	14.5%	8.6%	12.3%
	CBD	25.0	16.8	10.1	6.9	11.7	8.1	14.5%	8.6%	12.3%
	P-Spline	25.0	16.9	10.1	6.9	11.7	8.2	14.6%	8.6%	12.2%
	CMI	26.1	17.5	10.4	7.1	11.9	8.3	14.1%	8.4%	12.0%
EMSSA09: 2009	LC	28.6	21.0	14.4	7.7	13.2	10.5	12.9%	7.6%	9.6%
	CBD	28.5	20.9	14.3	7.7	13.2	10.4	13.0%	7.6%	9.6%
	P-Spline	28.5	21.0	14.5	7.7	13.2	10.5	13.0%	7.6%	9.5%
	CMI	29.9	22.0	15.0	8.0	13.5	10.7	12.6%	7.4%	9.3%

Notes: LC = Lee-Carter model; CBD = Cairns-Blake-Dowd model; CMI = CMI model.

Source: OECD (2014).

Table 6.7. **Cohort life expectancy, annuity values and payments at age 55, 65 and 75 – females**

Mortality tables		Life expectancy 2010			Annuity factors			Annuity payment		
		55	65	75	55	65	75	55	65	75
EMSSA97		29.3	20.6	13.0	8.1	13.3	9.8	12.3%	7.5%	10.2%
EMSSA09		34.0	24.3	15.1	9.5	15.0	11.1	10.5%	6.7%	9.0%
Modelled Mortality										
Population	LC	26.2	18.2	11.8	7.1	12.2	9.0	14.0%	8.2%	11.1%
	CBD	26.2	18.3	11.9	7.1	12.2	9.1	14.0%	8.2%	11.0%
	P-Spline	26.3	18.3	11.9	7.1	12.2	9.1	14.0%	8.2%	11.0%
	CMI	27.6	19.2	12.3	7.4	12.4	9.3	13.5%	8.0%	10.8%
Adjusted										
EMSSA97: 1997	LC	28.7	20.0	12.6	8.0	13.0	9.6	12.6%	7.7%	10.4%
	CBD	28.7	20.0	12.6	8.0	13.1	9.6	12.6%	7.7%	10.4%
	P-Spline	28.8	20.1	12.7	8.0	13.1	9.6	12.6%	7.6%	10.4%
	CMI	30.2	21.0	13.2	8.3	13.3	9.8	12.1%	7.5%	10.2%
EMSSA09: 2009	LC	32.9	23.6	14.7	9.3	14.7	10.9	10.8%	6.8%	9.1%
	CBD	32.8	23.5	14.7	9.2	14.7	10.9	10.8%	6.8%	9.2%
	P-Spline	33.0	23.7	14.8	9.3	14.7	11.0	10.8%	6.8%	9.1%
	CMI	34.3	24.5	15.2	9.5	15.0	11.2	10.5%	6.7%	9.0%

Notes: LC = Lee-Carter model; CBD = Cairns-Blake-Dowd model; CMI = CMI model.

Source: OECD (2014).

The analysis shows little to no potential shortfall in provisions. A proxy for the change in the liability value can be directly estimated by taking the ratios of the annuity values given by the models over those computed with the standard mortality tables. This corresponds to the change in reserves or funding needed to meet future pension and annuity payments as estimated by the alternative model. Figures 6.8 and 6.9 show the change in liability value given by the models studied based on the annuity values presented for the standard mortality tables and the adjusted model outputs in Tables 6.6 and 6.7. Both graphs show little to no potential shortfall in provisions. On the other hand, the recent low mortality improvements in Mexico result in a slight over-provisioning for longevity for annuities as measured here, as the improvements assumed are more conservative than recent population experience shows.

Figure 6.8. **Potential shortfall from EMSSA 97 tables for pensioners in Mexico**

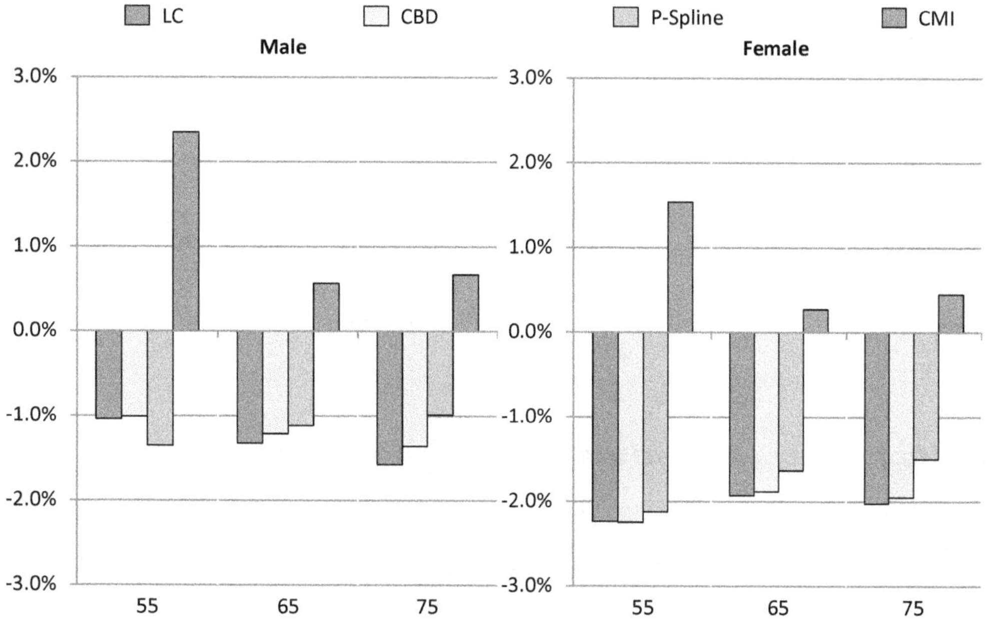

Notes: LC = Lee-Carter model; CBD = Cairns-Blake-Dowd model; CMI = CMI model.
Source: OECD (2014).

Figure 6.9. **Potential shortfall from EMSSA 09 tables for annuitants in Mexico**

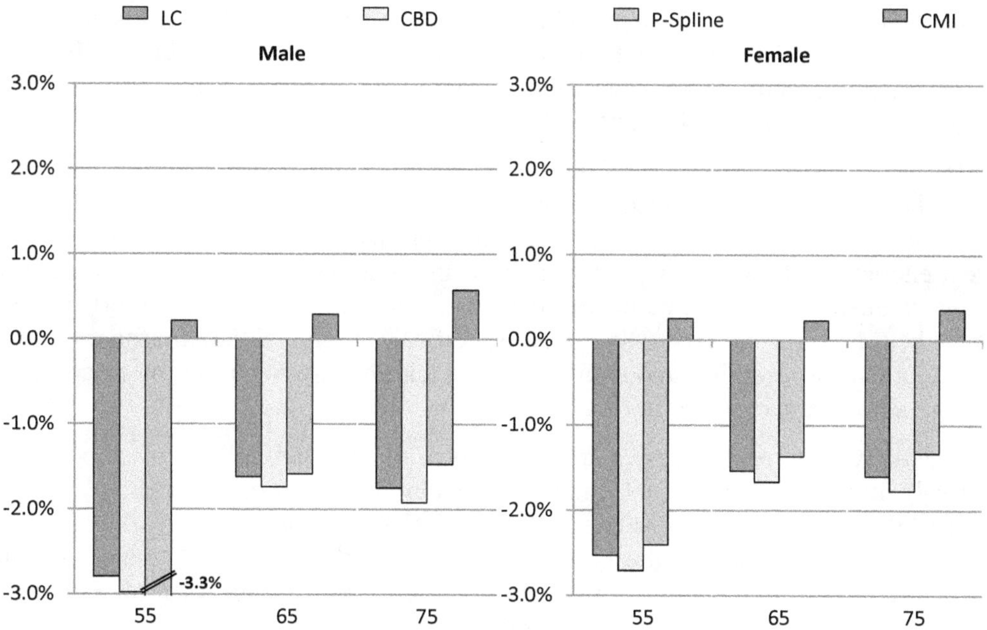

Notes: LC = Lee-Carter model; CBD = Cairns-Blake-Dowd model; CMI = CMI model.
Source: OECD (2014).

To put it in a nutshell, while the tables used by annuity providers in Mexico seem to sufficiently provision for expected mortality improvements for now, recent improvements in mortality have been slowing and the country currently has rather low life expectancy compared to other OECD countries. Therefore, the potential for longevity to accelerate in Mexico and life expectancy to catch up to other OECD countries exists, and mortality experience should be closely monitored for changing patterns to ensure that the tables remain adequate.

Occupational DB pension funds are not subject to any minimum mortality requirements, including using tables accounting for future improvements in mortality. A close monitoring of mortality is even more relevant for pension funds to make sure any mortality improvement acceleration is reported and assumptions updated accordingly.

6.4. Proposals to improve the design of the pay-out phase

6.4.1. Maximise the resources used to finance retirement

Allowing workers to withdraw part of their retirement savings to face contingencies can be seen as an incentive for workers to participate in the pension system. For individuals, a major worry about putting money into private pension arrangements, whether mandatory or not, is that they are not able to withdraw it until retirement. Yet, there may be cases where accessing some of those funds could help solvent a major shock, such as defraying health expenses that are not covered by the health system. For this reason, some countries allow withdrawals from retirement savings systems under specific, exceptional circumstances. For example, KiwiSaver plan members in New Zealand may withdraw all of their funds at any time in the event of serious illness or permanent disability, or if they face significant financial hardship (such as dependent's medical care or education). Similar rules on so-called hardship withdrawals apply in the United States for 401(k) plans, Individual Retirement Accounts and other qualified plans. In Mexico, partial early withdrawals from the individual retirement account are allowed in case of unemployment and marriage.

However, one needs to be careful as enabling access to savings may divert too much money that was initially intended to finance retirement and affect negatively retirement income adequacy. Considering this negative impact, marriage may not be a circumstance critical enough to allow for early withdrawals. In addition, allowing partial withdrawals in case of unemployment once every five years may be too frequent. Workers should access their pension savings only under specific, exceptional circumstances. Serious illness, permanent disability and significant financial hardship may be more appropriate causes to allow for early withdrawals.

Potentially large pots of assets are not used to finance retirement, possibly affecting negatively retirement income adequacy. For example, balances accumulated between 1992 and the date of the reforms (respectively 1997 for private-sector workers and 2007 for public-sector workers) in the housing sub-account and in the individual retirement account are always surrendered to workers upon retirement in the form of a lump sum. Transitional workers choosing a DB pension also get back the amount corresponding to the retirement insurance contribution in the retirement sub-account (2% of the base salary paid by the employer) as a lump sum. These assets have been accumulated in the pension system but are not combined with other retirement assets to buy a life annuity or get programmed withdrawals. Although such rule may be seen as an incentive for workers to participate in the pension system, diverting too much money that was initially intended to finance retirement many affect negatively retirement income adequacy.

These lump sum payments also increase public pension liabilities. In the case of transitional workers choosing to receive a pension calculated according to the old DB formula, the federal government is responsible for paying the pension. All the money accumulated in the pension system should therefore be transferred to the government and used to finance the DB pension, in particular the retirement insurance contribution. The federal government is also responsible for paying for the PMG once the assets in the individual retirement account are depleted and it is difficult to understand why all the assets accumulated in the pension system are not used to finance the minimum pension, leaving an additional burden on the state.

In addition, linking retirement age to life expectancy increases would allow keeping the cost of the PMG for the federal government constant. As said earlier, the federal government only starts paying the PMG at late ages, once the assets in the individual retirement account are depleted. The longer people live, the more likely is the government to finance a larger part of the PMG. In addition, if workers keep retiring at 65, the assets accumulated in the individual retirement account need to finance a longer retirement period as life expectancy increases. This would translate into lower pension payments and an increased likelihood to be entitled to the PMG.

Finally, pensioners should be allowed to choose an insurance company within the set of companies offering the same coverage and guarantees at the same price. This would limit pensioners' choice of the insurance companies providing disability and survivors' benefits but it would balance premiums to be paid by the social security institutes and the extent of the protection provided. As a result, pensioners could not choose insurance companies that provide the same coverage at a higher cost. Today, pensioners have a financial incentive to select the optimal choice (a lump sum of up to MXN 9 000), but there is no rule that prevent them from choosing an annuity provider charging a higher premium to the IMSS or the ISSSTE for the same coverage than other providers.

6.4.2. Improve prospects for the annuity market

Insurance companies should be allowed to offer different types of annuity products.[15] With only one annuity product available (a single premium inflation-indexed annuity), the annuity market in Mexico is unattractive to both insurance companies and plan members. On the one hand, annuity providers cannot compete by offering to people innovative annuity products. On the other hand, life annuities are usually perceived by people as costly. In addition, they are illiquid and inflexible, and do not allow for bequests. There are therefore strong incentives against taking-up a life annuity at retirement and choose a programmed withdrawal instead. This means a risk that workers retiring under the new DC system may be more exposed to longevity risk than those retiring today under the DB system.

An additional modality to allocate pension assets at retirement, achieving a balance between protection from longevity risk, flexibility, and liquidity, may reinvigorate the Mexican annuity market. Life annuities may need to be part of any default arrangement for the pay-out phase, depending on the overall pension system, as they provide insurance against longevity risk. A combination of programmed withdrawals with a deferred life annuity (e.g. starting payments at the age of 80-85) that offers protection against inflation could be seen as an appropriate default. This combination achieves a balance between protection from longevity risk, flexibility, liquidity, possibility of bequests, and access to portfolio gains.

The annuity market regulator should consider allowing a wider variety of annuity products to be offered in the market. The CNSF should make sure though that annuity providers adequately reserve for the potential additional risks that those additional annuity products may carry.

Finally, regulators should examine the possibility of changing the institutional set-up of annuity providers to bring economies of scale and risk diversification. Today, insurance companies need to create separate entities to offer annuities. This separated entity is regulated differently from insurance companies and cannot take advantage of economies of scale by merging its business with the parent company. Associating annuity providers and life insurance companies in the same branch could be considered. In addition, insurance companies in most other OECD countries can mitigate the life expectancy risk associated with the provision of life annuities by offering other products, such as life insurance policies. Indeed, while an increase in life expectancy increases the liabilities of the annuity provider stemming from life annuities (the annuitant will receive payments for a period of time longer than anticipated), it increases premiums paid in life insurance products and postpones the payment of the life insurance policy. In the same way, Mexican annuity providers should be allowed to diversify the range of products they can offer to diversify risks.

6.4.3. Better account for future improvements in mortality and life expectancy and improve the management of longevity risk

Following the main recommendations put forward by the OECD study on Mortality Assumptions and Longevity Risk (OECD, 2014) and the way annuity providers and pension funds in Mexico account for future improvements in mortality and life expectancy, the main recommendations are:

- Regularly update mortality tables to accurately reflect the most recent experience and avoid significant increases in reserves.
- Use the mortality experience of the relevant population to establish mortality tables.
- The Mexican government should facilitate the measurement of mortality for the purposes of assumption setting and the evaluation of basis risk of index-based hedging instruments. In this regard, accurate and timely mortality data should be publicly available, and mortality data by a socio-economic indicator should be made publically available when possible.
- Occupational pension funds should use mortality tables to calculate their liabilities and reserve accordingly. These mortality tables should include expected future improvements in mortality. They should use mortality tables in line with those used by annuity providers.

The Mexican regulatory framework should provide incentives to manage and mitigate longevity risk. For example, capital and funding requirements should be based on the risks faced in order to account for the specific exposure to longevity risk and allow institutions using instruments to hedge longevity risk to adjust their requirements accordingly. These requirements could be based on results from stochastic models, which provide probability distributions. Additionally, accounting standards should ensure the appropriate valuation of longevity hedging instruments.

Finally, the Mexican government should encourage the development of a market for instruments to hedge longevity following the approach laid out in OECD (2014), in order to ensure the capacity for pension plans and annuity providers to continue to provide longevity protection to individuals.

Notes

1. The annuity factor (*Unidad de Renta Vitalicia*) is defined as the actuarial value necessary to finance a unit of annual pension. The value of the URV changes periodically, due to updates to the mortality tables and to fluctuations in interest rates used to discount the future flow of payments.
2. The 12-month December to December evolution of the Consumer Price Index is used.
3. New entrants in the private sector after July 1997, new entrants in the public sector after April 2007, transitional workers choosing the DC system.
4. In case the worker chooses the programed withdrawal option, a survivor insurance annuity must still be purchased in order to pay the pension that arises from the pensioner's death.
5. The reference rate was defined periodically using a moving average of the level of real discount rates associated with a benchmark of selected long-term risk-free instruments of 10, 20 and 30 years.
6. Programmed withdrawals only apply for severance at old-age and old-age pensions.
7. This financial incentive is called "*Beneficio Adicional Único*".
8. See the OECD (2014) study on mortality assumptions and longevity risk.
9. According to CONSAR (2014), 49.6% of DB occupational pension plans use the EMSSA 97 table, while 27.3% use the EMSSA 09.
10. Indeed, annuity providers can use a table having as a minimum the EMSSAH-Rva-09 and as a maximum the EMSSAH-CMG-09 (for men) and the EMSSAM-Rva-09 and the EMSSAM-CMG-09 (for women). The tables EMSSAH-CMG-09 and EMSSAM-CMG-09 are used for capital purposes.
11. Period life expectancy makes no allowance for changes in mortality beyond the year in question, whereas cohort life expectancy is calculated taking into account future improvements in mortality and uses probabilities of death which follow a given group of the population. The cohort life expectancy shown here is the average given by four projection models. See OECD (2014) for more details.
12. Data for Mexico are based on Mexican population and death estimates from 1990 to 2009 published by CONAPO.
13. Figures are shown for age groups of five years, ages 55 to 110. It should be noted however that limited data is available at the very high ages and the improvements at these ages for the historical data are heavily dependent on the methodology used to extrapolate the mortality to these ages.

14. All annuities are calculated assuming a discount rate of 4.5%, and annuity values for age 55 are assumed to begin payment at age 65.

15. The new SAR Law approved by the Lower Chamber but stuck in the senate allows insurance companies to offer different types of annuity products.

References

CONSAR (2014), Estadísticas de Registro Electrónico de Planes Privados de Pensiones 2014.

OECD (2014), *Mortality Assumptions and Longevity Risk: Implications for pension funds and annuity providers*, OECD Publishing, Paris.
DOI: *http://dx.doi.org/10.1787/9789264222748-en.*

ORGANISATION FOR ECONOMIC CO-OPERATION AND DEVELOPMENT

The OECD is a unique forum where governments work together to address the economic, social and environmental challenges of globalisation. The OECD is also at the forefront of efforts to understand and to help governments respond to new developments and concerns, such as corporate governance, the information economy and the challenges of an ageing population. The Organisation provides a setting where governments can compare policy experiences, seek answers to common problems, identify good practice and work to co-ordinate domestic and international policies.

The OECD member countries are: Australia, Austria, Belgium, Canada, Chile, the Czech Republic, Denmark, Estonia, Finland, France, Germany, Greece, Hungary, Iceland, Ireland, Israel, Italy, Japan, Korea, Luxembourg, Mexico, the Netherlands, New Zealand, Norway, Poland, Portugal, the Slovak Republic, Slovenia, Spain, Sweden, Switzerland, Turkey, the United Kingdom and the United States. The European Union takes part in the work of the OECD.

OECD Publishing disseminates widely the results of the Organisation's statistics gathering and research on economic, social and environmental issues, as well as the conventions, guidelines and standards agreed by its members.

OECD PUBLISHING, 2, rue André-Pascal, 75775 PARIS CEDEX 16
(21 2015 03 1 P) ISBN 978-92-64-24592-1 – 2016

www.ingramcontent.com/pod-product-compliance
Lightning Source LLC
Chambersburg PA
CBHW061215240926
51846CB00006B/1235
* 9 7 8 9 2 6 4 2 4 5 9 2 1 *